From Cottage to Bungalow

Chicago Architecture and Urbanism

A series edited by Robert Bruegmann
Joan Draper
Wim de Wit
David Van Zanten

Other Volumes in the Series

Joseph Conners	*The Robie House of Frank Lloyd Wright*
Joseph Siry	*Carson Pirie Scott: Louis Sullivan and the Chicago Department Store*
John W. Stamper	*Chicago's North Michigan Avenue: Planning and Development, 1900–1930*
Sally A. Kitt Chappell	*Architecture and Planning of Graham, Anderson, Probst and White, 1912–1936: Transforming Tradition*
Robert Bruegmann	*Architects and the City: Holabird & Roche of Chicago, 1880–1918*

FROM COTTAGE TO BUNGALOW

Houses and the Working Class in Metropolitan Chicago, 1869–1929

Joseph C. Bigott

The University of Chicago
Chicago and London

Joseph C. Bigott is assistant professor in the Department of History at Purdue University, Calumet.

The University of Chicago Press, Chicago 60637
The University of Chicago Press, Ltd., London

Printed in the United States of America

10 09 08 07 06 05 04 03 02 01 1 2 3 4 5
ISBN: 0-226-04875-6 (cloth)

Works in Chicago Architecture and Urbanism are supported in part by funds given in memory of Ann Lorenz Van Zanten and administered by the Chicago Historical Society.

Library of Congress Cataloging-in-Publication Data

Bigott, Joseph C.
From cottage to bungalow: houses and the working class in metropolitan Chicago, 1869–1929 / Joseph C. Bigott.
p. cm. — (Chicago architecture and urbanism)
Includes bibliographical references and index.
ISBN 0-226-04875-6 (alk. paper)
1. Housing—Illinois—Chicago Metropolitan Area—History. 2. Working class—Illinois—Chicago Metropolitan Area—History. 3. Immigrants—Housing—Illinois—Chicago Metropolitan Area—History. 4. Minorities—Housing—Illinois—Chicago Metropolitan Area—History. 5. Architecture, Domestic—Illinois—Chicago Metropolitan Area—History. I. Title. II. Series.

HD7304.C4 B54 2001
363.5'09773'11—dc21

00-051208

∞ The paper used in this publication meets the minimum requirements of the American National Standard for Information Sciences—Permanence of Paper for Printed Library Materials, ANSI Z39.48-1992.

CONTENTS

ILLUSTRATIONS

TABLES

FIGURES

PREFACE

Recently, historians have reexamined accounts of the Great Chicago Fire, Pullman, the birth of the skyscraper, and the World's Columbian Exposition in an effort to reconstruct the imaginative world of literate Chicagoans at the end of the nineteenth century. In each case, historians have shown how an elite wished to assert its leadership by rebuilding the city in a manner that reflected its values and concerns.[1] They have also shown how ordinary citizens resisted attempts to impose a single culture on an increasingly diverse city. This resistance forced the elite to acknowledge, albeit grudgingly, its inability to control a disorderly and fragmented society. The result was a modern outlook that accepted "instability and change as conditions of life."[2]

This book explores the relationship between the ordered values of middle-class culture and the disorderly growth of working-class neighborhoods. To do so, it develops methods for analyzing the material culture of everyday life, especially the common house forms that served as building blocks for Chicago's neighborhoods. The built environment provides important physical evidence for interpreting the lives of people who did not leave written records. But historians have only recently considered the significance of common urban structures in a thoughtful and detailed manner.[3] Most historians continue to place less emphasis on the analysis of artifacts than on the analysis of written texts and quantitative data. Consequently, for traditional historians, material culture history remains "the scholarship nobody knows."[4]

Certainly, a cultural expression as complex as the built environment requires a broad analytical competence in order to test the authority of written texts, quantitative data, and artifactual sources, one source against the others.[5] The analysis in this book employs various types of evidence. But it assumes the primacy of artifacts in the study of the built environment. This assumption may raise difficulties for those unfamiliar with or opposed to the study of material culture. Artifacts derive from a different imaginative process, a visual, technological thinking, no less articulate than the verbal expressions that define more effectively the activities of elites and the middle class. The various forms of visual thought have affected profoundly the design and manufacture of the objects common to everyday life.[6]

I wish to demonstrate the value of examining these artifacts in a rigorous and substantive manner. While doing so, I seek a broad, and often traditional, historical audience. Consequently, I address debates and employ methods common to the history of cities, labor, immigration, politics, economics, architecture, technology, and culture. Specialists in these fields share an interest, both academic and personal, in a common built environment. It is hoped that competent analysis of diverse forms of evidence can overcome the barriers between fields in a manner that allows us to understand more fully the relationship between labor, artifacts, and capital in the modern world.

ACKNOWLEDGMENTS

I owe special debts to three persons. At the University of Notre Dame, Thomas Schlereth introduced me to the study of material culture. His teaching expanded tremendously my approach to the history of everyday life. At the University of Delaware, Richard Bushman provided an example of a social historian who produced work of the highest quality. He encouraged me to pursue the significance of the small, seemingly insignificant houses at the heart of this study. Robert Bruegemann became a great defender of this work. Always, I will remain in his debt for negotiating so expertly its transition from manuscript to book.

I wish to thank the friends who helped refine my thoughts. I can no longer recall all of the important conversations. But I am forever grateful to those who read portions of the manuscript, offering support, counsel, and criticism. These included Gerard Coop, Tim Gilfoyle, Philip Gleason, Bert Hindmarch, Carol Hoffecker, Tom Hubka, Ed Kantowicz, Ann Keating, Kris Kimball, Dennis Korchek, Saul Lerner, Chris Miller, Dominic Pacyga, Larry Peterson, Ellen Skerritt, and Pat Thatcher. At the University of Chicago Press, Susan Bielstein was both a wise and patient editor.

Three environments were important during the writing of the book. The research began at the Hammond Public Library. The library's staff provided continuous help for the man with the large photocopying account. In 1992, at a critical point in the development of the manuscript, I participated in a National Endowment for the Humanities Summer Seminar at the University of Virginia. Its director, Olivier Zunz, offered among the finest critiques of this work. He challenged me to discover a "winning" argument. At some point, it seems all Chicago historians interested in the city benefit from the Urban History Seminar held each month at the Chicago Historical Society. Its gracious hosts, Ann Keating, Russell Lewis, and Michael Ebner, continue to provide a collegial environment and a wonderful place to talk about cities.

Finally, I acknowledge the debt to my family. My wife Geri and my children, Katharine and Adam, remained patient and steadfast in their support, willing to sacrifice time and attention so the project could reach a satisfying conclusion. I hope they remember fondly the countless times we navigated portions of metropolitan Chicago in search of some neighborhood where I promised to take just one more photograph.

My greatest debt remains to my parents, Robert and Irene, to whom I dedicate this book about the virtues and failings of where we came from.

INTRODUCTION

From Cottage to Bungalow

As Americans entered the nineteenth century, the middle levels of society refined their manners and their surroundings. They improved their homes and adorned them with a host of beautiful things. The possession of refined objects and genteel manners defined the concept of respectability for an emergent middle class. Increasingly, ordinary people justified luxuries as a means of raising themselves to a higher plane. By midcentury, many "luxuries" had become necessities, leading Americans to believe that in the United States no one, no matter how humble, was beyond the reach of good manners and good taste. Under these circumstances, access to material goods became a liberating force, for many assumed the great division in society was not between the rich and everyone else but between those who lived in homes with parlors and aspired toward improvement, however modest, and those who did not.[1]

The rise of industrial cities challenged this assumption by widening the division between the haves and have-nots. Immigrants from southern and eastern Europe seemed far beyond the reach of well-mannered, polite society. A few generous reformers insisted that immigrants learn proper conduct under careful supervision.[2] But others argued for the futility of remedial efforts.[3] During the 1880s, American intellectuals described southern and eastern Europeans as "peoples that had the worst of the race wars for centuries," who possessed "neither the capacity nor the disposition to raise themselves above the lowest plane of industrial life," and who "represent the very lowest state of degradation to which human beings can be reduced by hopelessness, hunger, squalor, and superstition."[4] To prevent the increase of so degraded a population, they called for restrictions on immigration. Well into the twentieth century, respected social scientists warned "of one thing we may be sure: future man will have the characteristics of those who are superfecund, whether we like it or not."[5]

Few intellectuals freed themselves from the strident racial categories common at the beginning of the twentieth century. These preconceptions affected the analysis of the social problems originating in the nation's rapidly expanding cities. In Chicago, the housing reformer Robert Hunter believed that race suicide would occur if immigration continued unabated because the children of degraded southern and eastern Europeans would displace the native-born.[6] Hunter's 1901 survey of tenements claimed that Chicago's Polish section already contained a population density three times greater than "the most crowded portions of Tokio, Calcutta, and many other Asiatic cities." The survey hoped to awaken the "better" citizens of Chicago to the severity of the problem so they might overcome "a dangerous sort of apathy content to leave things as they are, a laissez faire policy which brings forth the fruit of unrighteousness."[7] Hunter considered public action the best means to prevent southern and eastern Europeans from becoming "breeders of children, who persist in the degeneration into which their fathers have fallen; and, like the tribe of Ismael or the family of Jukes, they have neither the willingness nor the capacity to respond to the efforts of those who would help, or force, them back into the struggle."[8]

The 1901 tenement survey profoundly influenced images of working-class Chicago because three generations of historians accepted Hunter's account as "careful, thorough, and forceful." They even suggested that Hunter regarded the ethnic origin of tenement dwellers as insignificant.[9] Such uncritical acceptance led historians to claim that "the landscape of working-class Chicago was dominated until the time of urban renewal by small, dark, difficult to heat, tinderbox cottages that were often crowded two or three deep on a single lot." According to this view, working people had "no choice but to live in unsafe, unsanitary, and overcrowded homes," creating an "inelastic demand for substandard structures" that was "the most fundamental obstacle" to reform in cities like Chicago.[10]

Of course, modern scholars renounced the explicit racial views so common at the beginning of the century. Later reformers, such as Edith Abbott, regarded attempts to distinguish the suitability of immigrants as "tedious meaningless discussion" that incorrectly stressed race above economics. Abbott argued that immigrants failed because a modern economy did not provide families with sufficient income.[11] Ironically, the transfer from racial to economic causation led to harsher criticism of working-class participation in the housing market. At the turn of the century, Robert Hunter had argued that, prior to the arrival of southern and eastern Europeans, one- and two-family frame cottages provided "excellent homes for working people." Unfortunately, single-family housing became unprofitable as land values and densities increased. So a slum of brick three- and four-story tenements replaced the earlier city of one- and two-family frame houses. In 1901, Hunter feared that these larger structures, and their immigrant populations, would spread outward from the core, like an infectious disease, creating a city of filthy streets, alleys, courtyards, and passageways that were "a menace to the coming century, a force for evil creeping into the newer cities while the citizens are unaware."[12]

A generation later, Abbott denied that cottages ever provided decent accommodation. She argued that city leaders erred when they rebuilt cottages for families who lost their houses in the Great Fire of 1871. The decision allowed for construction of thousands of poorly built, single-family cottages. More important, it reestablished a tradition of private ownership that did not provide safeguards for the poor. Consequently, when southern and eastern Europeans arrived, unscrupulous landlords took advantage of those least capable of protecting themselves.[13]

Despite greater racial tolerance, Abbott shared Hunter's conviction that southern and eastern Europeans would never improve substantially the quality of their lives. Like Hunter, she believed that "the real child of poverty ends life where he began it, without perhaps even lifting his hand toward the next round [*sic*] of the ladder. . . . Ignorant, incapable, and for the most part unorganized, they cannot help themselves." Abbott warned, "It must not be forgotten that the unskilled are a dangerous class; inadequately fed, clothed, and housed, they threaten the health of the community, and, like all the weak and ignorant, they often become the misguided followers of unscrupulous men."[14]

By the 1930s, Edith Abbott concluded that immigrant home ownership was a pathological behavior, dangerous to community welfare. She insisted that immigrant residences never resembled the "pleasant cottage home and garden of a sturdy artisan or mechanic who is on the thrifty road to independence and comfortable living."[15] Instead, immigrants compromised their families by withdrawing children from school, sending mothers to work, and depriving families of food, clothing, and comfort, all to purchase tenements and acquire status as landlords and property owners.[16] To remedy the problem, Abbott wished to withdraw the poor from the market by demolishing older housing and replacing it with newly constructed government housing. She considered public housing essential in a society where working-class consumers did not act in their own self-interest and where investors sought profit at the expense of the public good.[17]

This book refutes the summary dismissal of the working-class housing market that has dominated twentieth-century scholarship. It argues that a market for modest houses contributed to a fundamental transformation as Americans, both native and immigrant, refined the qualities of urban life. At the turn of the century, typical working-class houses in the Midwest were known as cottages. These structures existed in blighted tenement districts (fig. 1). But cottages were not residences limited to an illiterate, foreign-born underclass. In 1893, Edwin and Lillian Thompson built a seven-room cottage at 708 East Eighty-Ninth Street in Chicago. Thompson was a

Figure 1 A tenement cottage. (Source: Robert Hunter, *Tenement Conditions in Chicago: Report by the Investigating Committee of the City Homes Association* [Chicago: City Homes Association, 1901], 23.)

union carpenter from Ohio. He lived in this house with his wife for more than forty years. The exterior was ornamented with a porch, a bay window, and decorative shingles. Since the house sat close to the street, ample space existed for a backyard that was fenced for privacy (figs. 2–6). The furnishings suggest literacy and a high level of comfort by 1910. The family valued its phonograph, dishes, books, woodwork, lamps, photographs, prints, draperies, and numerous articles of furniture, including a piano not shown in these photographs. The images demonstrate that cottages were not universally substandard. They provided a range of accommodations, offering residences for prosperous as well as for poor members of the working class.

Figure 2 *(top left)* The home of Edwin C. And Lillian Thompson. (Source: author.)

Figure 3 *(top right)* Rear of Thompson home. (Source: author.)

Figure 4 *(left)* Lillian Thompson in her dining room. (Source: author.)

Figure 5
Thompson family's phonograph. (Source: author.)

Figure 6
Edwin C. Thompson in his study. (Source: author.)

Historians have overlooked the significance of respectable working-class houses because they have accepted the exaggerated claims of reformers.[18] With few exceptions, historians have argued that a privileged middle class was responsible for innovations in modern housing. In a highly acclaimed study, Kenneth Jackson assumed that social change began at the top of society and later filtered down as the fashions of the rich and powerful became "popular with ordinary people."[19] From this assumption, Jackson argued that upper- and middle-class suburban culture created the market for modern single-family housing. To support this view, he maintained that dramatic increases in urban home ownership occurred during the first decades of the twentieth century, when streetcars opened vast sections of land on the periphery to residential development.[20] The result was a suburban frontier of unprecedented affluence where the middle class created a distinctive style of life, a "haven in a heartless world," far from the impersonal concerns of business and industry.[21]

By the 1920s, images of affluent suburbs and middle-class culture dominated advertising and the media. They were critical elements of an emerging urban society. But historians have employed the middle-class suburban ideal as the basis for interpreting the significance of home ownership in the twentieth century. In doing so, they have been especially critical of the expansion of home ownership after World War II, when the federal government committed resources to create a suburban nation. Jackson argued that the federal government accomplished this goal by funding highway construction and insuring long-term mortgages that allowed young families to purchase new homes with small down payments and low monthly mortgage installments. These actions expanded the construction industry as developers rationalized the building process and made suburban life affordable for most white Americans.[22]

During the 1950s, contemporaries generally praised suburbia as a triumph of the private market, proof of a prosperity shared reasonably well among the population. But critics always questioned whether so comfortable a population would commit to higher social values.[23] The crises of the sixties suggested they could not. Suburbia and home ownership became symbols of excessive materialism. It seemed the refinements of middle-class culture would neither unite Americans nor make them more generous toward the poor. From this perspective, the suburbs became a monument to a satisfied and conformist people who lost the opportunity to create a just society because they preferred "little boxes made of ticky-tacky."[24]

While this interpretation holds enormous persuasive power, it fails to consider the relevance of high rates of working-class home ownership that existed in most cities by the beginning of the twentieth century.[25] The working class had access to affordable houses because major industrial districts at the periphery of cities created opportunities for employment and home ownership.[26] In Detroit, the working-class market was so large that home ownership at the turn of the century "was more an emblem of immigrant working-class culture than of the established middle-class native-white culture." According to Olivier Zunz, two markets existed: one for the middle class and one for the working class, with each operating independently from the other. Zunz concluded that the working-class market was at least as significant as the middle-class market in building the industrial city. Even Detroit's poorest immigrants experienced "a freedom of choice as to where they would live," a freedom that allowed immigrants to settle on the periphery, where opportunities for ownership provided the chance to establish autonomous neighborhoods with strong community institutions.[27]

Progressive reformers such as Edith Abbott believed that allowing immigrants the freedom to build was a mistake, an environmental and aesthetic tragedy, creating deplorable conditions that might have been avoided if society had acted to prevent the evils of bad housing.[28] The founding fathers of urban history offered similar criticisms, arguing that "twentieth-century urban America presents a picture of endlessly repeated failures," of an enduring tradition demonstrating the absence of "the desire, the power, the wealth, and the talent necessary to create a humane environment."[29] But the first generation of urban historians never bothered to examine for themselves the types of common housing built in American cities. Consequently, their accounts often degenerated to little more than pejorative aesthetic criticism and suggestions that the lack of forethought ingrained a taste for the vulgar among the general population.[30] Such criticism preferred utopian visions of model towns and experimental communities to detailed analysis of the common houses built in American cities. Recent works continue to rely on the work of Progressive reformers, assuming that the market failed and that unskilled workers "were not significantly integrated into the emerging consumer economy."[31]

This study assumes that no one can speak with authority about the evolution of common house forms without material evidence derived from analysis of the built environment.[32] Written sources, photographs, maps, and historical drawings reflect what was built, and proper analysis requires their use. But they assist in understanding what is primary: the houses themselves. Whenever possible, I have supported the analysis of material evidence and photographs with statistical evidence drawn from census materials, housing surveys, and fire insurance maps. Too often, urban historians have offered little analysis of the photographs appearing in their texts. Equally common, historians have used census records as statistical "proof" of housing conditions without considering the types or range of housing within a neighborhood. They assumed that one working-class house was as good as another or, more typically, as bad.

Effective combinations of material, visual, and statistical evidence are critical in challenging the authority achieved by

Progressive housing reformers in works published at the turn of the century. Their images remain the evocative symbols of an era. New combinations of evidence will make it possible to document the varied and changing conditions that existed in the first decades of the century. Historians then can challenge misleading ideas that govern the history of modern housing. Drawing on advice manuals and popular magazines, previous accounts have assumed that "owning one's home was evidence both of a certain level of income and of a particular outlook on life," an outlook decidedly native and middle class. But it is wrong to assume that "the middle-managerial ranks of clerks, shopkeepers, and professionals such as engineers and accountants . . . owned the majority of single-family dwellings during the past century."[33] It is also misleading to suggest that a shift occurred in the twentieth century "toward smaller, much simpler houses," as the middle class altered its conception of a proper home.[34] Perhaps persons born in very large Victorian houses lived in smaller houses in the twentieth century. But most people who purchased bungalows in the 1920s bought structures larger and more complex than the houses in which they were born. To suggest otherwise fails to recognize the effects of economic abundance and social mobility in the twentieth century.

Investigation of Chicago's built environment revealed that the evolution of modern housing could not be explained by suggesting that styles filtered down from the affluent to the masses. Modern housing resulted just as much from a bottom-up process, from the creation of a large market for working-class housing that increased in size and quality over time. Of course, privileged persons exercised cultural leadership. As Richard L. Bushman has demonstrated, "The exchange between high and low is anything but equal. . . . The fact remains that people at the top have an immense advantage in influencing cultural forms. To believe otherwise is to misunderstand the nature of power."[35] Clearly, advertising spread images of middle-class ideals throughout twentieth-century society. But advertising strategies cannot explain why so many goods were sold to so large and so inclusive a market.

It was not marketing that produced the achievement of the Ford Motor Company when, in a period of six years, it "wiped out all former notions of how things ought to be moved and assembled." Rather, it was the innovations in production and assembly at Ford that were revolutionary. Americans crossed enormous intellectual and technological barriers by creating a mass market for even complex consumer goods.[36] Modern housing was part of this transformation. It represented a confluence, the joining together of a pervasive and disseminating middle-class culture with a very large and improving low-end market. Assumptions derived from master categories of race, class, and aesthetics have prevented scholars from looking at common urban houses and acknowledging the confusing and often contradictory process by which the market evolved.

Instead, historians have examined the emergence of a modern American culture by focusing on dramatic events rather than on objects. Recently, studies of Chicago have shown how the Great Fire, the Haymarket tragedy, the Columbian Exposition, and the Pullman strike brought worldwide attention to the city. These events affected profoundly writers of various skills who struggled to make sense of the social disorders affecting the United States near the end of the nineteenth century.[37] Within this sequence, the Pullman strike has served as the culminating event, the epochal conclusion for the nineteenth century. Few stories equal the drama of George Pullman's attempt to create a model environment that would refine and control his workforce.[38] According to Jane Addams, Pullman was a modern King Lear whose actions led to a fundamental confrontation between American labor and corporate capitalism.[39]

Dramatic events always have served as the lifeblood for narrative history. However, when historians of everyday life attempt a similar type of narrative, they face a significant challenge. As Lawrence Stone has noted, the rise of the social sciences made the narrative tradition appear disreputable unless supported with statistical evidence. Whatever its literary merit, a historical narrative of everyday life must demonstrate that it represents a typical case rather than an exception to the rule.[40] By these standards, the story of George Pullman and his model town was an anomaly. Its history and appearance differed radically from the vast majority of Chicago's working-class neighborhoods. Indeed, the model town began as a simplified equation. When Pullman employed corporate wealth to build rental properties for his workers, he eliminated the portions of the local economy responsible for creating the dominant features of Chicago's residential landscape, the cottage and the bungalow.

Cottages and bungalows were built over a tremendous portion of metropolitan Chicago. The story of their creation lacks a central dramatic figure such as George Pullman upon whom to focus the narrative. Hundreds of thousands of people were responsible for creating Chicago's common residential landscape. A single work cannot develop intimate, narrative details for so large a population. Any study of this landscape must narrow its focus if it wishes to place the intimate experiences of ordinary people within an orderly narrative context. Consequently, I have chosen Hammond, Indiana, and West Hammond, Illinois, as appropriate locations for examining the evolution of the market for working-class housing during the critical period from 1869 to 1929 when houses became modern.

Inevitably, such choices are to a degree arbitrary and must be defended. In its favor, Hammond was among the early industrial suburbs of Chicago. From a historical perspective, age has tremendous value. Hammond's market for cottage housing developed prior to the establishment of corporate capitalism. Consequently, it provided a better location than later, more famous, counterparts such as Pullman or Gary for understanding the type of development most common during the earlier portion of the nineteenth century. However, like most of Chicago, Hammond entered the world of corporate capitalism rapidly. By 1910, corporate investments had transformed the southeastern portion of metropolitan Chicago from prairie and sand dune into one of the significant industrial districts of the world (fig. 7). This transformation was especially poignant in Hammond where

Figure 7
Map of the Calumet region. (Source: "The Greatest Steel Plant in the World," Iron Age 42 [January 7, 1909], 1.)

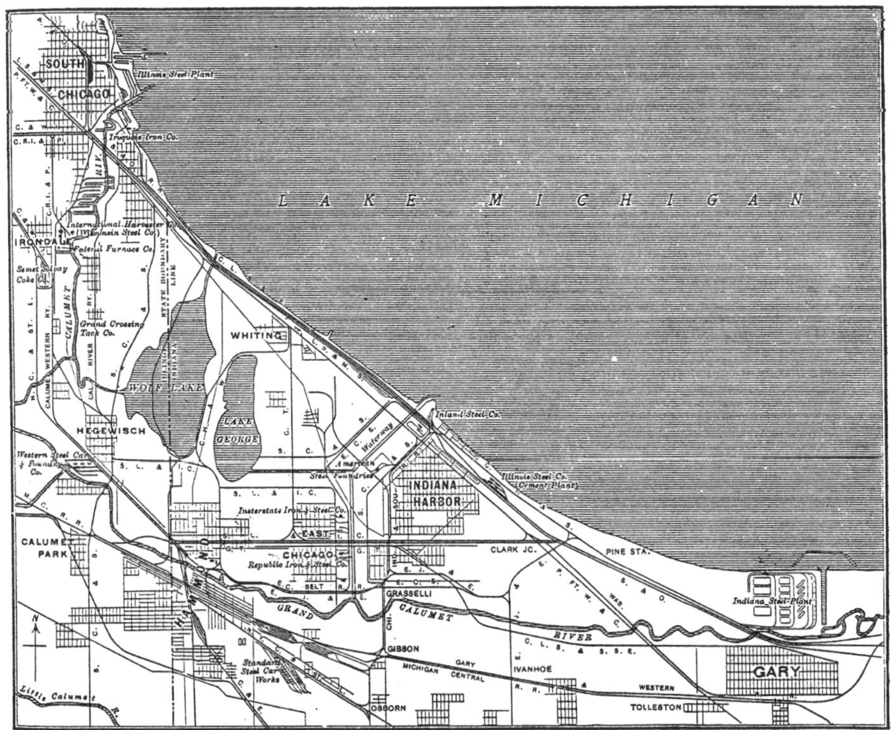

residents participated actively in a defining historical event, the Pullman strike of 1894.

Local sources provided detailed accounts of the strike and its participants. These accounts differed from the national perspective of leading newspapers and journals employed so effectively in recent cultural histories. Local stories described how ordinary people experienced the fundamental change as American capitalism became corporate. My analysis demonstrates how, by the end of the nineteenth century, dramatic national events could alter the nature of everyday life. The rise of corporate capitalism redefined the meaning of working-class home ownership in Hammond and other industrial communities. By developing narratives of critical events, both local and national, I wish to examine, in this study, that redefinition and to generate conclusions based on the "accumulation of historical description" rather than on theoretical structures imported from the social sciences. Such a focus follows an important trend in social history, which seeks "to connect everyday experience to the large structures of historical analyses and major changes of the past."[41]

It is hoped that, when making these connections, the narrative will avoid the awkwardness that often results from shifts back and forth between analysis describing the larger forces at work in society and intimate stories describing how local persons encountered these forces.[42] To avoid confusion, I will summarize the argument, stating the purpose of each of the book's four parts.

Part 1 provides an overview of common house forms in metropolitan Chicago from 1830 to 1930. It establishes the pattern that will be studied throughout the remainder of the book by explaining the transition from cottages to bungalows. Initially, common houses derived from rural, New England forms. But two major transformations occurred with, first, the proliferation of urban cottage housing after 1869 and, second, the adoption of the bungalow as the most common form of new construction from 1915 to 1929. Detailed analysis of building components and construction techniques show that an expanding market for common structures spurred the most significant innovations in the housing market. These improvements occurred incrementally as common houses began to include an increasing range of amenities. The total effect was substantial. Over a period of seventy years, an ancient form of rural hall-and-parlor house evolved into a modern suburban bungalow.

Part 2 presents an analysis of the development of the cottage market in Hammond from 1869 to 1904. In these chapters, I employ a wide range of evidence to examine the social and cultural implications of home ownership among a German working-class population prior to the establishment of a dominant corporate culture. Initially, Hammond prospered because local investors committed resources to creating a town with commercial and residential interests separate from the largest employer. Their actions produced a town with widespread home ownership, especially among unskilled German workers. Under these conditions, the market for cottages created a bond between the local middle class and the majority working-class population, both of whom supported the town's independence from the dominant employer.[43]

This analysis places the housing market within the context of an American labor history that portrays nineteenth century industrial towns as centers for a native radicalism opposed to the growing power of corporate capital.[44] The third chapter examines these values by describing local politics and Hammond's participation in the Pullman strike. In its aftermath, the meaning of home ownership changed radically as the triumph of corporate capitalism limited the power of local communities to control their destinies. Despite heroic support for labor during the strike, Hammond leaders recognized that no city could expand and profit if it possessed a reputation as favorable to labor. Within the course of a decade, corporate capitalism had disciplined local capitalism. Local leaders became brokers between capital and labor in a society where widespread home ownership no longer united local citizens against the values of corporate culture.

Part 3, like Chapter 1, describes the experience of a very large population. It provides an overview of community life among Poles in Chicago from 1880 to 1939, showing how the transformation from cottages to bungalows affected the city's poorest communities. This account challenges directly the views of housing reformers who argued that a dangerous, unorganized working class threatened the social order. It contends that, despite the dominance of corporate capitalism, affordable housing remained a dynamic force for social change during the period when Midwestern cities attracted unprecedented numbers of immigrants from southern and eastern Europe. These immigrants experienced a poverty far more severe than did earlier German immigrants. Their arrival placed enormous strains on the housing market, which adapted traditional forms to accommodate new levels of poverty.

In addition, as Polish immigration increased, social differences arose between new Polish arrivals and more established members of the community. By the twentieth century, the high tide of immigration pushed Chicago Poles in two directions: toward greater crowding in tenements and toward dispersion to newer, more comfortable areas of the city. By 1939, a variety of conditions distinguished Polish-American neighborhoods in Chicago, which ranged from old tenement districts to prosperous neighborhoods of bungalows and modern two-flats. The creation of new neighborhoods and the adaptations of the market redefined Polish-American life in a manner that allowed the community to maintain ethnic allegiances despite increasing social division among its members.[45]

Part 4, develops an intimate case study, once again, to show how ordinary persons experienced a fundamental social change. These chapters draw on the particular experience of two generations of Poles in West Hammond, Illinois. When Poles arrived in West Hammond in the 1890s, they were an organized community that established a Catholic parish and a separate settlement, where houses were affordable and where immigrants could maintain their culture. Chapter 5 shows that widespread ownership of cottage housing led Poles to participate in local politics. The first generation learned that political success depended on ethnic allegiances and on bread-and-butter issues of taxation. Polish politicians could not depend on continued support from fellow Poles if officials did not provide desired services at a reasonable cost.

Chapter 6 argues that after 1915 a new generation of American-born leaders expanded the concept of citizenship among Poles to include notions of good government, patriotism, and civic improvement. In part, these concerns derived from the influence of public campaigns by native-born, middle-class Progressive reformers. To date, the history of progressivism retains a decidedly middle-class perspective. It describes a world without aspiring working-class home owners. But reformers never represented the interests of Polish home owners in cities like Chicago. In West Hammond, reform resulted from the second generation's desire to improve the quality of housing and urban life. Second-generation leaders promoted the development of a bungalow district that contained a more prosperous population, the majority of whom were not Polish. Indeed, poverty among recent Polish immigrants made reform especially difficult.

Nevertheless, Polish-American leaders succeeded in rebuilding the city in a manner that encouraged a broader concept of citizenship. Most notably, they increased city services, established a public park, and secured a new high school for the city. Analysis of the intimate experiences of a particular community provides insight into the relationship between first- and second-generation Polish-Americans. While most Poles lacked the full range of amenities common in the bungalow districts, the children of even recent immigrants benefitted from the recreational and educational opportunities provided by a new civic culture, a culture unavailable to Poles before 1915.

The transformation from cottages to bungalows was part of a larger process of social change that brought respectability to groups in various cities throughout the United States. Critics often have dismissed the importance of modest respectability. Typically, they have argued that increasing levels of comfort promoted a materialism that destroyed a radical potential within society. They have viewed abundance as the product of "dominant elites—white, male, educated, affluent"—who employed the powers of advertising to make mass consumption "a cultural ideal" and "a hegemonic way of seeing."[46] More recently, Lizabeth Cohen has demonstrated that, contrary to usual assumptions, mass culture allowed workers to overcome racial and ethnic fragmentation and to mount effective political action by creating a common working-class culture.[47] Her work provides a counterweight to studies of mass culture from a decidedly middle-class point of view.

Unfortunately, it continues to be difficult to demonstrate even fundamental changes in attitudes of people who did not leave written records. Analysis of material evidence, especially the built environment, allows historians to penetrate the silence. Housing provides evidence of changes in everyday life as a diverse society embraced new forms of capitalism and developed complex identities as workers, home owners, and citizens.[48] To exploit this evidence, historians must reconsider the manner in which they present evidence. The images in this book do not illustrate ideas derived from the analysis of written texts. Instead, they serve as proof for my argument, communicating ideas that words do not adequately convey.

While this study employs new evidence, it addresses a traditional historical debate concerning the exercise of power and authority. Improvements for groups like the Poles were modest. Hard work, perseverance, and a booming economy allowed them to purchase houses, create decent lives, and sometimes achieve a level of comfort. Certainly, the virtues of immigrant life can be exaggerated. Even well-meaning people become sanctimonious when describing a social mobility that results from hard work. The immigrant working class was never independent. They were subject to the influence of elites, especially to coercion by employers and talented advertisers, and their well-being depended on a booming industrial economy over which they had no control. But much will be lost if we forget that at the beginning of the twentieth century there existed two dynamic cultures: one organized and increasingly national, led by educated middle-class professionals who were literate, and the other local and private, which allowed working-class immigrants a freedom to build houses, establish their cultures, participate in city government, and improve their condition.

The clash between cultures, one stressing management and order and the other freedom and opportunity, was a basic element in the development of industrial cities during the first decades of the twentieth century. The divisions were never reconciled. Even the most notable achievements seemed bargains with the devil.[49] Nevertheless, both cultures shared a common desire. They wished to create a positive vision of the American city. I argue that such a vision depended on a housing market that offered the working class increasing opportunities for a respectable life. The desire to improve their condition encouraged immigrant populations to overcome parochialism so they might achieve greater security and modest comfort. In pursuing these goals, immigrants broadened appreciably the concept of respectability, of who deserved recognition as a worthy member of society. The purchase and improvement of a house extended to new and different peoples the benefits of the cultural revolution that began in the nineteenth century when refinement first spread to the middle levels of society. To understand this achievement, historians must overcome bias and look closely at the material culture of everyday life and the role it played in allowing for a more tolerant society.

PART ONE

THE EVOLUTION OF COMMON HOUSE FORMS

CHAPTER I

The Evolution of Construction Practice and House Forms in Chicago, 1830–1930

A popular myth suggests that in 1833 a Chicago carpenter "invented" the balloon frame and revolutionized construction practice.[1] When the myth originated, the "first" balloon-frame structure no longer existed except in photographs that revealed little about its construction. But even if the building remained in pristine condition, it would prove nothing. This myth of a sudden invention resulted from a failure to interpret properly the origins of common housing. Individually, simple structures possess little historical value. One house does not provide sufficient evidence to tell a story. Common houses acquire historical value collectively and in sequence. When placed in a larger context, they form a linked series of events that demonstrates how builders responded to problems over time.[2]

For most of the nineteenth century, builders worked within a narrow field of problems, limited by what was known and available locally. Most builders did not strive to invent new forms and establish themselves as creative individuals. Instead, they solved problems by asking a simple question: What must I do to make what I know fit my needs?

Circumstances seldom required a builder to rethink the manner in which he worked.[3] So invention occurred incrementally, over the long haul, as people offered minor solutions to simple problems.[4] Under these conditions, construction practice evolved slowly, with the process accelerating after 1870 as builders struggled to meet the demands of an expanding urban market. As Chicago grew, the demand for large numbers of simple houses led to innovations in construction practice, real estate development, and the manufacture of building components. When combined, these innovations produced the bungalow, Chicago's first modern, urban house form. This chapter examines the transformation, as a traditional rural form evolved into a modern house.

Construction Practice in Illinois

Few structures built before 1850 exist within the city limits of Chicago. Fortunately, many remain near Chicago in the western suburbs along the DuPage and DesPlaines rivers. One of the oldest structures was a Tavern built along the plank road between Naperville and Chicago for one of Chicago's earliest settlers, Mark Beaubien (fig. 8).[5] The Beaubien Tavern occupies a position near the beginning of the sequence that defines construction practice in northern Illinois.[6] It employed a type of box frame common after the middle of the eighteenth century. These frames simplified construction by eliminating portions of the handwork associated with the traditional timber frame.[7]

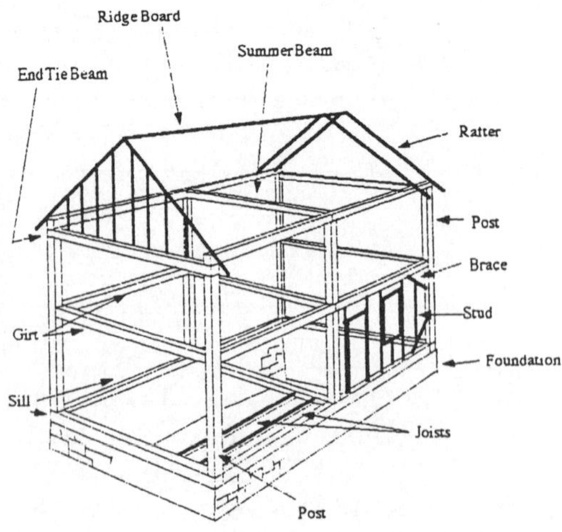

Figure 8
Beaubien Tavern and framing diagram. (Sources: author and "Beaubien Inn and Tollhouse Historic Structures Report," available at the Lisle Station Historical Park, Lisle, Ill.)

Aesthetically, the box frame was inferior to the heavily carpentered frames of eighteenth-century New England, which fascinated architectural historians early in this century. Documenting construction of these houses required elegant drawings to convey the talent of skilled carpenters who joined timbers of different sizes at various complex angles.[8] In contrast, the tavern's timbers were standard eight-by-eight, hand-hewn oak timbers joined by the simplest mortises and tenons. The tavern roof did not contain a timber. Instead, it employed a system of much smaller common rafters held in place by nails rather than joinery. The roof of the tavern simply rested on the lower portion of the frame. The rafters and top post were not joined intimately as they were in an older, more complex timber frame.

With its simplified frame and modest embellishment, the Beaubien Tavern lacked the aesthetic qualities of a romanticized eighteenth-century craftsmanship.[9] It resembled closely the standardized braced frame described in twentieth-century builders' guides (see fig. 9). The evidence shows that long before arriving in Illinois,

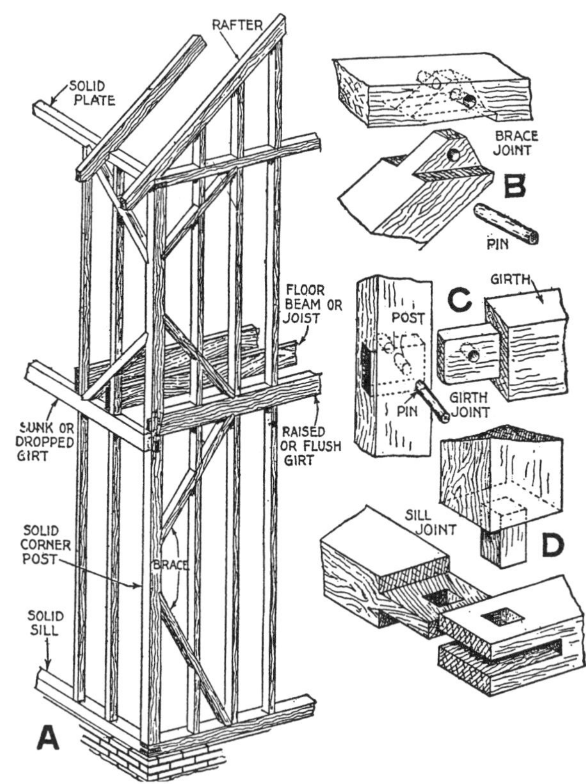

Figure 9
Braced frame, 1923. (Source: Frank D. Graham and Thomas J. Emery, *Audels Carpenters and Builders Guide: A Practical Illustrated Trade Assistant on Modern Construction for Carpenters-Joiners-Builders-Mechanics and All Wood Workers*, 4 vols. [New York: Theodore Audel & Co., 1923], 3:866.)

carpenters had simplified construction by standardizing structural components and eliminating complex joinery, especially in the framing of roofs.[10]

But simplification involved more than framing. By 1830, the manufacture of cast-iron stoves eliminated the need to build large masonry fireplaces.[11] Houses in northern Illinois were heated with stoves. Thomas C. Hubka described the significance of stoves when he compared two houses in North Yarmouth, Maine—one built in 1790, the other in 1857. The older structure contained a central chimney and derived its plan from the standard New England colonial residence, the hall-and-parlor house. The second house eliminated the fireplace, freeing the builder from the constraints imposed by a massive chimney at the center of the structure. Stoves were a more significant innovation than any change in framing practice, for the use of stoves allowed builders to reconfigure the floor plan of the common house by locating the kitchen in an attached ell away from the other rooms.[12]

During the first decades of settlement, most common residences in northern Illinois were traditional hall-and-parlor houses.[13] But they were built with balloon frames and were heated with stoves. Two houses built in Naperville in 1833 and 1834 by New Hampshire native John Stevens offer fine examples.[14] The smaller house was a one-story building with two rooms: a kitchen and a bedroom (fig. 10). The second structure was a four-room house of one-and-one-half stories (fig. 11). The first floor had a kitchen, bedroom, and a simple

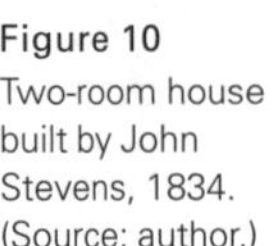

Figure 10
Two-room house built by John Stevens, 1834. (Source: author.)

Figure 11 George Martin house by John Stevens, 1833. (Source: Genevieve Towsley, *A View of Historic Naperville: A Collection of Articles of Historic Significance from the Sky-Lines,* rev. ed. [Naperville, Ill.: Naperville Sun, 1979], 19. Courtesy Sun Publications/Copley Newspapers.)

stairway that provided access to bedrooms on the second story. Neither structure included a large masonry chimney, and both were of balloon-frame construction.[15] They were built about the time a Chicago carpenter supposedly "invented" the balloon frame. More likely, carpenters came to Illinois with a repertoire that included the ability to construct both balloon and timber frames. Carpenters selected the method suited to the job.[16] Public buildings and elaborate houses allowed for more substantial construction, as witnessed by the Beaubien Tavern.[17] But a balloon frame sufficed for a simple farmhouse.

Typically, historians have conveyed the idea of a balloon frame with a single image copied from a carpentry how-to book.[18] But one image cannot account for the various practices common among carpenters during a transitional period of building that lasted from 1830 to about 1880. At first, a minimal difference existed between balloon frames, like the Stevens's houses, and box frames, like the one used for the Beaubien Tavern. In the tavern, timber girts supported second-story floor joists. They were tenoned, pinned, and braced to mortised corner posts. Stevens eliminated the timbers, mortises, and tenons for the girts by nailing a one-by-four-inch board called a ledger or ribband into vertical studs that ran continuously the height of the building (cf. figs. 9 and 12). The studs were notched so that the ledger fit into them. Joists for the second floor were also notched so they could hook on the ledger. The joists were then nailed to the studs.

While significant, a ledger was not a radically new idea. In seventeenth-century Virginia, carpenters employed a similar method

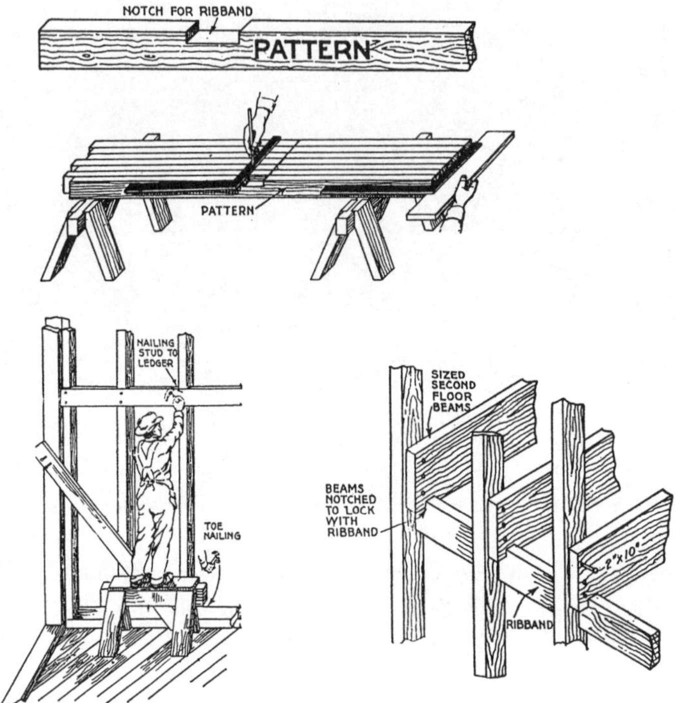

Figure 12 Marking studs, nailing the ribband, and placing second-floor joists. (Source: Frank D. Graham and Thomas J. Emery, *Audels Carpenters and Builders Guide: A Practical Illustrated Trade Assistant on Modern Construction for Carpenters-Joiners-Builders-Mechanics and All Wood Workers*, 4 vols. [New York: Theodore Audel & Co., 1923], 3:914, 916, 917.)

during a period when the fastest and simplest means of construction replaced the traditional, fully carpentered house.[19] Most important, carpenters in Illinois continued to use timber sills for fifty years.[20] These sills were elements of the traditional timber frame. Just as in the Beaubien Tavern, the sills were mortised, tenoned, and pinned together. Because of the large size of timber sills, floor joists and studs could not be nailed to them. So carpenters cut a simple tenon into every joist and stud just as they did in the tavern. The tenons fit into individual pockets cut in the sills: studs horizontally, joists vertically (fig. 13). The process was simple but consumed time.

Whatever the method, carpenters could not reduce drastically the handwork necessary for framing and finishing a house. Carpenters still used hand tools to produce their own windows, doors, and trim. Making component parts defined much of the rural carpenter's trade. During the winter, he spent time in his shop preparing components for the next building season.[21] (See fig. 14.) Of all the carpenter's work, the products of his shop are least likely to survive. Typically, frames remained intact despite remodeling and numerous additions. But interiors were gutted, the trim discarded. Fortunately, a

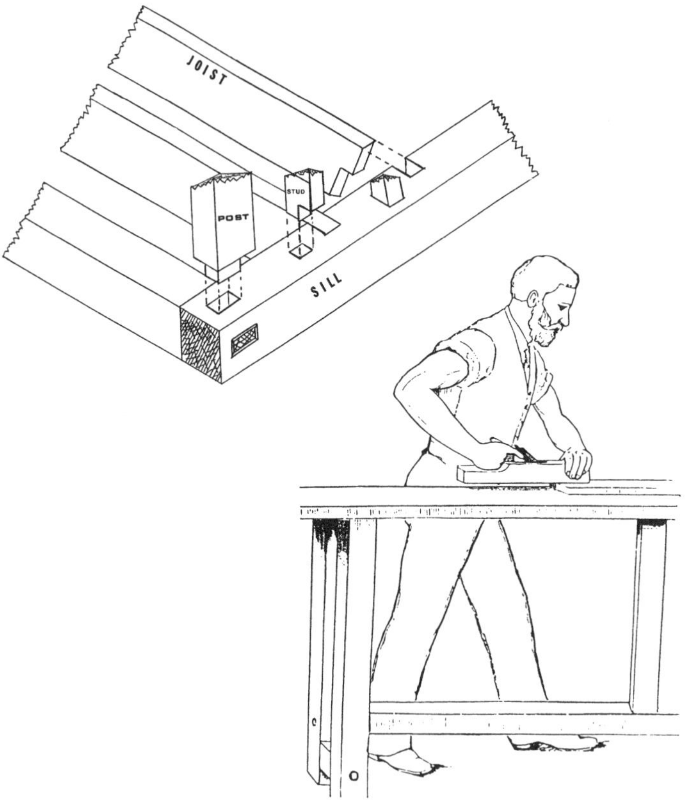

Figure 13
Timber sills with mortises; studs and floor joists with tenons. (Source: author.)

Figure 14
Hand-planing a board. (Source: Industrial School Association, *Wood-Working Tools: How to Use Them: A Manual* [Boston: D. C. Heath, 1887], 28.)

few interiors survive intact. The Murray House at Naper Settlement Museum Village provides a critical example for defining construction practice in northern Illinois prior to 1850.

John Murray was a lawyer in 1842 when the house was built in a common New England style (fig. 15). Like the Beaubien Tavern, the house employed a timber frame with stoves for heat. Prior to 1860, a one-and-one-half-story, two-room-deep house conveyed social distinction.[22] The size of the house and the local carpenter's handwork set it apart from its neighbors. Distinctions appeared in major features, such as the formal doorway and entry hall, as well as in smaller details, such as the hand-planed exterior corner boards (see figs. 16 and 41). The entry hall provided access to the first floor rooms, which included a parlor, a bedroom, a large kitchen, and a law office. A local carpenter made the baseboards, doors, windows, and trim for these rooms.[23] But the second-floor bedrooms remained unfinished when the building was first occupied.

Figure 15
Murray house exterior view, Naper Settlement, Naperville, Illinois. (Source: author; courtesy of Naper Settlement.)

Figure 16
Murray house: formal hall, Naper Settlement, Naperville, Illinois. (Source: author; courtesy of Naper Settlement.)

During the first decades of settlement, buildings reflected the skills of local carpenters, who created a wide range of structures, mostly simple three- and four-room houses. Before 1860, most of these structures contained only traces of the detailed work present in the Murray house. Most builders economized by eliminating handwork whenever possible. Carpenters smoothed only the front siding for a house and laid the remainder rough.[24] They built a ladder rather than stairs to provide access to a second story and constructed panel doors only for the front of the house and parlor, using unfinished batten doors for the remainder. Refinements came piece by piece. Most improvements were minor—for example, converting a two-room house that resembled the Stevens's house into a three-room structure (figs. 10 and 17). But additions could transform simple buildings into complex houses. In 1861 a common two-room house built by the

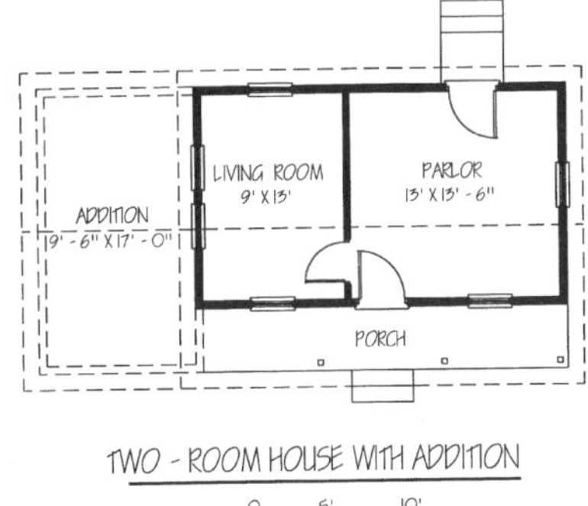

Figure 17
Converted three-room house and floor plan. (Source: author.)

Joseph Naper family received a major addition, a new wing that added a parlor and bedroom on the first floor and bedrooms on the second floor (fig. 18). Soon after, another addition increased even further the size of this once diminutive house.

The Stevens and Naper houses were examples of the New England influence writ large on the Midwestern landscape.[25] These structures evolved from hall-and-parlor houses to a form known as the upright-and-wing, the dominant rural house of the upper Midwest. This form derived from adding onto structures and transforming simple rectangular houses into buildings with a T- or L-shape. Over time, the upright-and-wing became a single, integral unit built from scratch and no longer the result of additions.[26] Variations of the upright-and-wing accommodated families from the modest to the prosperous (see fig. 19). Its popularity contributed greatly to the spread of genteel

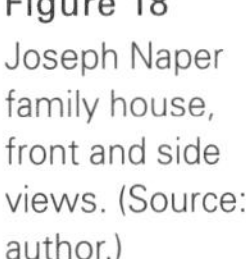

Figure 18
Joseph Naper family house, front and side views. (Source: author.)

Figure 19
R. Rathbun residence, DuPage County. (Source: Thompson Brothers & Burr, *Combination Atlas Map of DuPage County, Illinois* [Elgin, Ill.: Thompson Brothers & Burr, 1874], 111.)

manners throughout the middle levels of society, as increasing numbers of families added parlors to their houses, demonstrating that a measure of refinement was within reach.[27]

For most families, advances were limited so long as improvements depended on the handwork of local carpenters. In Naperville, carpenters did not confront the pressure to build rapidly as their counterparts would later, when urban populations doubled and tripled in a decade. Consequently, when local carpenters altered buildings, they produced irregularities. Figure 20 shows a peculiar method for splicing the studs of an interior wall in the Naper house, while figure 21 shows that the first addition did not include exterior sheathing. The carpenter nailed siding directly to the studs. The omission of sheathing reduced the structural integrity of the frame as well as the ability of the house to withstand weather. More important, it demonstrates the eccentricities of a rural market that had simplified but not standardized construction.

Factory-Produced Millwork and Component Parts

The finished qualities of common houses improved once factory products replaced the handwork of local carpenters. Of course, carpenters relied on sawmills as "the first essential of civilization."[28] But

Figure 20
Naper family house, spliced studs. (Source: author.)

Figure 21
Naper family house, exterior wall without sheathing. (Source: author.)

prior to 1865, sawmills produced only rough goods, such as lumber, sheathing, siding, and flooring; local carpenters still required tool chests with numerous hand planes, saws, and chisels for constructing windows, doors, and trim.[29] Once Chicago became the center for lumber distribution in the Midwest, the demand for new construction provided incentive for capital investments in sash, door, and blind factories (see table 1). By 1880, factory products dramatically increased the supply of building components available to local carpenters. No longer limited by the output of their shops, they built houses that were more elaborate than the Murray residence. In Naperville, these houses appeared in a district easily distinguished from the older section of town. Within this district, wealthier residents adopted national styles of architecture, from the Italianate to Queen Anne.[30] These styles introduced discontinuity on the landscape, testifying to class differences of considerable magnitude.

Manufactured components were critical to an expanding, middle-class culture that prized the refinements of the parlor. Advertisers promoted refinements aggressively, leading historians to argue that the power of advertising "inculcat[ed] a new set of social values into the culture."[31] However, the transformation was neither sudden nor driven principally by the market for expensive goods. Machines did not produce the lavish items advertised in trade catalogs. Michael J. Ettema has shown that mechanization affected the simple tasks involved in preparing stock and joining parts. Intricate products such as high-style Victorian furniture remained the province

Table 1 Capital Investment, Cost of Labor, and Value of Product for Sash, Door, and Blind Manufacturers in 1860, 1870, and 1880

	Nation	**Cook Country**
1860:		
Establishments	986	13
Average capital investment per establishment ($)	5,496	2,048
Average cost materials per establishment ($)	4,022	1,668
Average number of emplyees per establishment	7.5	4.0
Average total wages per establishment ($)	2,785	1,326
Average wage per worker($)	371	332
Average value of product per establishment ($)	9,664	4,362
1870:		
Establishments	1,605	17
Average capital investment per establishment ($)	13,234	18,782
Average cost materials per establishment ($)	10,954	22,041
Average number of employees per establishment	12.7	31.1
Average total wages per establishment ($)	6,268	17,914
Average wage per worker ($)	494	577
Average value of product per establishment ($)	22,446	51,444
1880:		
Establishments	1,288	30
Average capital investment per establishment ($)	15,883	41,435
Average cost materials per establishment ($)	16,142	55,222
Average number of employees per establishment	17.0	67.3
Average total wages per establishment ($)	6,631	27,008
Average wage per worker ($)	390	401
Average value of product per establishment ($)	28,433	99,242

Source: Department of the Interior, *Manufactures of the United States in 1860; Compiled from the Original Returns of the Eighth Census, under the Direction of the Secretary of the Interior* (Washington, D.C.: Government Printing Office, 1865), 87, 740, and *The Statistics of the Wealth and Industry of the United States, Embracing the Tables of Wealth, Taxation, and Public Indebtedness; of Agriculture; Manufactures; Mining; and the Fisheries* (Washington, D.C.: Government Printing Office, 1872), 473, 649; Joseph D. Weeks, Special Agent Tenth Census, Department of the Interior, Census Office, *Report on the Statistics of Wages in Manufacturing Industries; with Supplementary Reports on the Average Retail Prices of Necessaries of Life, and on Trades Societies, and Strikes and Lockouts* (Washington, D.C.: Government Printing Office, 1886), 70, 213.

of skilled workers with hand tools. High-priced goods set trends and served as models for less expensive items. But common goods were the bulk of the trade. They resulted from a new system of design that manufactured simple goods with the capabilities of machines in mind. This system responded to a market where more people could afford furniture.[32]

The manufacture of millwork resembled the manufacture of furniture. Skilled hands produced high-priced goods in small specialty shops that did custom work for hotels, restaurants, banks, offices, churches, and expensive houses.[33] But common doors, windows, flooring, and moldings were the bulk of the trade. Less costly as individual items, common goods were greater in total value due to the quantity of their manufacture. More than high styles, advertising, and whims of fashion, the large demand for simple goods led to capital investments in mechanized production. As early as 1881, Albert S. Bolles understood the importance of a market for common goods. He considered it "obvious that inventions are more likely to take place when the quantities handled are very large, than when but little is done from year to year. Thus if a few houses are built occasionally, the want of great facilities will not be so marked as when twenty hundred million feet of lumber is to be worked up every year for building purposes, mostly in the construction of dwellings."[34]

Bolles understood that high-volume, component manufacture required the subdivision of labor for each part of an object. He described insightfully the relationship between subdivision, demand for common products, and mechanization: "A pattern being once fixed upon, all the parts of that pattern are given out to workmen, who confine themselves each to the manufacturing of the part he undertakes. The parts so produced are made in the best manner. In this minute subdivision of labor, there is a constant tendency to resort to machinery, because that [*sic*] where there is a great demand to be supplied, the various parts can be produced more rapidly and in many cases more perfectly by machinery than by manual labor."[35]

Woodworking industries were the first to adopt systems of sequentially arranged machines that produced large quantities of standard parts for a common product. Again, progress was evolutionary rather than sudden and dramatic. As early as 1793, the Englishman Samuel Bentham patented general purpose planing, boring, molding, rebating, mortising, and sawing machines, as well as special purpose machines for producing window sash and carriage wheels. In 1803 at the Portsmouth Dockyards, Bentham and Marc Brunnel developed forty-three machines employed in sequential operations to produce 100,000 wooden pulleys required each year by the British Navy.[36] A jewel of British technology, this system anticipated the more complex armory practice that manufactured rifles for the American military.[37]

But private manufacturers lacked the resources of the British and American governments, and their markets were neither sufficiently large nor sufficiently stable to warrant capital investments for creating systems of sequentially arranged, special purpose machines. Consequently, manufacturers increased production by hiring more workers and employing inexpensive general purpose tools.[38] Since few woodworking industries employed water or steam power, these tools operated manually by foot pedals or hand levers with movements that resembled the hand tools they displaced.[39] A simple tenoning machine operated with two levers that engaged cutters that shaved wood like a rabbet plane. Inexpensive mortising machines employed a lever and chisel-like cutting tool. The tool formed a mortise by moving across a firmly secured workpiece with a harsh reciprocating action (fig. 22). Sash, door, and blind factories employed machines to cut mortises and tenons because they were the nuts and bolts of joinery, essential for creating rigid frames. Simple, manually powered machines remained common among small manufacturers into the twentieth century.[40] But larger concerns introduced steam-powered machines to meet increasing demand. When accommodating these machines, woodworking industries confronted fundamental problems with shafting, bearings, gearing, machine placement, and work sequences. Manufacturers adapted or redesigned general purpose machines to produce standard parts such as door panels and window sash more rapidly.[41] However, sash, door, and blind factories also purchased

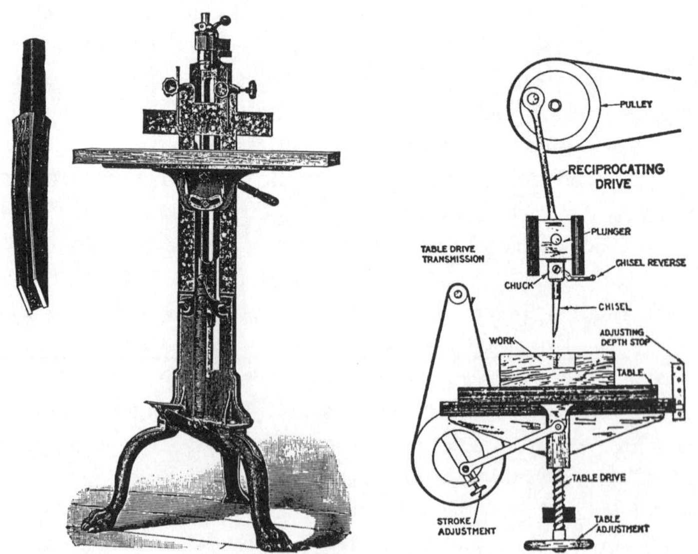

Figure 22
Foot-powered mortiser. (Source: Frank D. Graham and Thomas J. Emery, *Audels Carpenters and Builders Guide: A Practical Illustrated Trade Assistant on Modern Construction for Carpenters-Joiners-Builders-Mechanics and All Wood Workers,* 4 vols. [New York: Theodore Audel & Co., 1923], 4:1,466.)

Figure 23
Sash sticking machine. (Source: "Sash Sticking Machine," *Carpentry and Building* [April 1893], xxii.)

special purpose machines (fig. 23) from established tool companies who sold their products to manufacturers throughout the industry.[42]

By 1876, Greenlee Brothers and Company of Chicago manufactured various machines to perform specific tasks for making windows and doors. These machines no longer mimicked hand tools. The company's tenoning machine employed circular saws set at right angles, an arrangement faster and more accurate than earlier designs that resembled chisels (fig. 24). Clamping machines employed a treadle to engage a series of clamps that trued and joined windows and doors. The machine reduced the time required for fitting and assembling each piece. The most ingenious machine was a mortiser capable

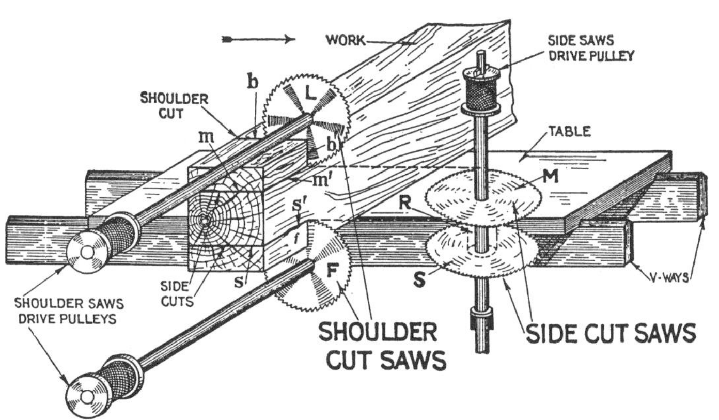

Figure 24
Circular saw and rotary tenoners. (Source: Frank D. Graham and Thomas J. Emery, *Audels Carpenters and Builders Guide: A Practical Illustrated Trade Assistant on Modern Construction for Carpenters-Joiners-Builders-Mechanics and All Wood Workers*, 4 vols. [New York: Theodore Audel & Co., 1923], 4:1,476, 1,480.)

of boring a square hole. The machine combined a high-quality tool-steel hollow chisel with a high speed auger bit (fig. 25).[43] The bit removed the space for the mortise while the chisel squared the hole. The design eliminated the jarring action of earlier mortising machines.

According to *Industrial Chicago*, capital investments in new machines and work sequences allowed for "a very superior and greatly improved class of goods."[44] Edward W. Byrn claimed that prior to mechanization, dwellings of the middle and poorer classes were crudely made with "uncouth and clumsy doors, windows and blinds." He argued that mechanization democratized the decorative arts so that "to-day nearly every cottage has beautifully molded trimmings, paneled doors, handsomely carved mantels and turned balusters, all furnished at an insignificant price."[45] While exaggerated, Byrn's point was valid. The supply of finished building components increased tremendously once manufacturers replaced the skills of craftsmen with the precision of machines.

Nevertheless, the nature of markets limited mechanization in most woodworking industries. Furniture makers confronted constant

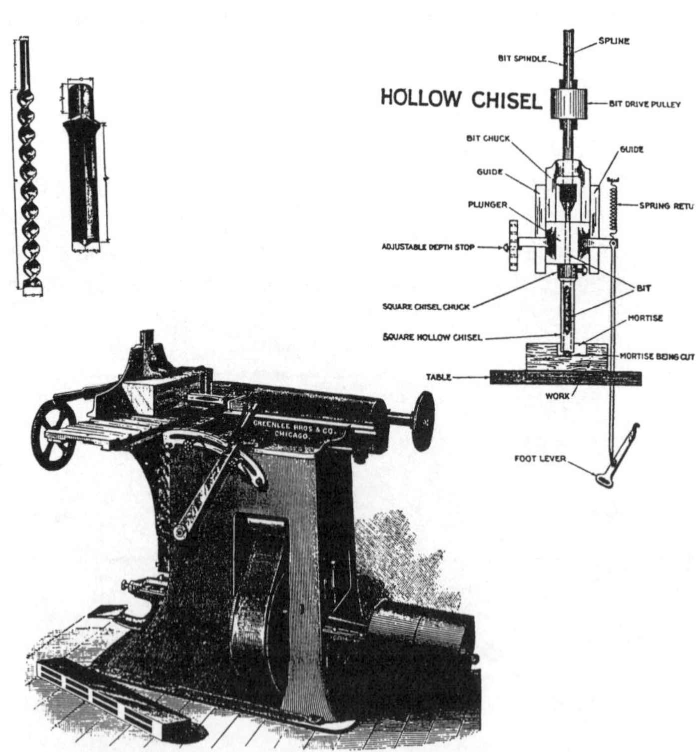

Figure 25 Core-boring hollow chisel mortiser. (Sources: "Core-Boring Hollow Chisel Mortiser," *Carpentry and Building* [December 1886], 235; Frank D. Graham and Thomas J. Emery, *Audels Carpenters and Builders Guide: A Practical Illustrated Trade Assistant on Modern Construction for Carpenters-Joiners-Builders-Mechanics and All Wood Workers*, 4 vols. [New York: Theodore Audel & Co., 1923], 4:1,469.)

shifts in fashion. To meet consumer demands, they created varied product lines that changed frequently. Under these conditions, even the most advanced manufacturers never justified costly investments in special purpose tools because they never produced a large quantity of a standardized product for a long period of time. Manufacturers sacrificed economies of scale for a flexible system of manufacture capable of responding to changing fashions with greater scope and versatility.[46] Fashion affected the manufacture of building components less than it did furniture. But the industry adopted flexible systems because of frequent booms and busts in building cycles. In boom times, Chicago factories could not satisfy local demand. As winter approached, demand subsided and sometimes collapsed when building did not resume the following spring. In so volatile a market, manufacturers considered it risky to invest too much capital in expensive systems of special purpose tools for quantity manufacture.[47] It was safer to hire workers when the product was in demand and release workers when demand subsided.[48] Just as in the furniture industry, manufacturers sacrificed economies of scale for systems adapted to the fits and starts of the market.

In addition, as lumbering depleted the forests of Michigan and Wisconsin, the production of building materials shifted to southern and western states.[49] The result was a complex industry that defied easy generalization. Urban manufacturers continued to produce windows, doors, and trim. But production fluctuated dramatically. In Chicago, between 1890 and 1900, the annual value of product for planing mills and sash, door, and blind factories fell from $17,604,494 to $7,350,387 as production shifted to smaller cities in Wisconsin, Michigan, and Iowa.[50] By the twentieth century, clear distinctions emerged between centers for the production of lumber and centers for remanufacture. During the 1920s, southern and western lumber accounted for half the total value of product for all planing mills. Washington state produced and also remanufactured lumber. But even large southern companies seldom produced windows, doors, and other forms of millwork. So despite the decline of the Midwestern lumber industry, Iowa and Wisconsin retained niches and continued to manufacture millwork.[51]

The result was a decentralized industry that adjusted to booms and busts of building cycles. Certainly, some manufacturers became substantial. By 1916, the catalog for the M. A. Disbrow Company of Clinton, Iowa, advertised a wide variety of products, from simple windows, doors, and trim to very elaborate staircases. But Disbrow did not manufacture all the products it sold. To create a comprehensive catalog, the company depended on thirty-five suppliers scattered throughout the United States.[52] By 1920 the Gordon-Van Tine Company of Davenport, Iowa, produced a catalog of 117 house designs for precut houses. Like Aladdin Homes, its Michigan competitor, Gordon-Van Tine claimed to provide better building materials for lower cost by the use of scientific methods for design and assembly. But precut houses never accounted for more than half the firm's business. Most sales were individual orders for lumber, hardware, sash, doors, and trim. The company was primarily a large wholesaler with mills in Washington and Mississippi and factories for remanufacturing and assembly in Iowa and Missouri.[53]

Despite limitations, the manufacture of building products affected carpentry profoundly. Carpenters debated the effects of an increasing subdivision of labor as inside carpenters produced doors, windows, and trim in factories while outside carpenters relied on these products to build a house at a specific site.[54] Given these conditions, *Carpentry and Building* warned that "no man is safe in his trade knowing only one thing. He may be a house joiner of exceptional ability, and having met with success in his trade for a term of years, feels secure. But a change occurs, and . . . he is displaced by men who are his inferiors."[55] Others welcomed the division of labor arguing that it spurred invention, allowed for greater output of higher quality, and, most important, allowed employers to avoid paying skilled labor for commonplace work.[56]

In 1880 a carpenter from Quincy, Illinois, claimed that builders would lose money making their own doors, sash, blinds, moldings, and stairs. A better and cheaper job resulted when builders purchased millwork from a factory and then hired separate classes of men to install it. Less skilled men could do the same work more efficiently by concentrating on a single task, such as laying shingle or hanging doors.[57] *Carpentry and Building* even suggested that new machinery and the subdivision of labor benefitted the trade by doing away with antiquated forms of apprenticeship. The journal suggested that a ready supply of factory products eliminated "the drudgery with which apprentices used to be charged and bored, resulting in a loss of much of their time without learning anything. The world has found out that it is much better to keep boys at school a longer time, when, after having received a more complete education, they will on entering a modern shop at a maturer age, learn more of the business in three months than very young apprentices in former times learned in three years."[58]

Streamlined construction also provoked debates about common building methods. In August of 1885, a Canadian carpenter, Thomas Sorby, argued for a "rough-and-ready" construction that employed lumber "brought to the site ready for immediate fixing" and eliminated skilled labor and hand tools other than a saw and hammer.[59] Like most advocates of a simplified frame, he suggested traditional practices were unnecessary, remnants of what Solon Robinson called "old-foggeyism."[60] For example, Sorby considered it foolish to notch the joists over the ledger board for "there is little practical advantage to be gained by this great accession of labor."[61] Yet, as late as 1923, *Audels Carpenters and Builders Guide* insisted that the omission of notches in second-floor joists "cannot be too strongly condemned."[62] (See figs. 26 and 27.) These lingering debates testified to variations in practice that occurred for two generations after the introduction of the balloon frame in northern Illinois.

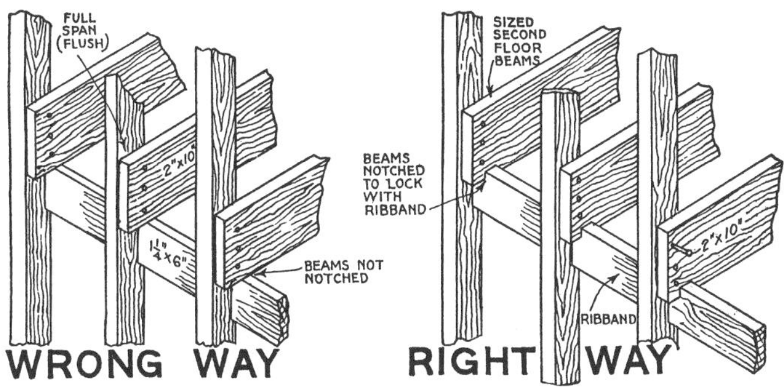

Figure 26
Notched second-floor joists. (Source: Frank D. Graham and Thomas J. Emery, *Audels Carpenters and Builders Guide: A Practical Illustrated Trade Assistant on Modern Construction for Carpenters-Joiners-Builders-Mechanics and All Wood Workers*, 4 vols. [New York: Theodore Audel & Co., 1923], 3:917.)

Figure 27
Lyman Bridges' ready-made house. (Source: Lyman Bridges Company, *Illustrated Catalogue: Lyman Bridges Building Materials and Ready-Made Houses* [Chicago: Rand McNally, 1870].)

Despite these variations, the examination of old structures in neighborhoods throughout metropolitan Chicago revealed that a significant change occurred after 1880. Over a period of ten years, carpenters throughout Chicago accepted manufactured components and a more streamlined balloon frame that replaced timber sills with box sills of dimensional lumber. Before 1880, even manufactured houses were balloon frames with mortised timber sills and tenoned studs and joists. (See figs. 27 and 13.) These structures resembled the balloon frames built in Naperville in the 1830s. By 1889, the T. H. Harvey Lumber Company manufactured a balloon frame of all-nail construction using only standard dimensional lumber and boards. The sills and joists were two-by-eights, butt-jointed and nailed, the simplest of processes (see fig. 28). Carpenters no longer cut a mortise and tenon for each stud and floor joist. These two illustrations demonstrate wonderfully the change in carpentry following increased

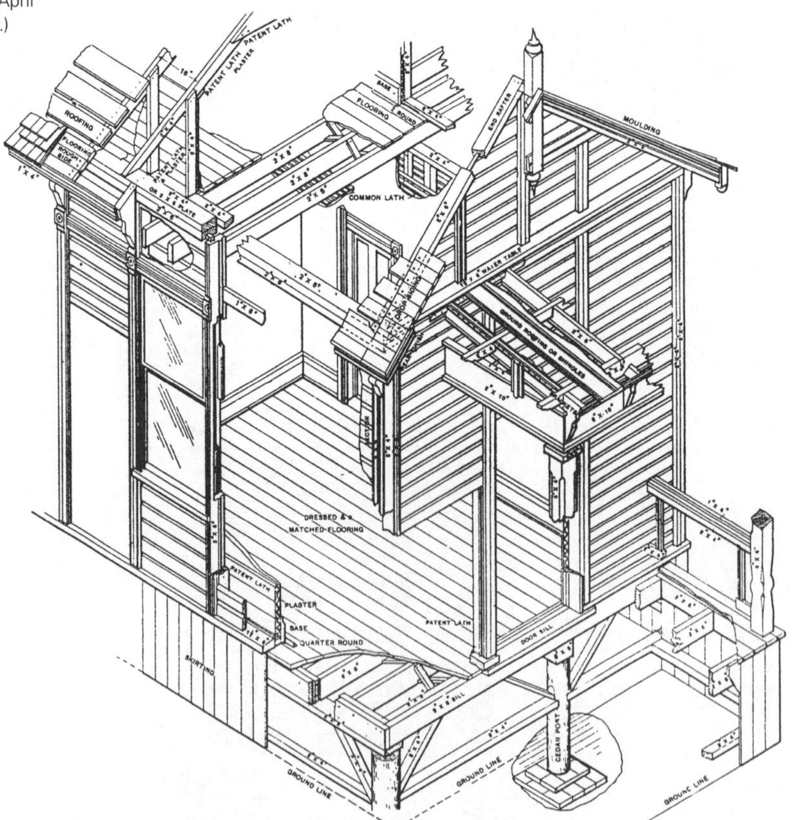

Figure 28
T. H. Harvey's ready-made house. (Source: "Ready Made Houses," *Carpentry and Building* [April 1889], 67.)

capital investment in planing mills and sash, door, and blind factories. Harvey's ready-made house signaled the coming together of standardized building components, manufactured millwork, and simplified construction practice. It was the product of both the sawmill and the factory.

Indeed, Turlington Harvey's career as a Chicago lumberman paralleled the advent of modern construction methods. Harvey arrived in the city in 1854 when he was nineteen. Quickly, he became foreman at the city's largest sash, door, and blind factory. Within five years, he established a small planing mill that developed into one of the city's largest lumberyards with capital stock valued at $1 million. By 1880, the company owned 40,000 acres of pine lands in Michigan and Wisconsin, with mills at Marinette, Wisconsin, and four sailing vessels. The firm occupied 2,400 feet of dock in Chicago's lumber district, where it operated ten planers powered by a 250-horsepower engine. These machines dressed 300,000 feet of lumber a day, while ten kilns dried from 50,000 to 75,000 feet.[63] In 1887, the firm established a construction department with a factory for producing trim and woodwork for Chicago and its suburbs. Harvey specialized in large contracts of "ready-made houses" promising to "furnish on short notice lots ranging from 10 to 100 houses of one kind."[64]

The demand for common buildings created opportunities to establish larger, more highly mechanized, capital-intensive manufacture as the Harvey Company did. These manufacturers produced dimensional lumber with tighter tolerances. Prior to 1880, two-by-eight floor joists varied considerably. One joist might measure seven and five-eighths inches and another eight and one-fourth. To adjust for differences, carpenters fitted each joist into a pocket cut in a timber sill.[65] After 1880, kiln-dried lumber varied only one-eighth inch in either direction, allowing carpenters to place the joists on a dimensional lumber sill without fitting and still achieve a relatively smooth surface for the floor above.[66]

The accumulated innovation of fifty years prepared Chicago to meet the demand for housing during the great real estate boom of the 1880s. Advances in manufacture allowed for faster, cheaper, and higher quality construction. Rapid growth also forced wealthy citizens to recognize a social as well as an economic imperative to build. In 1890, Turlington Harvey organized a syndicate of investors to create the industrial suburb of Harvey, Illinois. In some respects, the town resembled the model community of Pullman, where industrialist George Pullman hired an architect to design an entire city built of brick and based on the principles of science and aesthetic harmony.

To achieve his goal, Pullman established a paternalistic order, securing better living conditions by granting corporate authorities power over most aspects of life. Pullman did not allow saloons in his model town nor did he permit employees to own houses. He believed the corporation provided best for the welfare of employees if it was both employer and landlord.[67]

Like Pullman, the Harvey syndicate intended to reshape the conditions under which people worked and lived by prohibiting saloons and establishing a well-equipped local government with a handsome commercial section (fig. 29). But the syndicate avoided autocratic rule by selling workers small lots and simple frame cottages (fig. 30). To encourage sales, the syndicate sought employers who promised to hire and retain home owners first. They promoted Harvey as a town offering full employment "in a well-regulated vil-

Figure 29 French block, Harvey, Illinois. (Source: Harvey Land Association, *The Town of Harvey, Illinois Manufacturing Suburb of Chicago Aged Two Years* [Chicago: Harvey Land Association, 1892].)

Figure 30 $500 cottage, Harvey, Illinois. (Source: Harvey Land Association, *The Town of Harvey, Illinois Manufacturing Suburb of Chicago Aged Two Years* [Chicago: Harvey Land Association, 1892].)

lage with all the modern conveniences made possible by waterworks, improved drainage, electric light and electric transit," as well as "absolute protection from the evils which spring from drinking places, gambling hells and low resorts."[68]

Most industrial towns were neither so paternal nor so pure. In an excellent study, Ann Durkin Keating showed how during the 1880s a new breed of aggressive developers became catalysts for shaping Chicago's real estate practices.[69] Short on cash and strong on nerve, they developed large tracts of land as quickly as possible. To do so, they created strategies for selling cheap lots to a working class hungry for property but short on cash. Unlike Harvey or Pullman, most syndicates did not pave streets, plant trees, or provide water and gas.[70] Development was haphazard, sometimes producing the horrors described by reformers. Typically, however, industrial towns occupied positions in between, exhibiting a range of advantages and disadvantages that shifted with time. None of these towns has received the attention Pullman has. While volumes have described the origins of the model town, no one has written of the great majority. But buildings endure, testifying to the range of circumstances that resulted as housing markets evolved from isolated and rural to concentrated and urban.

From Rural to Urban Forms

Even before 1880, urban working-class houses broke with the tradition of the hall-and-parlor house. In effect, builders turned the earlier rectangular form ninety degrees and located the front and rear doors on the narrow gable ends of the structure. Like the hall-and-parlor house, these cottages derived from New England, where side-hall houses of one-and-one-half stories with Greek Revival details became popular after 1830, most with front entry halls (figs. 31–33).[71] Similar houses with a front-gable entry appeared in Naperville, Joliet, and Lockport, Illinois, before 1850. They ranged from stylish to very plain (fig. 32).

In the western suburbs of Chicago, derivatives of the traditional rural upright-and-wing remained the dominant house form. Owners adapted front-gable houses as they had side-gabled, hall-and-parlor houses. The structure in figure 33 was built as a five-room, side-hall house for a German resident of Naperville in the 1870s. Soon afterward, the house was modified to an upright-and-wing. Traditional rural forms persisted even in western suburbs that became

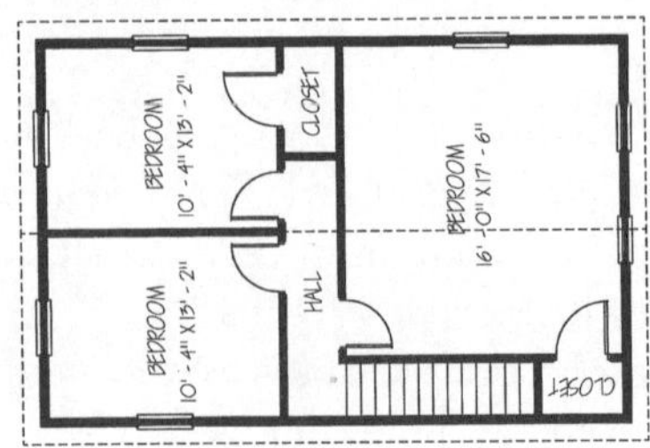

SECOND FLOOR PLAN

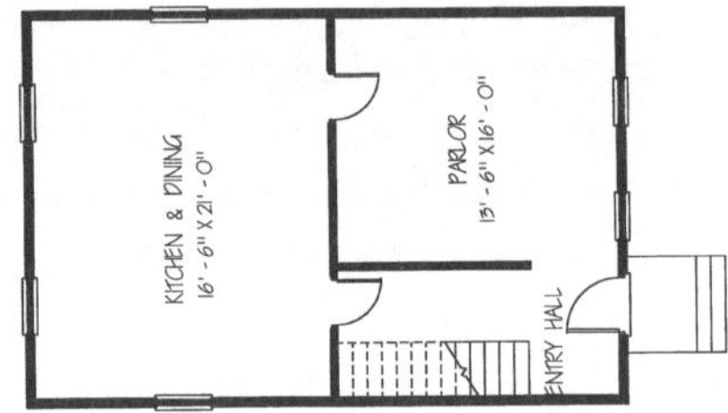

FIRST FLOOR PLAN

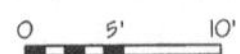

Figure 31 *(top left & right)* Side-hall house and floor plan, Naperville. (Source: author.)

Figure 32 *(center left & right)* Side-hall houses, Naperville. (Source: author.)

Figure 33 *(bottom right)* Adapted side-hall house, Naperville. (Source: author.)

industrial. Polish immigrants in Lemont built very modest upright-and-wing houses of either three, four, or five rooms. The location of the stairway distinguished this form (fig. 34). Identical structures were built fifty miles south, near Kankakee in the rural community of Saint Anne, Illinois (fig. 35).

Rural forms persisted for good reason. Compared with the one-story cottage, hall-and-parlor houses offered larger rooms for a

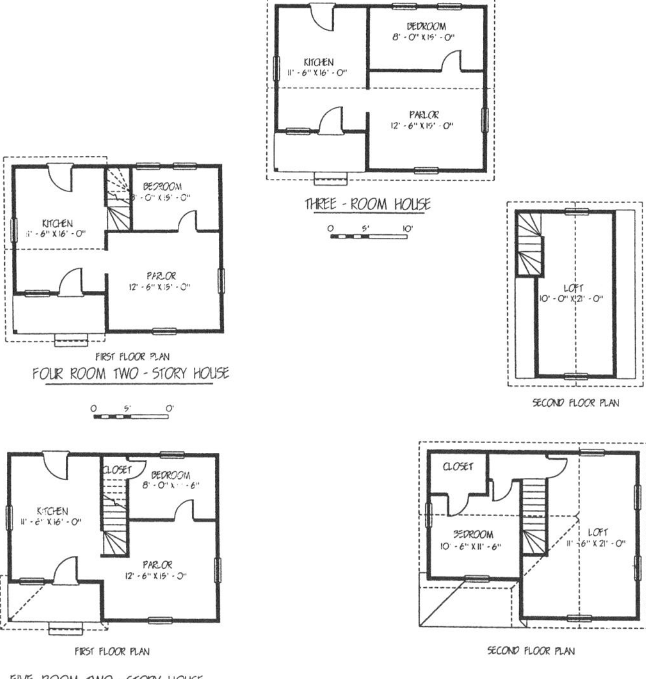

Figure 34 Upright-and-wing floor plans, Lemont, Illinois. (Source: author.

Figure 35 *(bottom left & right)* Upright-and-wing, St. Anne, Illinois. (Source: author.)

given amount of space, as seen by a comparison of a twelve-by-twenty-four-foot hall-and-parlor house with an eighteen-by-thirty-foot cottage (fig. 36). The comparison raises questions of economy. The expense of building a stairway and second floor was probably less than the cost of constructing a larger one-story building to contain an equal number of rooms. But in most working-class neighborhoods, standard lots measured twenty-five by 125 feet. Only the smallest hall-and-parlor house fit on a typical urban lot since the long end of the house faced the street. The Poles who settled in Lemont lived in upright-and-wing houses because their lots were fifty feet wide. However, in urban neighborhoods where land was expensive and lots were narrow, it made economic sense to place the shorter gable end of the house toward the street and to build a longer, single-story structure without a staircase. Cottages became the dominant housing form for Chicago's working class because they accommodated narrow city lots.

In 1870 the Lyman Bridges Company manufactured a range of houses that demonstrated the variations among cottages.[72] Most

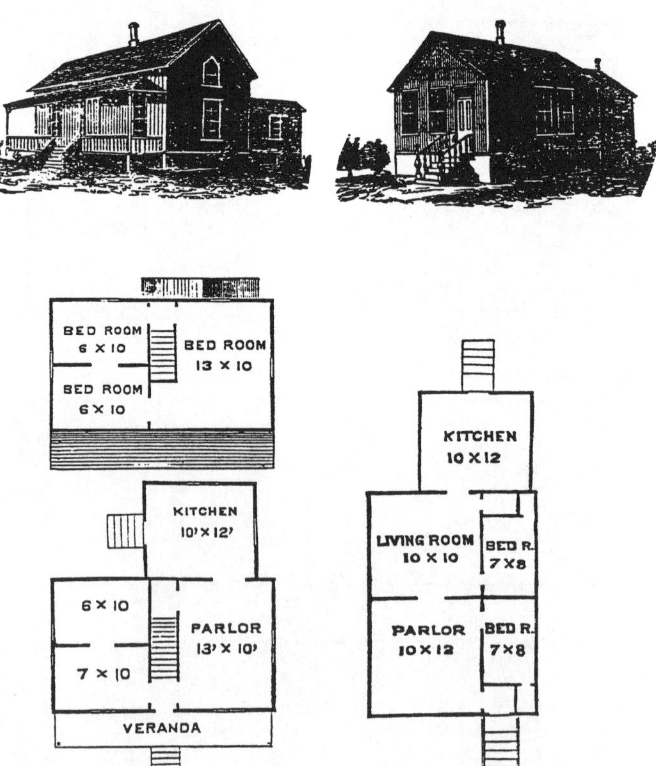

Figure 36
Comparison of a hall-and-parlor house with a cottage. (Source: Lyman Bridges Company, *Illustrated Catalogue: Lyman Bridges Building Materials and Ready-Made Houses* [Chicago: Rand McNally, 1870].)

cottages were one-story structures of four, five, or six rooms (fig. 37) The smallest cottage measured eighteen by twenty-four feet. Larger five-room cottages added a kitchen to the rear of the structure and came in two sizes, while six-room cottages came in three sizes, the largest measuring twenty by thirty-six feet. Despite variations in size, cottages followed a standard floor plan. The parlor, dining room, and kitchen were on one side of the house, the bedrooms on the other.

The catalog offered two more spacious versions of the cottage. The one-and-one-half-story cottage contained seven rooms, with a rear stairway leading to two bedrooms on the second floor away from the public rooms of the house. The first-floor arrangement resembled the five-room cottage, but the second story was awkward since one bedroom lacked a separate access. Builders often located the stairs between the two first-floor bedrooms allowing for a small hall on the second floor that provided access to each bedroom. In both cases, the inconspicuous location of the stairway eliminated the need for an expensive formal staircase in a hall at the front of the house.

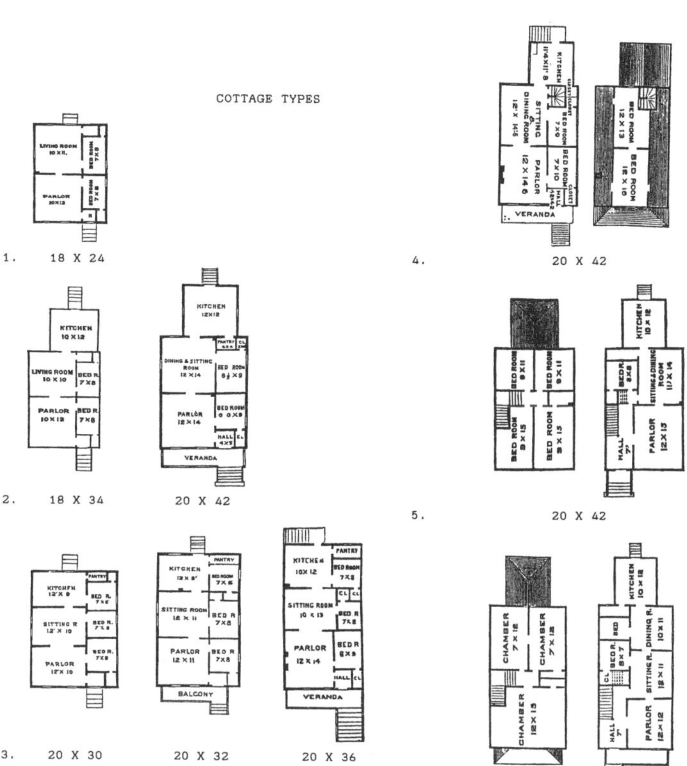

Figure 37
Floor plans for cottages. (Source: Lyman Bridges Company, *Illustrated Catalogue: Lyman Bridges Building Materials and Ready-Made Houses* [Chicago: Rand McNally, 1870].)

Larger, more expensive two-story cottages contained formal halls with stairs. These buildings were three to four times the size of a four-room cottage and were beyond the means of most working-class home owners. The presence of a hallway suggested important social distinctions. The etiquette and expense of the hall and stairs were a part of polite middle-class culture.[73] But visitors entered the parlor of working-class houses directly. In most working-class neighborhoods, two-story cottages served as apartments with living space for two separate families. They were equivalent to placing one small cottage on top of another, with the front stairway providing entry to the top apartment.

An extraordinary collection of houses dating to the 1850s in the southern suburb of South Holland documents most clearly the adoption of machine-made millwork and the cottage form. In 1847 a few Dutch families purchased land along the Calumet River south of Blue Island.[74] One early settler, Gerrit Van Oostenbrugge, recalled that residents built "cheap dwellings constructed of timbers from the neighboring woods and of lumber brought by oxen from Chicago." The houses were fourteen feet high and measured either twenty by twelve or twenty by fourteen feet, providing space for three or four rooms. Harry Eenigenburg remembered that in the fall of 1853 his father built a sixteen-by-twenty-four-foot house near South Holland that was one-and-one-half-stories high with a small attic where the children slept.[75]

Many structures built before 1870 remain in South Holland, including two remarkably well-preserved properties administered by the local historical society. One is the house Van Oostenbrugge built for himself when he arrived in 1858. Despite being of Dutch origin, Van Oostenbrugge built a balloon frame much like those erected by Yankee carpenters in Naperville. The structure was a simple hall-and-

Figure 38 Van Oostenbrugge house, South Holland, Illinois. (Source: author.)

Figure 39
Van Oostenbrugge house, interior. (Source: author.)

parlor house with two rooms on the first floor and four very small rooms above (fig. 38). Van Oostenbrugge made the doors, windows, and millwork on site with hand tools (fig. 39). Later, he added a kitchen ell to give the building its T-shape. Twenty similar structures remain in the village, all very modest houses.

The second property is the house of Peter Paarlberg, the son of one of the first settlers. Paarlberg built a basic one-and-one-half-story hall-and-parlor house in 1870 (fig. 40).[76] It contained a kitchen and parents' bedroom on the first floor, with a ladder providing access to a hall and two children's bedrooms above. The structure was a balloon frame with timber sills. Like the Van Oostenbrugge house, it offers a fine example of a common house built prior to the availability of inexpensive, machine-made millwork. The windows and doors were made by a local carpenter, who hand-planed the exterior corner

Figure 40
Paarlberg house: front and side views. (Source: author.)

boards (fig. 41). As in most simple houses before 1870, the carpenter economized by using board-and-batten doors inside the house (fig. 42).

In 1894, Paarlburg built a major addition that differed radically from the earlier simple house. The addition contained machine-made products inside and out. Interestingly, South Holland carpenters did not distinguish interior from exterior millwork. The same product used for casing an interior doorway was used to case an exterior window (figs. 43 and 44). After 1870, rebuilding occurred throughout the

Figure 41
Paarlberg house: hand-planed corner boards. (Source: author.)

Figure 42
Window and door, original Paarlberg house. (Source: author.)

village, as the Dutch replaced plain hall-and-parlor houses with more stylish cottages. Evidence of the transformation exists especially in portions of the village where fathers and sons lived near each other. Parents resided in older houses and grown children in cottages (fig. 45). The cottages were larger than original hall-and-parlor houses. By 1910, six- and seven-room houses were standard, whether residents were American-born and more established or newly arrived from Holland. The new houses contained parlors with factory-produced millwork. Typically, they also had dining rooms and bay windows (fig. 46). But most did not have a basement.

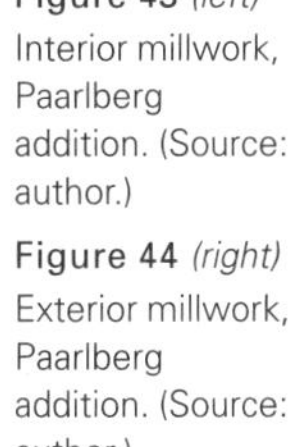

Figure 43 *(left)* Interior millwork, Paarlberg addition. (Source: author.)

Figure 44 *(right)* Exterior millwork, Paarlberg addition. (Source: author.)

Figure 45 Van Drunen family houses. (Source: author.)

Figure 46
Cottage with bay window. (Source: author.)

As South Holland prospered, a few families built larger one-and-one-half-story cottages with entry halls. These structures were more elaborate than simple, low-end houses (fig. 47).[77] Builders also introduced a more elegant version of the bay window. In addition, most families modernized by adding plumbing, electric and gas service, and central heating. When sociologist Linden Seymour Dodson studied South Holland in 1930, he found that nearly every family owned an automobile and that most listened to the radio.[78] However, nothing demonstrated the transformation of the common landscape more clearly than the rapid adoption of the bungalow, a decidedly urban house.

Bungalows were the first common houses built from scratch with all the modern amenities. They represented a national style with identical houses built in different sections of the country. More stylish than the cottage, the bungalow combined a wider range of factory

Figure 47
One-and-one-half-story cottage with bay window and formal entry hall. (Source: author.)

components with streamlined methods of construction. By 1920, younger farmers in South Holland were building bungalows rather than cottages, just like their urban counterparts (fig. 48). However, bungalows were not sudden intrusions on the landscape.[79] The distinctions between modernized cottages and more stylish bungalows were minimal since most bungalows followed the same floor plan as a six-room cottage (fig. 49).[80] The shift from cottage to bungalow was so subtle that a manufacturer, such as Aladdin Homes, could change the catalog description of its ready-made house, "The Princeton," from a cottage to a bungalow without having to alter a single feature in the design.[81]

As well as any portion of metropolitan Chicago, the built environment of South Holland demonstrates the incremental process

Figure 48
Modest and mid-range bungalows, South Holland. (Source: author.)

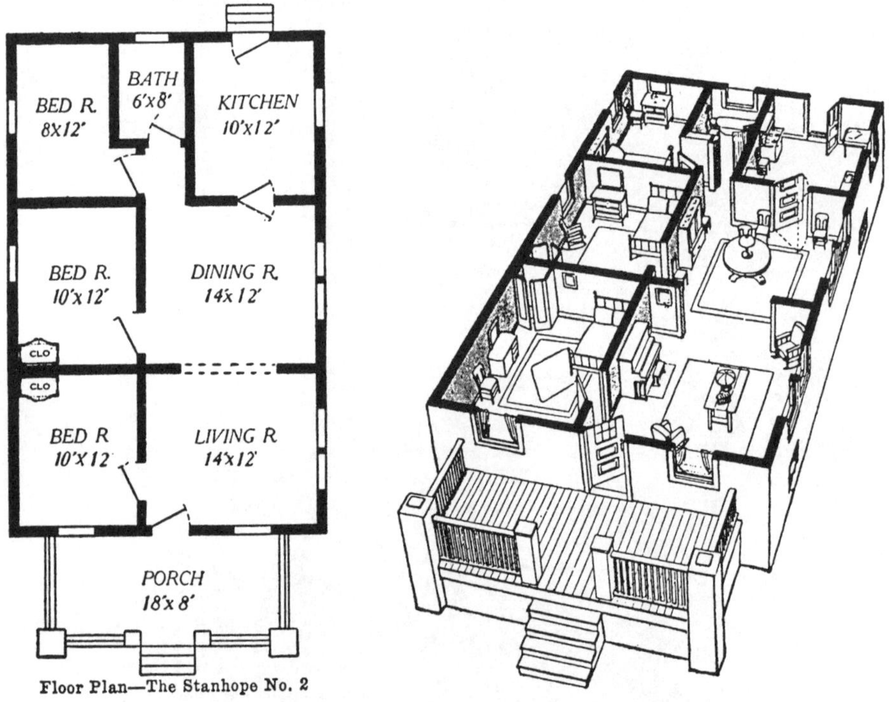

Figure 49
The Stanhope bungalow floor plan. (Source: Aladdin Company, *Aladdin Homes* [Bay City, Mich.: Aladdin Homes, 1917].)

that defined the evolution of common house forms from a variant of an ancient hall-and-parlor house to the construction of a modern suburban bungalow. The transformation occurred over a span of seventy to eighty years. During this period, builders and manufacturers searched for the most economical methods to create a range of simple houses. Initially, reliance on local craftsmen limited advances to a wealthy few. After 1880, the growth of urban markets accelerated change, allowing for the manufacture of components in quantity. The housing market became more varied. The best common houses embraced the full range of amenities associated with parlor culture. But most families remained aspirants, acquiring bits and pieces of a more comfortable life as their tastes gradually changed. Nevertheless, the lower end of the market shared the exhilaration from having improved, albeit modestly, their circumstances.[82] The modest improvements of a great number of families expanded the urban housing market, creating dynamic social and economic relationships that allowed for the transformation from cottage to bungalow.

PART TWO

LOCAL CAPITALISM AND THE ORIGINS OF THE WORKING-CLASS MARKET

CHAPTER 2

Creating Hammond

Traditionally, the adoption of a new house form has followed a broad historical change when altered social relationships led society to redefine the qualities of the built environment. Most often, wealthy families constructed new houses to separate themselves from their neighbors. In colonial America, the construction of Georgian houses occurred when the gentry developed patterns of life more refined than the lives of common people.[1] Similarly, in the nineteenth century, urban-oriented agriculture altered the rural class structure, allowing for new construction that distinguished prosperous persons who managed farms from those who toiled in the fields.[2]

The adoption of cottage housing occurred during an especially dynamic period of American history. As cities expanded, the absence of building regulations allowed workers to establish neighborhoods free from the oversight of social and economic superiors. After 1865, opportunities for working-class home ownership increased as industries built facilities on the undeveloped periphery of the city.

These areas provided potential home owners with greater access to cheap land. The rise of corporations accelerated this trend since highly capitalized, modern industries required large amounts of space to operate efficiently. Since corporations seldom played major roles in developing residential properties, most neighborhoods derived from the efforts of a local developers who profited from the sale of real estate.

Local developers promoted new neighborhoods in a haphazard manner, responding to the booms and busts of a volatile economy.[3] Consequently, most developments lacked a coherent physical or social plan. Nevertheless, near the end of the nineteenth century, the proliferation of working-class residential areas raised serious questions about ordinary people and their roles as employees, citizens, and home owners. The reconciliation of these roles proved difficult since two dynamic forms of capitalism, one corporate and the other local, existed simultaneously, side by side, uncertain of each other.

When corporations attempted to impose their will on local communities, they encountered a "subculture of opposition" based on the values of social equality and mutual assistance.[4] In Hammond, the market for inexpensive cottages contributed to this opposition by generating a bond between resident, middle-class developers and working-class home owners.[5] As citizens, they shared notions of local proprietorship that were contrary to the interests of newly established but extraordinarily powerful corporations. In response to the corporations, local communities defended their right to live and prosper in the towns they struggled to create.[6] In doing so, they objected to the influence of employers whose interests extended beyond the local community.[7]

This chapter examines in a detailed fashion the social and economic origins of a nineteenth-century market for cottage housing that was sensitive to the needs of a working-class population. The following chapter explores the political dimension of nineteenth-century home ownership. It shows how the unexpected strengths of local communities forced corporations to discipline industrial towns. By the twentieth century, the extraordinary power of corporate capital compelled local leaders to accept the authority of a centralized economy controlled by outsiders. The recognition of corporate power destroyed the militant notions of proprietorship that had distinguished industrial communities in the nineteenth century. In doing so, it redefined the social meaning of home ownership in a manner critical to an understanding of the history of modern capitalism.

The Creation of an Industrial Site at Hammond

Shortly after the Civil War, William Davis, a Detroit merchant, told Caleb Ives, a local banker, of his success shipping fish, vegetables, and fruits long distances in railroad cars containing boxes of ice. Ives spoke to George Hammond, a Detroit butcher, who agreed it might be profitable to ship beef to Eastern cities using refrigerated cars. The plan would reduce the cost of meat significantly because it allowed for the slaughter of cattle in the West before shipment East, thereby eliminating the waste that occurred when live cattle traveled long distances by rail. Ives built a refrigerated car and assumed the risk for the first shipment. Hammond selected the cattle, butchered and packed the beef, and arranged for its shipment to Boston where Marcus Towle, a butcher and acquaintance of Hammond, arranged for its sale.[8]

The first shipment arrived safely in April of 1869. Ives, Hammond, Towle, and a fourth investor, George Plummer, then formed a partnership in a plan to send regular shipments East using refrigerated cars. The four men invested a total of $6,000. Hammond and Ives invested $2,000 each, Towle and Plummer $1,000 each. They decided to establish operations near the Chicago stockyards. The following summer, the partners traveled to Chicago, rented a horse and wagon, and drove south from the yards. They chose Hohman's Bridge as a site appropriate for a slaughterhouse. While remote and unpopulated, the site offered rail connections with eastern cities as well as an inexpensive supply of ice from nearby lakes.

By September of 1869, the George H. Hammond Company had purchased fifteen acres of land for $750 and made arrangements for the arrival of three boxcar loads of building materials and eighteen workmen. The workmen built a slaughtering plant and a boarding house. Operations began within a month, allowing thirty-year-old George Hammond to return to Detroit where he conducted the firm's business with the railroads and with Eastern wholesalers. Twenty-eight-year-old Marcus Towle remained at the slaughterhouse, where he supervised daily operations. His wife managed the company boarding house.[9]

The firm prospered immediately, as the use of refrigerated cars transformed meatpacking into a complex industry with a centralized system of distribution. By 1873 the company was doing business in excess of a $1 million a year. Two years later the figure doubled, and in the 1880s business exceeded $12 million a year.[10] Despite financial success, Hammond and Towle disagreed over whether to create a permanent site for their operation. Hammond was responsible for establishing a centralized system of distribution for a perishable product.[11] He worked constantly to protect the low cost of his product against the high shipping rates imposed by railroads, who wished to protect investments in facilities for transporting live cattle. If necessary, Hammond planned to abandon the present slaughterhouse for a new location where he could secure better shipping rates.[12]

As plant manager, Marcus Towle encountered a different set of problems. He could not retain skilled butchers at a site so remote and barren. During the week, butchers from Chicago resided at the boarding house. But after paydays, they returned to their families in Chicago. Many failed to report for work the following week. To stabilize the workforce, Towle suggested as early as 1873 that the company build housing for workers. Hammond refused. He claimed indications of a permanent settlement would lessen the company's bargaining position with its only rail outlet, the Michigan Central.[13] For Hammond, the decision of whether to build housing was a business matter. For Towle, the problem was as much personal as financial.

Marcus Towle was a wealthy man living in a disorderly slaughterhouse town. For four years, he and his wife operated the boarding house until he built a more suitable private residence in 1873. The following year, the first of their three children was born at a time when the town lacked the amenities essential for a comfortable life. The water supply was poor. There were no doctors, stores, churches, or schools, and nothing impeded fierce winds when they blew from the north. It is difficult to exaggerate how bleak it must have been in the winter. One visitor described the slaughterhouse as "almost out of the civilized world, there was no effort made to set an exemplary example, and for quite a little time slaughterhouse work went on seven days in the week, no Sunday being observed, no Sabbath being kept."[14]

In April of 1875, regardless of objections, Towle purchased sixteen acres of land adjacent to the packinghouse and platted "The Original Town of Hammond," naming the town for the partner who expressed no interest in its welfare. The plat consisted of four blocks with 112 lots, each having a frontage of fifty feet (fig. 50). Towle priced the lots at $200, often loaning workers the money and lumber for construction. He arranged for repayment in monthly installments of ten dollars. Within two years, Towle had established a lumberyard on the north side of the Calumet River, where he operated a small sash, door, and blind factory.[15]

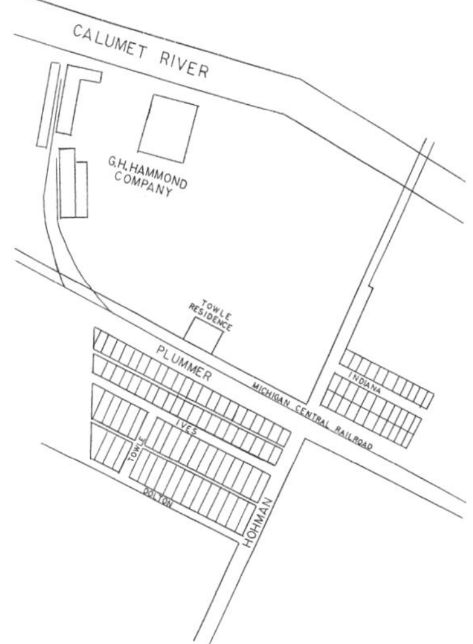

Figure 50
The original town of Hammond, 1875. (Source: author.)

Hammond remained a small, isolated community. But following Towle's first investments, it evolved from a place dedicated entirely to production to one that possessed local commercial and residential interests as well. Once Towle invested in real estate, his concerns turned increasingly to developing the town. He did so without a grand social plan. In all likelihood, he wished only to create a reasonable community where he could live comfortably with his wife and young children. Residence in Hammond offered a wealthy man few attractions other than the opportunity to build a town and profit from its expansion. Evidence of Towle's pride can be seen in a series of photographs that show the first subdivision approximately five years after his decision to build homes for workers (figs. 51 and 52).

Figure 51
Plummer Street south of the packing house. (Source: Calumet Room, Hammond Public Library.)

Figure 52 Hohman Street south of the Michigan Central Tracks. (Source: author.)

By 1880 Hammond had 689 residents. The majority (87 percent) were members of families. They included parents, children, and in a few cases a grandparent, an uncle, or a cousin. The census listed 136 heads of households, 128 of whom were men. Fifty percent of the heads of families were of German ancestry, 31 percent were born in the United States of American-born parents (hereafter identified as American-born), and 19 percent were a mixture of Irish, Swedish, and English immigrants. Nearly one of every four families had no children, while another one-third had only one or two.[16] In all likelihood, primitive conditions and the absence of a school affected the decision of whether to raise a family in Hammond.

Surprisingly, most heads of families, especially the German and American-born, did not work for the Hammond Company (table 2). The town's ten merchants and eight farmers made up a significant

Table 2 The Number of All Male Heads of Households, All Male Family Members, and All Male Boarders Employed by the Hammond Company in 1880

	Heads of Households		Family Members		Boarders		Total	
	Number	%	Number	%	Number	%	Number	%
German	16 of 64	25	11 of 30	37	11 of 28	39	38 of 122	31
American	10 of 40	28	5 of 12	42	8 of 13	62	23 of 65	35
Other foreign born	17 of 24	71	5 of 5	100	18 of 34	53	40 of 63	63
	43 of 128	34	21 of 47	45	37 of 75	49	101 of 250	40

Source: The information derives from the author's analysis of manuscripts for the Tenth Census of the United States, 1880, Population, Indiana, Lake County, North Township, Enumeration District 66.

portion of those who did not depend directly on the packinghouse for a livelihood. But skilled tradesmen, including blacksmiths, masons, carpenters, and teamsters, also provided services useful to local residents as well as to the slaughterhouse. David Nason derived income from a variety of sources. He did carpentry for local families and businesses, he owned and rented two houses from which he received rent of twelve dollars a month, and he loaned tools to local workmen for a fee. Nason worked for the Hammond Company only during the peak months of September through December, when wages were highest. During these months he earned an average of $1.75 a day.[17]

Circumstances differed for the seventy-five male boarders and the forty-seven family members who were part of the workforce. While boarders composed 11 percent of the population, they represented 30 percent of the workforce. Unlike the heads of families, boarders and family members concentrated in unskilled positions (table 3). Nearly one-half of the boarders worked as unskilled laborers at the packinghouse and another one-fourth as day laborers, who found jobs on a temporary basis wherever they could, most likely including frequent labor at the packinghouse. The presence of so many boarders created a population where males outnumbered females, 398 (57 percent) to 300 (43 percent).

The gender disparity contributed to Hammond's reputation as a place of wild amusements.[18] In her diary, Caroline Hohman told of a woman from Crown Point so frightened by the reputation for violence near the slaughterhouse "that when her husband, a lawyer, came over to our little town she nearly worried herself to death until he came home, on account of the desperadoes around the State Line Slaughterhouse."[19] In 1882 the absence of law and order astonished the editor of the *Lake County Star*. He claimed "men [were] dragged out and knocked down and pounded within an inch of their lives by bullies of the corner." Newspapers attributed the violence to a few "notorious" saloons.[20] The *Crown Point Register* reported that these saloons operated "like the Gospel gates, open night and day, every day of the year."[21]

The first photographs of the town showed that most buildings on Plummer and Hohman were two-story commercial structures or boarding houses rather than cottages for single families (figs. 51 and 52). These early structures provided owners with an income. A comparison of residents whose names appeared in the 1880 census and the 1891 city directory provide additional support regarding the importance of commercial investment among early residents.[22] For a brief period, Hammond offered the working class considerable opportunity

Table 3 The Family Status and Occupation of Hammond's Workforce in 1880

	Heads of Households	Family Members	Boarders	Total
Unskilled labor:				
G. H. Hammond	28	13	34	75
Day laborers	25	15	20	60
Other laborers	8	6	5	19
Total	61 (48)	34 (72)	59 (79)	154 (62)
Skilled labor:				
Butchers	11	5	3	19
Building trades	19	0	4	23
Farmers	8	0	0	8
Other	11	2	5	18
Total	49 (39)	7(15)	12 (16)	68(27)
Businessmen and professionals:				
Businessmen	11	1	2	14
Professionals	4	2	1	7
Clerks	3	3	1	7
Total	18 (14)	6 (13)	4 (5)	28 (11)
Total number in the workforce	128	47	75	250

Source: The information derives from the author's analysis of manuscripts for the Tenth Census of the United States, 1880, Population, Indiana, Lake County, North Township, Enumeration District 66.

Note: Numbers in parentheses are percentages.

to enter the business class. Of the 250 men who constituted the workforce in 1880, ninety-six (38 percent) were listed eleven years later in the city directory. The overwhelming majority belonged to families. One-half of the heads of households and their family members (eighty-eight of 175) remained, compared with only 11 percent (eight of seventy-five) of the boarders. Fifty-five of the heads of households who remained were listed in the 1880 census as either skilled or unskilled workers. Of these, thirty (55 percent) became businessmen of some sort by 1891, seventeen from among the unskilled and thirteen from among the skilled.

Opportunities existed because the rapid expansion of the slaughterhouse attracted workers to Hammond. By 1890, the plant employed 1,000 workers. The complex factors that produced the increase were beyond the control of Hammond residents. The town grew because a revolution in corporate capitalism transformed American society. Nevertheless, residents affected the form of development. From September of 1879 to March of 1882, local developers platted twelve subdivisions, including one across the state line in Illinois. In four years, the population quadrupled, reaching 2,960 in 1883.[23] At this time, residents incorporated as a city and elected Marcus Towle mayor. Soon afterward, Towle sold his interest in the slaughterhouse so that he could invest in Hammond and the surrounding region.[24]

During the 1880s, Marcus Towle was "the soul of Hammond and the source of its great prosperity."[25] He established the first Sunday school, started the first newspaper, and organized the first bank and the first cemetery. He secured a federal post office for Hammond, created the local masonic order, and built a hotel costing $40,000, a roller skating rink costing $25,000, and later an opera house seating 1,400. Towle contributed to the building of the first churches, without regard to denomination, and attempted to diversify the local economy by establishing a number of small industries. These included a flour mill, a distillery, a spring works, a carriage factory, and a nail mill. Unfortunately, these industries suffered serious losses from fires that plagued Hammond during the 1880s.[26]

But one investment affected development decisively. In 1886 Towle financed construction of the Chicago and Calumet Terminal Beltline Railroad, which provided rail facilities essential for continued growth in North Township. Until 1886, Hammond remained a town with a single outlet, the Michigan Central, just as it had been the day Hammond and Towle arrived (figs. 53 and 54). Other railroads passed to the north and south of town. So Hammond possessed no advantage over alternative industrial sites scattered throughout Chicago's periphery. The competition for industries became especially fierce when four new railroads entered Lake County: the Monon, the Erie, the Grand Trunk, and the Nickel Plate.

The beltline connected Hammond with Whiting, a small settlement bordering Lake Michigan at the extreme northwestern tip of Indiana. Figure 55 shows the Chicago and Calumet Terminal Beltline (CTB) as a right angle whose arms intersect at East Chicago. In a single stroke, the road made North Township a significant rail junction since it tied together all the lines entering Chicago from the south and east while providing Hammond and East Chicago with access to Lake Michigan.[27] For two decades, advertisements promoted

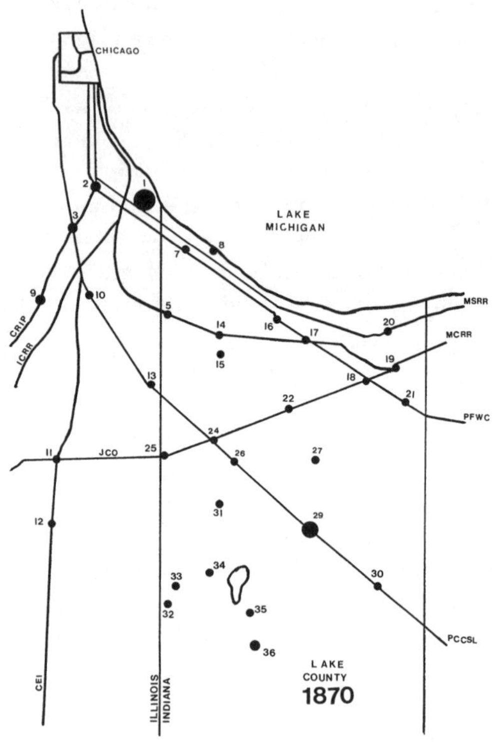

Figure 53
Railroads entering Lake County, 1870. Numbers represent towns and villages, abbreviations are railroad lines. Key: 1 = South Chicago; 2 = Englewood; 3 = Washington Heights; 4 = Hegewisch; 5 = Hammond; 6 = East Chicago; 7 = Robertsdale; 8 = Whiting; 9 = Blue Island;; 10 = Dolton; 11 = Chicago Heights; 12 = Crete; 13 = Lansing; 14 = Gibson Station; 15 = Hessville; 16 = Clarke; 17 = Tolleston; 18 = Liverpool; 19 = Lake Station; 20 = Miller Station; 21 = Hobart; 22 = Ross; 23 = Griffith; 24 = Hartsdale; 25 = Dyer; 26 = Shereville; 27 = Merrillville; 28 = Deep River; 29 = Crown Point; 30 = Leroy; 31 = St. Johns; 32 = Klassville; 33 = Brunswick; 34 = Hanover Center; 35 = Cedar Lake; 36 = Lowell; MCRR = Michigan Central (1851); MSRR = Michigan Southern (1851); JCO = Joliet Cutoff (1854); PFWC = Pittsburgh, Fort Wayne, & Chicago (1858); PCCSL = Pan Handle (1865); B&O = Baltimore & Ohio; GTRR = Chicago & Grand Trunk; NPRR = Nickel Plate (1882); CERR = Erie (1882); LNAC = Monon (1882); EJE = Elgin, Joliet, & Eastern (1888); CTB = Chicago & Calumet Terminal Beltline (1888). The dates indicate the year the railroad entered Lake County, Indiana. (Source: drawn by the author from Timothy Horton Ball, *Lake County, Indiana 1834 to 1872* [Chicago: J. W. Goodspeed, Printer & Publisher, 1873].)

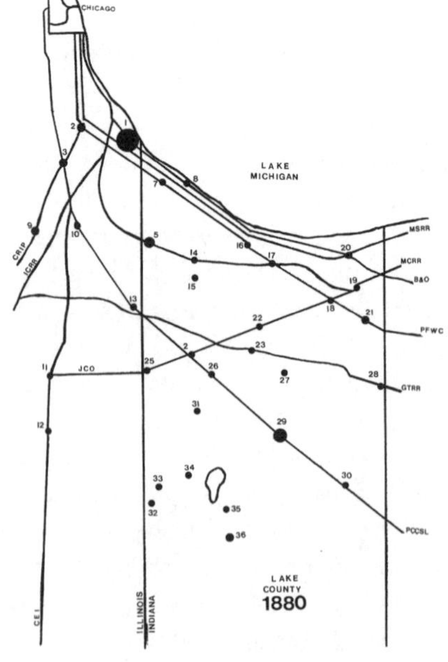

Figure 54
Railroads entering Lake County, 1880. Numbers represent towns and villages, abbreviations are railroad lines; see figure 53 for key. (Source: drawn by the author from Timothy Horton Ball, *Northwestern Indiana from 1800 to 1900; or A View of Our Region through the Nineteenth Century* [Crown Point, Ind.: n.p., 1900].)

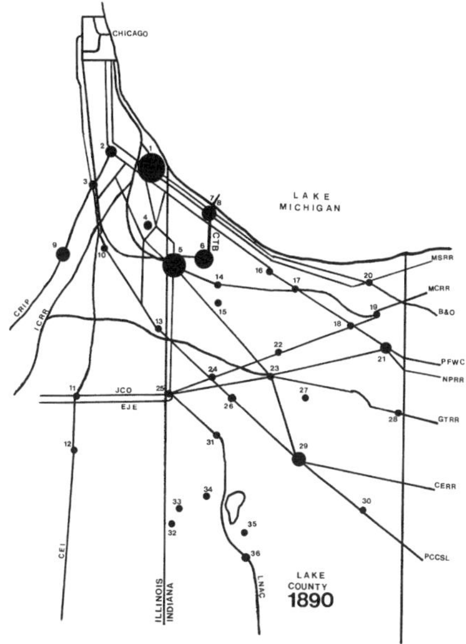

Figure 55 Railroads entering Lake County, 1890. Numbers represent towns and villages, abbreviations are railroad lines; see figure 53 for key. (Source: drawn by the author from Timothy Horton Ball, *Northwestern Indiana from 1800 to 1900; or A View of Our Region through the Nineteenth Century* [Crown Point, Ind.: n.p., 1900].)

the region by boasting of the rail facilities provided by its beltline system (fig. 56).

By 1900 Hammond, East Chicago, and Whiting contained eighty-five industries representing a capital investment of $21.8 million. These industries paid 6,535 employees $3.6 million in annual wages.[28] Figure 57 shows the extent to which industries opened sections of land to real estate development. In Hammond, developments included lands one mile north of the Calumet River and one mile west of the Illinois state line. In 1904 U.S. Steel eclipsed all previous plans by announcing its intention to build the largest steel mill in the world at the site it named Gary.

The arrival of U.S. Steel transformed the Calumet region into one of the world's great industrial districts.[29] From a larger perspective, this development represented a small portion of the changes that transformed the United States. Marcus Towle was an actor in a play written elsewhere by men whose interests resembled those of George Hammond and the officers of U.S. Steel. Nevertheless, the local story was significant, for close attention to a place like Hammond demonstrates how ordinary people experienced the large structural changes of modern life.[30] For ordinary persons, the familiar world of local capitalism provided the context for judging the transformation of America into a corporate society.

Figure 56
Advertisement for the Chicago Terminal Transfer Railroad. (Source: Calumet Room, Hammond Public Library.)

Chicago Terminal Transfer Railroad Co.

General Offices—Grand Central Passenger Station, Chicago, Ill.

E. D. ADAMS, Chairman of the Board.......New York	E. R. KNOWLTON, Superintendent ....Chicago
J. N. FAITHORN, President and Gen'l Manager....Chicago	HENRY S. HAWLEY, Traffic Manager ....Chicago
J. H. McCLEMENT, Comptroller....Chicago and New York	F. E. PARADIS, Chief Engineer...................Chicago
S. L. PREST, Ass't Comptroller................ Chicago	J. B. BARTON, Attorney ....Chicago
GEO. P. BUTLER, Sec'y and Ass't Treas.........New York	W. B. MALLETTE, Purchasing Agent...............Chicago
HENRY S. HAWLEY, Treas. and Ass't Sec'y........Chicago	J. A. LAHEY, Roadmaster ....Chicago

Chicago— Belt Line connecting with EVERY RAILROAD entering Chicago, thus furnishing a route for ALL Through Freight.

Terminal— Owning the Grand Central Passenger Station—the finest passenger station in Chicago; also extensive yards and sidings located in the heart of the city, and furnishing passenger and freight terminals to the Baltimore & Ohio R. R., Chicago Great Western Ry., and Wisconsin Central Lines.

Transfer— Handling Cars between ALL Railroads and between Industries and Railroads.

Railroad— Operating 244.5 miles of track in Chicago and vicinity, upon which are located the leading Industries, Manufacturing Plants, Elevators and Warehouses.

MAP OF THE CHICAGO TERMINAL TRANSFER RAILROAD AND CONNECTIONS.

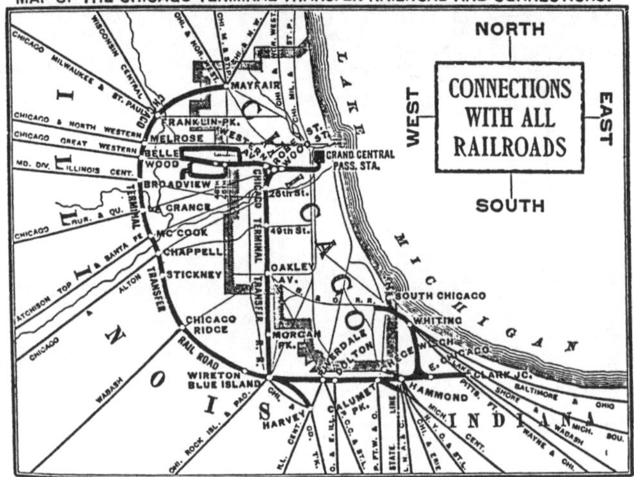

Figure 57
Map of Hammond, Whiting, East Chicago, and West Hammond, 1900. (Source: drawn by the author from a map in Frank E. Gero, *Frank E. Gero's Hammond City Directory for 1891–1892* [Hammond, Ind.: Calumet Printing & Publishing Co. Printers, 1891].)

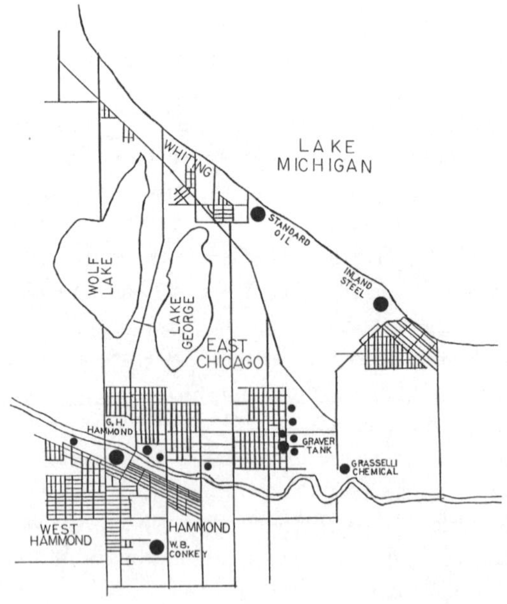

Local Capital

In Hammond, a local form of capitalism, small in scale and with specific interests in the community, affected intimately the lives of ordinary people. Locally, Towle became more than a manager of a modern industry. He was creator of a regional economy. He and others who prospered shaped local society and its institutions by establishing the essential elements of an urban community. When Towle donated to the first churches, built a first-class hotel and an opera house, and established small industries, a cemetery, and a bank, he provided momentum for further investments that allowed Hammond to establish a downtown with commercial buildings of considerable value (figs. 58 and 59).

Figure 58
Towle Opera House. (Source: Calumet Room, Hammond Public Library.)

Figure 59
Hohman Street, 1904. (Source: Calumet Room, Hammond Public Library.)

Aside from Towle, Thomas Hammond contributed most to the town's development. Brother of George Hammond, the founder of the packing company who was ambivalent about the creation of a permanent town, Thomas Hammond became assistant superintendent of the slaughterhouse in 1875 when he was thirty-two. Like Towle, he raised a family amid the privations of an isolated slaughterhouse town. Not surprisingly, he also wished to improve conditions. His opportunity came in 1886 when he resigned his position at the slaughterhouse following the death of his brother and the sale of the Hammond Company to a syndicate of English investors.[31] After 1886 neither Towle nor Thomas Hammond held a financial interest in the packinghouse. They invested in local commerce and real estate, while the English syndicate hired outsiders to manage the slaughterhouse. In the spring of 1888, Thomas Hammond platted the largest of the early subdivisions and built forty-eight homes for workers. That same year, he became the first Democratic mayor, defeating the Republican incumbent, Marcus Towle. Hammond won reelection twice and then served a term as a U.S. representative. During this time, he established the largest bank in Hammond and replaced Towle as the town's wealthiest citizen.[32]

Opportunities also existed for German residents during the 1880s. Ernest Hohman was a tailor who emigrated from East Prussia in the 1840s. After a brief stay in Chicago, he purchased forty acres on the north bank of the Calumet River in 1851 for $260. At thirty-four, Hohman settled in North Township with his wife Caroline, building a bridge across the river where they operated a tavern and stage stop. Ernest Hohman died in 1873, but his family profited from the sale of their land. In 1883, ten years after her husband's death,

Figure 60
Hohman block. (Source: Calumet Room, Hammond Public Library.)

Caroline Hohman built the town's first brick office block. The Hohman Block was a risky investment that expressed confidence in the city's future.[33] The structure differed radically from the frame commercial buildings that preceded it (see figs. 52 and 60).

Gottlieb Muenich and Anton Tapper sold local farms to invest in Hammond. They prospered by developing various real estate and commercial interests (fig. 61). Jacob Rimbach was among the older residents of North Township at the time of Hammond's first real estate boom. He had worked for the Michigan Central Railroad for twenty-five years. In 1880 he invested $1,500 in real estate. This land became part of the downtown, where Rimbach built a brick office block and the town's largest store (fig. 62). These investments increased the value of downtown real estate, generating wealth at a time when local investors lacked capital.

Figure 61
Tapper's first store. (Source: Calumet Room, Hammond Public Library

Figure 62
Rimbach block. (Source: Calumet Room, Hammond Public Library.)

Charles Heimbach, William Kleihege, Charles and August Mayer, George Drackert, and Fred Mott were Germans who worked for the Hammond Company in 1880. Heimbach worked as a butcher, Kleihege as a carpenter, Charles Mayer as a millwright, and Drackert, August Mayer, and Mott as common laborers. As the city boomed, each invested in its development. Heimbach organized the first livery and paved the first streets. Kleihege built office blocks and residences. Charles Mayer manufactured a soft drink with his brother August and his brother-in-law Drackert. They expanded their investments to include an ice company, a brewery, a coal yard, and an asphalt company, as well as banking and real estate interests. Mott earned his fortune in a classic way. He worked his way up from common laborer to become head bookkeeper. Then he married Ernest and Caroline Hohman's daughter, a union that allowed him to resign from the packinghouse to oversee the family's real estate.[34]

In Hammond, ordinary men profited because the city lacked the basic structures of urban life. The German families who benefitted from the creation of these structures formed a core group that exercised influence over local politics for a generation. However, most of those who prospered did so on a smaller scale. They became saloon owners, grocers, or some other kind of merchant, conducting business in one of the many small commercial structures scattered throughout the city (fig. 63).[35] Their businesses were ubiquitous features of the landscape, more numerous than the office blocks clustered at the center of town.

Figure 63
Hardware store. (Source: Calumet Room, Hammond Public Library.)

The American-born middle class differed from the German middle class. While most Germans were farmers and members of the working class who arrived early and prospered as merchants, a large portion of the American-born middle class were professionals. Doctors, lawyers, teachers, business managers, newspaper editors, dentists, and ministers were accorded status immediately on arrival (see table 4). Most of these men came from rural backgrounds, and like Abraham Lincoln, they were self-educated, self-made men without much formal training. In 1891 American-born professionals accounted for about one-fifth of Hammond's middle class. A few, like William C. Belman, the first school superintendent, became wealthy and locally prominent.[36] But their population was unstable. A majority of the clergy, physicians, teachers, and businessmen listed in the 1891 city directory did not appear in the 1900 city directory or in the

Table 4 The Ethnicity and Occupations of Members of Hammond's Middle Class in 1891 Who Remained in Hammond until 1900

	Number Remained		Percent			Other
	1891	1900	Remained	German	American	Foreign-Born
Saloonkeeper	67	49	73	35	6	8
Grocer/butcher/baker	65	35	54	28	5	2
Dry goods merchant	31	16	52	13	1	2
Other merchant	26	6	23	3	2	1
Total	189	106	56	79	14	13
Livery	31	17	55	7	8	2
Hardware/Express/ Building contractor	36	19	53	9	10	0
Total	67	36	54	16	18	2
Real estate/insurance	27	15	56	6	6	3
Physician/dentist	19	6	32	0	6	0
Lawyer	11	6	55	1	5	0
Clergy/teacher	39	16	41	2	9	5
Manager/clerk	64	16	25	8	6	2
Total	160	59	37	17	32	10
Total	416	201	48	112	64	25

Sources: Frank E. Gero, *Frank E. Gero's Hammond City Directory for 1891–1892* (Hammond, Ind.: Calumet Printing & Publishing Co. Printers, 1891); and author's analysis of manuscripts for the Twelfth Census of the United Stated, 1900, Population, Indiana, Lake County, North Township, Enumeration District 34 and manuscripts for the Twefth Census of the United States, 1900, Population, Illinois, Cook county, Thornton Township, enumeration District 1, 189.

manuscripts of the federal census taken that same year. Most professionals resided briefly in Hammond.[37] Their skills allowed mobility, and other locations offered better opportunities than an isolated industrial town like Hammond.

Hammond also provided opportunities for Edward C. Minas and A. Murray Turner, the American-born sons of merchants from Crown Point, the county seat fifteen miles southeast of Hammond. Minas was the son of a shoe merchant. He came to Hammond as a young man to work as a clerk in Marcus Towle's general store. In 1890 Minas opened a hardware store, which he expanded until, according to the *Hammond Daily News*, he sold "anything and everything that the average mind can conceive as needed to furnish the modern home." In 1913 Minas opened a department store valued at half a million dollars (fig. 64). By that time, he and Turner were among the four men, all American-born, who controlled Hammond's largest banks.[38]

A. Murray Turner played an even more prominent role in the city's development. He was the son of David Turner, a Lake County pioneer who arrived as a child in 1837, among the first white settlers in the region. David Turner became Crown Point's leading merchant, a state senator, and president of the First National Bank of Crown Point. As a result, Murray Turner was one of the few in Hammond

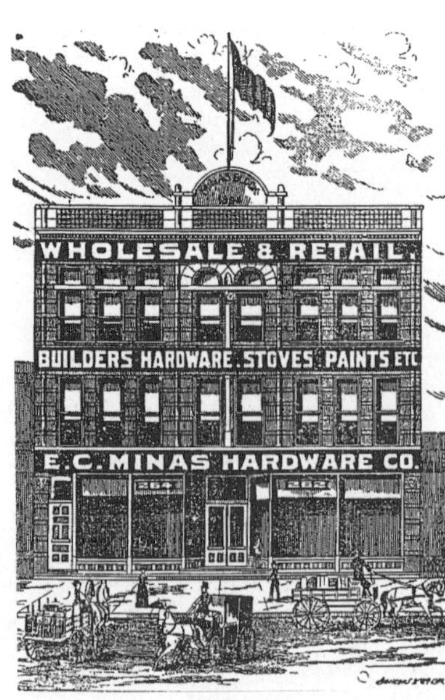

Figure 64
Minas hardware store. (Source: "Industrial Edition," *Hammond Daily News*, December 1904; reprinted as Hammond Historical Society, *The Hammond Historical Society Presents the Famous 1904 Edition of the "Hammond Daily News,"* [Hammond, Ind.: Hammond Historical Society, 1954], 11–16.)

who claimed a privileged upbringing. But he did not attend college. Instead, he worked for his father until he was thirty-three, at which time he settled in Hammond. Quickly, Turner made wise investments, developing Hammond's street railway and the Northern Indiana Gas and Electric Company. In 1909 he became the city's wealthiest resident by combining the two largest banks to form the First National Bank of Hammond, the county's largest financial institution.[39]

By 1900 Hammond contained a few wealthy American-born entrepreneurs, a small and unstable group of American-born professionals, and numerous merchants, saloon owners, and small businessmen, a majority of whom were German. Since most of the middle class prospered from investments that affected everyday life in Hammond, their importance cannot be calculated simply by counting the upwardly mobile and classifying them into categories. As Herbert Gutman observed, "Such studies often describe with some precision regularities in behavior. But they fail to explain them."[40] Explanations require judgments about the way the local middle class invested resources.

Marcus Towle and Thomas Hammond, for instance, prospered because of their knowledge of a trade, butchering, and because of their ability to manage others engaged in that trade. But butchering changed fundamentally once George Hammond, J. Ogden Armour, Gustavus Swift, and Edward Morris transformed it into an enormous enterprise. The extent of change was evident in Hammond by 1890, when the slaughter occupied only a small portion of the plant. Most employees were unskilled laborers involved with the by-products of slaughter and the refrigeration and transportation of beef.[41]

After 1886, Hammond and Towle no longer worked to develop the meatpacking industry. Neither wished to be a corporate manager. Instead, they developed local interests by transforming undeveloped land into real estate.[42] In 1896 their efforts attracted the town's second large employer, the W. B. Conkey Publishing Company. A prominent Chicago publisher, Conkey required a modern manufacturing site with excellent rail facilities that would allow for construction of a rationally designed one-story plant (fig. 65). Local investors provided Conkey with a site at no cost, promised low property taxes, and contributed money for construction of the plant. The investors then profited from the sale of residential properties surrounding the plant, which offered employment to 1,000 workers by 1898.[43] Thus, common housing served as the basis for a dynamic local economy in which a resident middle class profited by responding to the needs of the dominant working-class population. Their ability to

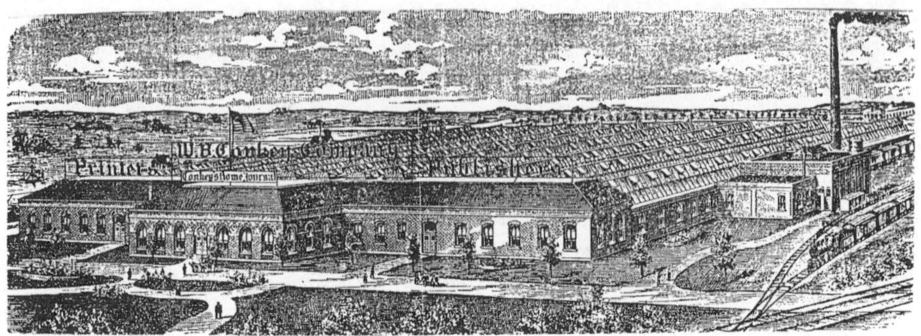

Figure 65
W. B. Conkey Company. (Source: "Industrial Edition," *Hammond Daily News*, December 1904; reprinted as Hammond Historical Society, *The Hammond Historical Society Presents the Famous 1904 Edition of the "Hammond Daily News,"* [Hammond, Ind.: Hammond Historical Society, 1954].)

do so affected decidedly the landscape of working-class towns like Hammond.

The Housing Market in Hammond

The 1890 federal census described Hammond's residents as predominantly foreign-born. Immigrants and their children accounted for three-fifths of the city's 5,428 residents. The census also reported that 973 residential buildings housed 1,098 families. In other words, nine structures existed for every ten families.[44] This ratio suggests that most houses were for single families. Unfortunately, the 1890 census offered no further information since fire destroyed the manuscripts. But Hammond published a city directory in 1891 that provided a reasonable account of an overwhelmingly working-class population (table 5).

Sixty percent of workers (1,501 of 2,494) were unskilled, while another 24 percent (589) were semi-skilled or skilled. In 1880, heads of families made up only 37 percent of the Hammond Company workforce, while family members constituted 18 percent and boarders 45 percent. Eleven years later heads of households accounted for 68 percent of the workers at the slaughterhouse, family members 13 percent, and boarders only 19 percent. These figures are rough estimates at best. But the point is clear. As Hammond matured, most families were headed by laborers who worked for the dominant industry. This population was relatively stable. Historians have shown that typically about two of every five families listed in a census remained in that same city for a period of at least ten years, so they could be counted again in the next census.[45] In Hammond, 41 percent of the heads of households listed in the 1891 directory remained until at least 1900.

Table 5 Occupations for Male Heads of Households, Male Family Members, and Male Boarders in Hammond in 1891

	Heads of Households	Family Members	Boarders	Total
Unskilled labor:				
Hammond Co. labor	412	81	112	605
Other manufacturing	168	68	148	384
Day laborers	181	59	104	344
Other labor	75	33	60	168
Total	836 (55)	241 (75)	424 (66)	1,501 (60)
Skilled labor:				
Building trades	228	26	79	333
Other skilled labor	158	16	82	256
Total	386 (25)	42 (13)	161 (25)	589 (24)
Business and professional:				
Small businessmen	200	11	16	227
Professionals	63	5	16	84
Managers/clerks	46	22	25	93
Total	309 (20)	38 (12)	57 (9)	404 (16)

Source: Frank E. Gero, *Frank E. Gero's Hammond City Directory for 1891–1892* (Hammond, Ind.: Calumet Printing & Publishing Co. Printers, 1891).

Note: Numbers in parenthses are percentages.

Three-fourths of the 634 heads of households who remained were working class (table 6). Many of these families owned houses. The 1900 federal census provided the first reliable information on home ownership. By 1900 the towns of Hammond and West Hammond, its newly created Illinois neighbor, were populated by 2,817 families, with 1,214 (43 percent) of these families owning the houses in which they lived. Forty-eight percent of unskilled laborers who were heads of households owned their homes, 36 percent of skilled workers, and 45 percent of businessmen and professionals. But a more detailed analysis of manuscripts for the census showed that ownership rates were highest among the foreign-born working class, especially the unskilled, and low among the American-born population (table 7). Sixty percent of unskilled German laborers owned their houses, compared with 25 percent of the American-born population. The figures were even higher for German families who resided in Hammond for nine or more years. Among these families, 77 percent of the unskilled owned their house, 69 percent of the skilled, and 80 percent of the business and professional class.

Table 6 Heads of Households in Hammond in 1891 Who Remained and Did Not Remain in 1900

	Total in 1891	Remained in 1891	Did Not Remain	Percentage Who Remained
Unskilled labor:				
Hammond Co. labor	412	170	242	41
Other manufacturing	168	61	107	36
Day laborers	181	48	133	27
Other labor	75	37	38	49
Total	836	316	520	38
Skilled labor:				
Building Trades	228	87	141	38
Other Skilled Labor	158	64	94	41
Total	386	151	235	39
Business and professional:				
Small businessmen	200	119	81	60
Professionals	63	28	35	44
Managers/Clerks	46	20	26	44
Total	309	167	142	53
Total	1,531	634	897	41

Sources: Frank E. Gero, *Frank E. Gero's Hammond City Directory for 1891–1892* (Hammond, Ind.: Calumet Printing & Publishing Co. Printers, 1891); and author's analysis of manuscripts for the Twelfth Census of the United States, 1900, Population, Indiana, Lake County, North Township, Enumeration District 34 and manuscripts for the Twelfth Census of the United States, 1900, Population, Illinois, Cook county, Thornton Township, enumeration District 1, 189.

In Hammond, inexpensive houses were built rapidly. In 1900, one-half of all home owners had arrived after 1891. The experience of the Polish community in West Hammond demonstrated the speed with which communities established themselves. Poles first settled in West Hammond in 1891 when a Chicago investor opened a 320-acre subdivision one mile south of the packinghouse. Within nine years, 1,233 Poles lived in West Hammond. Seventy-two percent of the 233 families owned their houses, a tribute to the ability of the market to accommodate quickly new residents from among the financially least secure. This ability continued into the twentieth century. In 1930, three of every five residential buildings (14,269 of 24,195) in Hammond, West Hammond, Whiting, and East Chicago were owned by an occupant, and 63 percent of the foreign-born families in the region owned their houses (table 8). Clearly, from the

Table 7 The Nativity, Occupational Status, and Home Ownership Rates in 1900 for All Residents of Hammond and West Hammond and for Those Families Residing in the Cities since 1891

	All Residents		Resident for Ten Years	
	Number	Percent Home Owners	Number	Percent Home Owners
German:				
Unskilled	575	60	157	77
Skilled	339	50	67	69
Business class	246	58	94	80
Total	1,160	57	318	76
American:				
Unskilled	261	16	61	38
Skilled	354	26	67	33
Business class	225	35	49	82
Total	840	25	177	48
Other foreign:				
Unskilled	431	50	40	58
Skilled	250	30	26	59
Business class	136	39	21	86
Total	817	42	87	65
Total population:				
Unskilled	1,267	48	258	66
Skilled	943	36	160	52
Business class	607	45	164	81
Total	2,817	43	582	66

Source: Frank E. Gero, *Frank E. Gero's Hammond City Directory for 1891–1892* (Hammond, Ind.: Calumet Printing & Publishing Co. Printers, 1891); and author's analysis of manuscripts for the Twelfth Census of the United States, 1900, Population, Indiana, Lake County, North Towenship, Enumeration District 34 and manuscripts for the Twelfth Census of the United States, 1900, Population, Illinois, Cook county, Thornton Township, enumeration

earliest period of development, Hammond established a market for immigrant, working-class home ownership.

The success of the market depended on affordable cottage housing. Fire insurance maps from 1887 suggest that four of every five residential buildings (396 of 507) were cottages. Forty-six percent of all residences were one-story cottages, 13 percent one-and-one-half-story, and 19 percent two-story. Nearly all were frame, and most were built on narrow lots of twenty-five by 125 feet.[46] The least expensive

Table 8 Statistics regarding Home Ownership, Nativity, and Population in 1930 for Hammond, West Hammond/Calumet City, East Chicago, and Whiting

	Hammond	West Hammond	East Chicago	Whiting	Total
Population in 1930	64,560	12,298	54,784	10,880	142,522
Total dwellings	12,948	2,295	7,272	1,680	24,195
% one family	88	84	68	77	81
% two family	9	11	19	17	13
% three or more	3	5	13	6	6
Total families	15,478	2,878	11,525	2,227	32,108
% native with native parents	50	30	20	30	37
% native with foreign parents	22	32	12	19	20
% foreign-born	28	38	48	51	38
% other	...	...	11	...	5
Ratio of families per dwelling	1.20	1.23	1.58	1.33	1.32
Total home owners	7,573	1,578	4,069	1,049	14,269
% native with native parents	35	21	11	15	25
% native with foreign parents	24	30	10	17	20
% foreign-born	41	49	5	...	53
% other	...	...	5	...	2
% of all families who are home owners	49	56	35	47	45
% native with native parents	35	39	19	23	31
% native with foreign parents	53	53	30	42	47
% foreign-born	72	71	54	63	63

Source: U.S. Department of Commerce, Bureau of the Census, *Fifteenth Census of the United Staates: 1930 Population*, vol. 6, *Families* (Washington, D.S.: Government Printing Office, 1932), 424–25.

one-story cottages, without lots, cost as little as $500, even less if the owner built the house and avoided the expense of a carpenter.[47] However, the cheapest cottages lacked ornament and appeared in subdivisions without paved streets, gas and electric service, sidewalks, or sewer and water connections.

More expensive cottages employed standardized building components inside and out. These components included larger windows, porches of various sizes, and interior moldings that enhanced the appearance of the house. But amenities were limited. Working-class houses seldom had indoor toilets or central heating until the twentieth century. Most early cottages were illuminated by oil lamps and heated by stoves, while waste was disposed of in backyard privies.

In Hammond, cottages of two full stories usually provided owners with an income. Two-story residential buildings were the equivalent of placing one cottage on top of another. Similarly, two-story commercial cottages offered space for a business on the first floor and a residence above (see fig. 63). The combination residence and business reduced the cost of operating a small business. So not surprisingly, 56 percent (seventy-nine of 142) of Hammond's grocers, saloon owners, and dry goods merchants listed their business and residence as the same address in 1891.[48]

Analysis of manuscripts for the 1900 federal census showed that 84 percent of families in Hammond and West Hammond lived in structures housing one family, 14 percent in structures housing two, and only 2 percent in structures with three or more families. Rates varied slightly depending on ethnic background and occupation (table 9). But, clearly, Hammond never experienced the crowding found in the infamous tenement districts of Chicago where reformers considered cottages incapable of being updated to accommodate modern circumstances. Indeed, owners in Hammond often improved their homes.

Three houses built in 1895 by Minrad Kaelin demonstrated the capacity to improve working-class cottages (fig. 66). When these structures were built, Kaelin was a forty-three-year-old immigrant from Switzerland who had lived in the United States for fifteen years. He worked at the packinghouse earning about $1.50 a day. Kaelin built the three four-room cottages on Wentworth Avenue in West Hammond, one-quarter mile from Hammond's downtown, in a neighborhood occupied predominantly by German laborers. The house in the foreground housed Kaelin, his wife, and two children. The houses farther from the camera were rental properties from which the Kaelins derived an income. Each of the rental homes cost about $800 to build, while the family home cost about $1,200.

The three houses were built on five lots, with a vacant lot on each side of the family's house. The fifth lot cannot be seen in figure 66, but its function was clear. Open spaces allowed breezes to cool the house in the summer. Other features distinguished the family's house from the rental properties. It rested on a taller foundation allowing space for a cellar. The large window on the front of the house was of finer design than the double-hung windows on the front of the rental properties. The front porch provided a more attractive entry as well as a place to sit and watch traffic as it passed the house. By 1904, when the photograph was taken, a wooden fence and sidewalk surrounded the properties. But the street was not paved.

Table 9 Home Ownership Rates and the Percentages of Families Living in Structures Housing One, Two, and Three or More Families in Hammond and West Hammond in 1900

	One Family		Two Families		Threee or More		Total	
	Number	% Own	Number	% Own	Number	% Own	Number	% Own
German:								
Unskilled laborers	502	63	65	43	8	13	575	60
Skilled laborers	295	53	34	11	10	10	339	58
Total	1,016	60	123	46	21	24	1,160	57
% of type		87		11		2		
American:								
Unskilled laborers	209	16	47	13	5	20	261	16
Skilled laborers	288	30	58	14	8	. . .	354	25
Business class	199	38	25	12	1	. . .	225	35
Total	696	28	130	17	14	7	840	25
% of type		83		17		7		
Others foreign:								
Unskilled laborers	345	53	73	36	13	31	431	50
Skilled laborers	203	34	40	18	7	14	250	30
Business class	117	47	13	37	6	33	136	39
Total	665	45	126	37	26	27	817	42
% of type		81		15		4		
Total								
Unskilled laborers	1,056	51	185	32	26	23	1,267	48
Skilled laborers	786	39	132	20	25	8	943	36
Business class	535	48	62	23	10	50	607	45
Total	2,377	46	379	26	61	11	2,817	43
% of type		84		14		2		

Sources: The information derives from the author's analysis of manuscripts for the Twelfth Census of the United States, 1900, Population, Indiana, Lake County, North Township, Enumeration District 34 and manuscripts for the Twelfth Census of the United States, 1900, Population, Illinois, Cook county, Thornton Township, enumeration District 1,189.

Figures 67 and 68 show the family house and the fifth lot in 1912. Located on the corner of an irregular city block, the fifth lot provided space for trees and a small garden. Figure 69 shows the fifth lot and the house in 1920. By this time, the family had adapted their house from a four-room to a six-room cottage. The extension included the area beyond the narrow window located toward the rear of

Figure 66
Kaelin cottages, 1904. (Source: author.)

Figure 67
Kaelin cottage, 1912. (Source: author.)

Figure 68
Kaelin property, 1912. (Source: author.)

Figure 69
Kaelin house, 1920. (Source: author.)

the house. By 1920, the city had paved the streets and sidewalks and installed water, gas, and electrical services.

This example shows that, while similar to one another, cottages were not identical. Variations allowed for a range of housing as families transformed simple structures by adding amenities over time. Within a generation, the Kaelins expanded their house and added the electric, gas, and water services requisite for a modern home. Fred W. Peterson has shown how rural families often built homes in two or more stages, adding substantial additions as a farm became profitable. The process allowed for radical alterations, transforming modest homes into elaborate residences.[49] Urban families seldom made such dramatic improvements because they could more easily move to another house.

Most new construction after 1900 improved the city's housing stock. In 1897 Martin and Rose Kunkel built a four-room cottage in the Polish neighborhood of West Hammond. Kunkel was a thirty-three-year-old laborer at the packinghouse with four children. He had lived in Chicago for eleven years. The house was similar to Kaelin's rental properties (figs. 70 and 66). Within fifteen years, the family's fortunes improved, allowing them to purchase three lots and build a better house across the street from their first residence (figs. 71 and 72). The new house was a one-and-one-half-story cottage with a large front porch and full basement. It resembled the houses of more prosperous American-born, working families (see fig. 2). Like most homes built after 1910, it had plumbing, gas, and electric services.

During the first generation of settlement, the cottage market allowed Hammond to expand rapidly and provide housing that could

Figure 70
Martin Kunkel and the family cottage, 1900. (Source: author.)

Figure 71 *(left)*
The new Kunkel house, 1910. (Source: author.)

Figure 72 *(right)*
Martin and Rose Kunkel. (Source: author.)

be improved with time. From 1890 to 1910 the population of Hammond and West Hammond quadrupled. Yet construction kept pace. In 1890, 973 dwellings housed 1,089 families, a ratio of one dwelling for every 1.12 families. Twenty years later, 4,621 dwellings housed 5,315 families, a ratio of one dwelling for every 1.15 families.[50] In the heavily industrial cities of Whiting and East Chicago, a larger percentage of families lived in residences housing more than one family (see table 8). But the percentages of owner-occupied residences were about the same as in Hammond and West Hammond. In all four cities in 1930, occupants owned three of every five residential buildings.[51]

In crowded areas, closer to industrial plants, immigrants were often landlords. They owned buildings with at least two separate apartments, one typically occupied by the owner. Within these neighborhoods, home ownership provided an income. But regardless of circumstances, the percentage of houses owned by immigrants was greater than the percentage of immigrants among the general population of the region. While immigrants accounted for 38 percent of all families in the four cities in 1930, they were 53 percent of all home owners.[52] These houses were seldom the crowded and dilapidated structures made famous by reformers. Certainly, as Hammond grew, housing near the downtown became congested. But it remained in good condition and often improved, as witnessed by changes in the Kaelin house. Furthermore, with open spaces common, new construction provided larger, more modern houses than in older residential districts. By 1910, Hammond provided a varied residential landscape that accommodated a diverse working-class population.

Conclusion

During the nineteenth century, markets for cottage housing evolved because of relationships between middle-class populations, with fortunes tied to a community, and majority working-class populations. In Hammond, a flourishing market transformed the region from swamp and sand dune into urban real estate. As the end of the century approached, similar developments on Chicago's periphery created a patchwork landscape that offered a striking alternative to the ideal expressed in the model town of Pullman. At Pullman, the built environment testified to the authority of the modern corporation. It exhibited what Richard T. Ely described as "benevolent, well-wishing feudalism."[53] In contrast, the cottage market remained open-ended as it faced two dramatic challenges, which the remaining chapters examine in detail. First, it confronted the increasing power of corporate capital so evident at Pullman. Second, it confronted the arrival of immigrants from southern and eastern Europe whose poverty raised serious doubts about the ability of a private market to sustain a traditionally high American standard of living.

CHAPTER 3

Local Politics and the Pullman Strike

Documenting changes in everyday life requires attention to trivial events and minute details that accumulate and acquire significance over time. Fortunately, social historians may also draw on a handful of dramatic events that served as turning points in the nation's history. These events provide windows that expose ordinary people as they encountered the large structural changes that transformed the modern world. During the Pullman strike of 1894, the nation confronted for the first time the full extent of corporate power. For a brief moment, Hammond residents defended their convictions on a national stage. Their story demonstrates how corporate capitalism altered social relationships in local societies and reconfigured the meaning of community development and home ownership in the modern world.

Local Politics and Community Development in Hammond

The growth of Hammond required investments from many persons, who in a manner unplanned, risky, and haphazard, attempted to create a stable city offering employment and modest comfort. At first, the process was painfully slow. For a decade, Hammond did not so much as establish a church. But when real estate boomed in the 1880s, local developers presented congregations with gifts of land and building materials. By 1900, the city had four Catholic churches, three Lutheran, two Methodist, a large Baptist church, and four smaller Protestant denominations.[1] Residents also established various social organizations including orders of Masons, Foresters, Odd Fellows, Knights of Pythias, Sons of Veterans, Daughters of Rebekah, the Grand Army of the Republic, Knights of Macabees, the Royal League, the Women's Christian Temperance Union, a Chautauqua Literary and Scientific Circle, a German singing society, a German athletic association, various labor unions, and a number of saloons.[2]

Most organizations were exclusive, illustrating various divisions within the community. The Masons limited membership to the Protestant elite, especially native-born professionals.[3] In contrast, the Foresters included almost every group within the city. But to do so, they required four separate assemblies: one for native Protestants, one for German Protestants, one for German Catholics, and one for Catholics who were not German.[4]

The most significant social division existed between native Protestants, who favored temperance, and Germans, who celebrated Sundays with picnics organized by saloon owners.[5] The picnics attracted large crowds who drank beer, gambled, danced, listened to music, and enjoyed fireworks. A few native citizens took offense because the picnics violated Indiana law prohibiting the sale of alcohol on Sunday. In response, the saloonkeepers moved the picnics across the state line separating Hammond and West Hammond. But Henry Kendall, a native-born Protestant lawyer, continued to attack the picnics as "immoral." He claimed they attracted hoodlums and prostitutes, "who could they wash themselves in the soap lakes of Dakota for a thousand years could not be clean enough to commingle on the same platform with pure women and innocent children."[6]

Following one Fourth of July picnic, which included a shooting and brawl, Kendall argued that saloon owners should not take refuge behind the claim that picnics were common in Germany. According to Kendall, "The conduct of the better classes of the people in all Christian countries differs but little in essentials. There is not a self-respecting citizens of foreign birth in all this town who will point with pride to that beerbesotted babel and say this is the way good people do in the fatherland."[7]

Despite these differences, Hammond residents shared common concerns that were vital to the future of the community. Most notably, during the 1880s and 1890s, the city struggled to provide adequate police and fire protection. For a considerable time, Hammond seemed "hoodooed by the fire fiend." The first major fire occurred on Christmas Eve in 1883 when twenty-one businesses in Marcus Towle's first subdivision burned to the ground. Two months later, fire destroyed a business block and several houses. In response, the city equipped its first volunteer fire department. But it proved insufficient as losses continued, including Marcus Towle's distillery, carriage works, and roller skating rink. In 1889, the Hammond Company suffered two fires so severe that 800 men were put out of work. On one occasion, vats of animal fats burst, releasing tons of grease into the Calumet River, which caught fire. After firefighters extinguished the blaze, a layer of grease two feet deep floated on top of the river.[8]

The police also struggled to maintain order. Initially, Hammond elected a town marshal. However, one man could not enforce the law. Newspapers told of victims robbed and beaten after spending an evening in one of Hammond's notorious saloons. Drunk and bloodied, they were dragged to the prairies outside town where despite cries they would not be discovered until morning. In one instance, a mob of a hundred armed sportsmen arrived unexpectedly on an afternoon train to attend a prize fight to be held that evening just outside town. One resident claimed Hammond would remain powerless before such mobs until the city established a force of "at least one hundred drilled armed police, that can be called when wanted in a moment's notice." After the city established a more modest force, petty theft remained so common that the mayor ordered the arrest of any suspicious persons found on the streets after midnight.[9]

From 1884 until 1888, Marcus Towle and a small group of fellow Republicans controlled city government. During this time, residents elected five native-born managers from the slaughterhouse, all but one Republican. In 1888, Thomas Hammond defeated Towle in the race for mayor, signaling a shift in power, as German merchants and saloonkeepers of the Democratic party gained control of the government. After 1888, the town elected only one packinghouse official, the Democrat Patrick Reilly, an Irish-American Catholic with a liberal attitude toward labor.[10] In turn, the local Republican party divided allegiance between Towle and Kossuth H. Bell, the superintendent of the slaughterhouse hired by the English syndicate that owned the packinghouse.[11]

Every two years as elections approached, the native-born

editor of the *Lake County News* would proclaim that the Democrats were the party of labor, opposed to K. H. Bell and rule by the English syndicate. This stance appealed to the working class, who constituted an overwhelming majority of voters and who often voiced opposition to the policies of the Hammond Company. Soon after the English syndicate took charge, the *Crown Point Register* reported that citizens were outraged that a full corps of men worked all winter on average only three and a half days a week. The short week did not provide sufficient income to support a family. As a consequence, the entire town suffered, including "landlords, grocers, coal dealers, doctors, merchants, and all who supply necessaries of life, . . . all to cater to the greed of the present management of the slaughterhouse."[12]

By the 1894 election, support for labor and opposition to the English syndicate had provided local Democrats with three consecutive mayoral victories. During the campaign, the Democrats boasted they were "the party of the whole people," committed "to equal rights and special favors to none." Their platform listed the public improvements initiated under Democratic administrations, including new streets, sewers, and sidewalks, an improved fire alarm system, enlarged fire and police departments, a street lighting system, and the purchase of land for a public park. The Democrats considered each improvement a monument to progress in Hammond.[13]

In contrast, the Democrats claimed that Kossuth Bell bribed and coerced workers to vote Republican, warning that submission insured the domination of the packinghouse in all facets of life. They also informed German voters that Indiana Republicans supported the American Protective Association (APA), which was hostile to immigrants, especially Catholics. The Democratic paper reported that local Republicans, sympathetic to the APA, promised antisaloon voters that if elected they would close saloons on Sundays. Following the primary, the Democrats denounced the Republican nomination of two German Protestants, Fred Mott for mayor and William Kleihege for treasurer, as a move to sway local Germans, without whom the Republicans could not win.

In 1894, the Republicans countered with charges of fiscal mismanagement. They argued that the Democrats provided physical improvements at too high a cost, inflating the special assessments levied on property owners to pay for new streets, sidewalks, water mains, and sewers. In addition, the Republicans claimed that excessive patronage raised the cost of city services, especially in the water department. Nevertheless, the Democrats predicted victory at a rally that included a parade with eighty-five mounted horsemen and two marching bands. On election day, the Republicans won the races for mayor, clerk, treasurer, marshal, water trustee, and three of four aldermanic posts. Fred Mott defeated the Democratic candidate for mayor, Patrick Reilly, 1,091 votes (53 percent) to 955 (47 percent).[14]

Following the election, the Democrats suggested that Kossuth Bell had bribed voters.[15] More likely, home owners resented high special assessments, as the Republicans claimed. Many property owners could not afford streets, sidewalks, and sewers. As home owners, voters were sensitive to charges of financial mismanagement. The Democrats corrected their mistake by 1898 when Reilly defeated the Republican candidate, Marcus Towle, 1,311 (61 percent) to 849 (39 percent).[16] As in previous campaigns, the Democrats stressed independence from the packinghouse and opposition to special privilege. However, their earlier defeats had taught the Democrats an important lesson. They also promised a fiscally responsible government that would not burden taxpayers with costly improvements.

Politicians who defended labor could not retain power if they discounted the opinions of home owners regarding services. Quality and cost of construction were issues vital to families who paid for improvements as cities extended systems of streets, sidewalks, and sewers.[17] Passionate over local issues, working-class home owners often voted against prominent citizens.[18] Consequently, local authorities responded to voters' concerns. These responses provided ordinary people with a sense that they could control to some degree the affairs of their community. As a result, citizens developed a sense of ownership, a proprietary interest in their town, which they assumed was as legitimate as the interests of the corporations that provided employment. Initially, few working-class home owners imagined the extent to which their interests conflicted with an increasingly powerful corporate society. However, during the summer of 1894, the citizens of Hammond learned in dramatic fashion that they were no match against the power and influence of corporate capital.

The Origins of the Pullman Strike

As Hammond experienced its first real estate boom, George Pullman attracted international attention by creating a model suburb on the outskirts of Chicago. Pullman believed an enlightened capitalism could improve the quality of everyday life and overcome the problems associated with the growth of cities.[19] He shared with most reformers a belief that urban populations must be disciplined, their base instincts curbed and channeled to higher pursuits.[20] However, unlike the reformers, Pullman controlled wealth sufficient to build what others only imagined. In four years, he established an orderly town of 8,000 residents that exhibited an "all-pervading air of thrift and providence," with "splendid provision" for the material comforts of its predominantly working-class population.[21] The corporation paved the streets, planted shade trees, trimmed lawns, and provided sewers as well as gas and plumbing for nearly all residents. The company also built attractive residences, mostly brick row houses, that accommodated various grades of employees.

Because of these efforts, residents never debated the provision of services nor did they suffer tragic losses from fires or crime. The corporation provided everything considered essential and prohibited everything Pullman considered harmful.[22] Workers could not own houses. Instead, they rented accommodations from the corporation because Pullman believed the corporation better equipped than residents to maintain the integrity of a planned community. In creating a model town, corporate "philanthropy" denied a local middle class an independent role in civic affairs. In Pullman, no separation existed between commercial interests and the dominant employer. They were one and the same.

Not surprisingly, Pullman heightened rather than diminished the class consciousness of workers. His policies led to a strike in 1894 that remains one of the seminal labor disturbances in American history. An event like the Pullman strike may be viewed from many perspectives. Certainly, the strike demonstrated the weakness of benevolent paternalism.[23] Following the strike, employers avoided large investments in residential properties. Few employers wished to repeat Pullman's tragic error. The violence associated with the strike led reformers like Richard Ely to renounce any taint of radicalism. While opposed to paternalism, Ely never supported unsupervised actions by the working class. He feared the mob more than the corporation.[24] But most significantly, the Pullman strike signaled the end of a locally controlled economy and the emergence of a corporate form of capitalism where ultimate power resided at a distance far removed from local control.

The strike originated in 1893 when a depression reduced the demand for new freight cars. At first, Pullman took orders at a loss to keep his workforce employed. But as the depression worsened, the company reduced wages. By May of 1894, workmen no longer earned a wage sufficient to support a family. They asked for a return to the old wage rates or a reduction in rents for the housing owned by the corporation. The corporation claimed that business conditions did not warrant a return to old wages, and it refused to lower rents. Pullman insisted that no relationship existed between conditions affecting rents and those affecting wages. The corporation regarded the shops and housing as separate investments. The profitability of one did not affect the other.

Pullman workers began their strike on May 11, 1894. As it continued into June, George Pullman distanced himself from the conflict, refusing to speak to representatives from labor. Newspaper reporters flocked to the model town and provided accounts of an entire community on strike. Initially, they portrayed the strike as a moral contest between George Pullman and his employees.[25] The reporters questioned whether one man should have so great an economic, political, and social power over workers. Most agreed with Richard Ely that the model town represented an un-American ideal, offering "the gilded cage as a substitute for personal liberty."[26]

The nature of the strike changed dramatically beginning June 12, when the newly formed American Railway Union (ARU) held its quadrennial convention in Chicago. Eugene Debs had formed the ARU in February of 1893. Debs intended to unify railroad workers regardless of skill in one large union, so its membership included unskilled workers new to the labor movement. Until this time, unions were composed overwhelmingly of skilled workers who expressed little concern for those who lacked skills. From the beginning of the convention, ARU delegates expressed sympathy for Pullman workers and called for actions against the corporation that would force arbitration. Debs favored a cautious policy. He believed that the union must perfect its organization and improve its finances before it attempted to demonstrate power. An experienced labor leader, Debs knew that ARU members throughout the country were unfamiliar with the demands of conducting a major strike.[27]

Nevertheless, Pullman remained the talk of the convention, and Debs reluctantly followed the dictates of the inexperienced delegates. On June 15, he sent representatives to the Pullman Company to discuss grievances. The company refused to negotiate. In fact, Pullman was adamant since the corporation did not recognize the ARU as the representative of workers in the car shops. The ARU responded with a resolution that unless the Pullman Company agreed to arbitrate by noon on June 26 the ARU would boycott Pullman cars, its members refusing to work with any train that hauled a Pullman sleeper. The measure threatened to interrupt rail traffic across the country. But the company still refused to bargain.[28]

The General Managers Association (GMA) opposed the ARU with even greater resolve. The GMA comprised officials of the twenty-four railroads that had terminal facilities in Chicago. Its members pledged to pursue a common policy toward labor. At no time did they intend to bargain, or allow Pullman to bargain, with the ARU. The GMA regarded the strike as an opportunity to crush a potentially dangerous labor organization. Consequently, the GMA prepared for battle with the poorly organized and weakly financed ARU. The association pooled its immense resources and hired John Egan, a former general manager of the Chicago and Great Western Railroad, to create a central office that served as headquarters during the strike. Egan received an unlimited budget and a staff that operated twenty-four hours a day for the duration of the strike. He established offices throughout the East to search for men to replace workers who walked off their jobs. Egan also hired detectives to infiltrate among strikers and report their activities to the GMA.[29]

Just prior to the deadline, the GMA announced that the railroads would honor contracts with Pullman and place sleeper cars on trains regardless of the boycott. As a result, the Pullman strike was transformed by the end of June into a battle between two very large national organizations, one representing labor, the other corporate power. This conflict overshadowed completely the earlier struggle between George Pullman and the workers in his model town.

The Pullman Strike in Hammond

Once it became clear that the GMA opposed the boycott with all the power at its disposal, Debs knew the ARU stood small chance of victory. The union possessed little more than the conviction that George Pullman treated workers unjustly. Nevertheless, when the deadline passed on June 26, Debs escalated the strike. He ordered ARU members to refuse to inspect, switch, or haul any train containing a Pullman car. If an ARU member was fired after refusing to work with a Pullman and a man was hired to take his place, Debs instructed all members who worked for that railroad to walk off their jobs. Few imagined that workers unfamiliar with the conduct of a strike could unite in support of a cause that did not affect them directly. Yet, within four days, 125,000 men walked off their jobs. The willingness of workers to strike surprised even Eugene Debs.[30]

On Wednesday, June 27, at five o'clock in the evening, Hammond ARU men and their supporters stopped an Erie train hauling two Pullman sleepers. After uncoupling the Pullmans, they pushed the cars onto the siding just as Charles Friedrich, the sheriff of Lake County, arrived with twenty-eight deputies from Crown Point. Powerless before the larger crowd of men, reported to be in the hundreds, the sheriff counseled the train's engineer to do what was best to protect himself and the property of the railroad. The crowd then pushed the Pullman cars to the Paxton Smith lumberyard, recoupled the train with its remaining cars, and told the engineer he was free to leave. At this time, an attorney for the Erie arrived, who instructed the engineer not to proceed without the Pullman cars.[31]

Already delayed several hours, the passengers demanded the train be taken into Hammond where they could get food and water. The attorney refused, insisting the train not move an inch until the Pullmans were recoupled. He offered the passengers the use of the sidetracked Pullmans for the evening and no more. Silas Swaim, editor of the *Lake County News*, reported the passengers were furious with the attorney and sympathetic with the strikers, blaming their delay on the railroad for not allowing the trains to proceed without the Pullmans.[32]

That evening strikers stopped and boarded four more trains, including a Monon train from which four Pullmans were detached. Once again, the railroad refused to permit the trains to move without the detached cars. By morning, 1,000 passengers were stranded outside Hammond, and rail traffic halted at one of the newest and most important junctions entering Chicago. The only relief came when Charles Heimbach, a Hammond politician and owner of a livery stable, brought barrels of ice water for the stranded passengers. Like most Hammond residents, Heimbach, a former butcher at the packinghouse, supported the strikers.[33]

Three days into the boycott, Hammond was an exciting place. Although the city contained no Pullman workers and fewer than 100 ARU members, most residents supported the strike. In May and early June, they had held parades, baseball games, and concerts to raise funds for striking Pullman workers. Once the boycott began, city officials and the local ARU counseled citizens to avoid conflict. On Friday afternoon, nine Illinois deputies patrolling the state line tried to persuade a group of Hammond ARU men to cross into Illinois where the deputies were authorized to arrest lawbreakers. When the men refused, two deputies crossed the line into Indiana to incite them. Officer Fred Prohl of the Hammond police arrested the Illinois deputies and charged them with impersonating Indiana officials. The deputies appeared before Judge Charles Morlock of Hammond, who set a court date for the following Monday. Morlock confiscated the deputies' watches and their money as bail. That evening, Hammond citizens chased two strangers from town after rumor spread they were Pinkertons hired to spy on Hammond residents.[34]

At this time, the federal government became involved in the strike. On June 28, U.S. Postmaster General W. S. Bissell reported to Attorney General Richard Olney that the boycott had delayed the mail in Hammond; Cairo, Illinois; Hope, Idaho; San Francisco; and a few other locations. On Friday, June 29, Olney ordered federal marshals to Hammond with warrants for three ARU members. They included Alex Shields, a railroad engineer at the packinghouse who was president of the Hammond ARU; Walter St. John, a worker at the packinghouse; and John Roscoe, an employee at an ax manufacturing plant located in Hammond.[35] The men were charged with obstructing the mails and impeding interstate rail traffic.[36]

The following morning, Saturday, June 30, marshals escorted Shields, St. John, and Roscoe to Indianapolis by special train for a meeting with Governor Claude Matthews. Matthews told Shields that he would send militia to Hammond if strikers continued to stop trains. He also provided Shields with a list of names of Hammond residents who might be charged as conspirators in obstructing the mails. Matthews said those found guilty of obstruction would receive fines of $100 and jail terms of up to two years.[37] Debs had advised locals not to provoke the use of militia at any cost. Apparently, Shields believed Matthews would send troops if necessary, for Shields wired the Hammond ARU to release all trains and to stop no others until he returned from Indianapolis.[38]

Upon receiving the telegram, members of Hammond's ARU argued that allowing free traffic would "give up all the advantages they had gained."[39] Philip Haxall, acting president of the local in Shields's absence, wired Debs and asked for instructions. Immediately, Debs sent word to release the trains and take no action that would bring out the militia or alienate the general public. For his part, Governor Matthews sent Lieutenant Thomas DeFries of the U.S. Army to Hammond to warn strikers that militia would arrive unless the trains moved freely.

On Saturday afternoon before DeFries arrived, the local ARU voted to allow traffic to proceed. But they sent committees to each of the trains entering Hammond to ask the crews hauling Pullman cars to walk off their jobs in support of the boycott. The crews refused. But the Erie train that had been stopped on Wednesday night proceeded without attaching its two sidetracked Pullmans. After seventy hours, all that remained of the halted trains were two Pullmans resting beside the Paxton Smith lumberyard.[40] No property had been harmed.

Even though Hammond's ARU obeyed authorities promptly, Chicago newspapers vilified the union. The *Chicago Inter Ocean* claimed that a howling mob controlled Hammond's switching towers, that nonunion men had been tied to railroad tracks and beaten, that strikers had vandalized signal wires, switches, and trains, and that Pullman cars had been pushed into the Calumet River. The *Inter Ocean* wrote that Hammond citizens spoke freely of burning railroad cars and that, in response, Governor Matthews ordered troops to the city, insuring bloodshed by morning.[41] Silas Swaim, editor of Hammond's *Lake County News*, denied each charge. He regarded the *Inter Ocean*'s account as "an outrage upon truth, decency, the reputation of the city, and an injury to the cause of the ARU."[42]

Bias resulted from the influence of the GMA on the reporting of the strike. The GMA hoped stories of riot and anarchy would draw the federal government into the strike. Indeed, the attorney general of the United States, Richard Olney, anxiously awaited accounts of violence, however minor, in Hammond and in other cities on the outskirts of Chicago, especially Blue Island. For much of his life, Olney was a lawyer for the railroads. He considered the boycott "an attack against railroad property, corporate control, and all that his world held dear." So he employed his representatives, the U.S. district attorneys and the U.S. marshals, against the ARU, especially in Chicago.[43]

Silas Swaim denounced the GMA and opposed federal action against strikers. He claimed representatives of the GMA were collecting information to convict anyone who interfered with the mails in Hammond. One representative told Swaim that the railroads planned to stop traffic completely if necessary to defeat the ARU, even if it meant halting commerce and placing the nation in chaos. To avoid so drastic a policy, Swaim suggested that the government assume control of the railroads. While he regarded government control as deplorable under normal conditions, Swaim considered extraordinary measures necessary to preserve the rights of ordinary people. He stated his views in an editorial addressed to the citizens of Hammond:

> Labor is now waging a battle that if won will free the shackles of labor. If lost—then the iron hand of capital will

> for years more firmly crush down the man who labors for his bread. While we can but deplore that labor must resort to such actions to gain its point yet the struggle is of such importance as to make extreme methods necessary.
>
> Cool heads and conservative action is advisable and if pursued must win, as the laborers constitute the great percentage of the people of the country. Sympathy and help are with them.[44]

Most Hammond citizens shared these views. Supporters of the ARU included skilled butchers from the packinghouse who voted to uphold the boycott. Soon afterward, workers at the slaughterhouse, both skilled and unskilled, walked off their jobs in support of the ARU, shutting down Hammond's largest industry for nearly two weeks. The workers did not have a grievance with the Hammond Company.[45] In fact, ARU president Alex Shields agreed to stand guard over packinghouse property to ensure the company suffered no damage. City officials also chose ARU men to serve as deputy marshals with responsibility for ensuring safe passage of the mail through Hammond. The officials reasoned that the ARU could maintain order among strikers, and men on strike need the wages the government paid deputy marshals.[46]

Throughout the strike, a variety of minor acts demonstrated local support for the ARU. A Nickel Plate passenger train sat idle for an entire day because no one would scab and spike the switch, not even Dennis Ryan of Hammond's switching tower, said to be the largest in the world. Ryan and two associates walked off their jobs, an action that slowed tremendously the passage of trains through town and drew cheers from a large crowd "highly elated over the new victory for the boys." Workers for the Chicago and Calumet Terminal Beltline united so strongly in favor of the strike that the railroad's engines remained in the roundhouse. As a consequence, manufacturers in Hammond, Whiting, and East Chicago, including Standard Oil's huge new refinery, could not ship goods. One week into the boycott, Hammond had become the terminus for westbound Erie and Monon trains. These roads unloaded passengers in Hammond and transferred them to streetcars to complete their trip to Chicago.[47]

A few acts of vandalism occurred. During the first week of the boycott, groups of men placed freight cars across tracks and drained locomotives of water. However, Silas Swaim reported, "no rioting or violence of any kind occurred and the depredations in regard to freight cars were not committed by home people nor were sanctioned by the ARU."[48] Unfortunately, crowds were not as controlled ten miles west in Blue Island, where strikers gathered along the tracks and prevented passage of the mails. Their actions provided Attorney General Olney with an opportunity to intervene.[49] On July 2, Olney secured a court injunction from Federal Judges William A. Wood and Peter S. Grosscup charging that strikers had prevented nonstriking workers from doing their jobs and, therefore, delayed the mails. To secure passage of the mail, the injunction declared it illegal for strikers to gather near the railroad or the property of the railroad. In addition, it forbade union leaders from sending messages that might encourage members to stop work and join the strike.[50]

The *New York Times* called the injunction "a gatling gun on paper" because it limited so effectively the ability of the ARU to conduct the strike. When marshals read the injunction before 2,000 strikers in Blue Island on July 1, the crowd remained on railroad property. After marshals tried to disperse the crowd, they telegraphed Olney to report their failure and request federal troops so that they could carry out the injunction. Olney advised Grover Cleveland to send the cavalry to Chicago to insure passage of the mails.[51]

Illinois Governor John Peter Altgeld regarded Olney's conduct and the approval of President Cleveland as a usurpation of constitutional rights guaranteed the states. Altgeld insisted that police and state militia could maintain order in Illinois. Certainly, the injunctions favored the railroads. Most important, the injunctions escalated once again the significance of the strike, for the GMA now played a less visible role. With the issuing of injunctions against the strikers, the contest was transformed from a battle between the ARU and the railroads to a battle between the strikers and the U.S. government.[52]

Federal troops arrived in Chicago on July 4. Silas Swaim warned "all friends of labor to keep cool, be cautious and in no way become involved." But on Friday, July 6, violence broke out at rail junctions around Chicago causing $340,000 in damages. No violence and no damage occurred in Hammond. Most of the loss resulted from a fire that destroyed 700 freight cars at the Pan Handle Yards ten miles northwest of Hammond.[53] Newspapers claimed anarchy erupted throughout the city. The press vilified Debs as a dictator willing to promote violence and portrayed Illinois Governor John Peter Altgeld as unwilling to use troops to quell riots, protect property, and restore order.[54]

The most lurid descriptions identified strikers as foreigners and thugs. In *Harper's Weekly*, the artist Frederick Remington drew sharp comparisons of the heroic cavalry with the uncontrolled, anarchistic mob. Remington expressed his position clearly when he described a cavalry march through the Chicago stockyards:

> When infantry must walk through a seething mass of smells, stale beer, and bad language, such as my picture indicates, they don't at all understand. The soldier idea would be to create about eleven cords of compost out of the material at hand. And, again, the soldier mind does not understand this Hungarian or Polack, or whatever the stuff is; he will talk to a real American striker in an undertone and tell him it is best to go home and not get shot, but he tells me in his simple way, "Say, do you know, them things ain't human—before God I don't think they are men."[55]

Remington informed readers that the "true American workman" supported a violent response against strikers, including shooting blindly into crowds if necessary. He reported favorably an incident that occurred after the cavalry pursued a crowd:

> After the malodorous crowd of anarchistic foreign trash had run as far as its breath would hold out and the cavalry halted, a real workman came out on a window landing of a big factory and shook his fist at the fleeing mob. "Kill em—, kill every one of 'em, you soldiers; they are cowards; they ain't got no wives and children; they are cowardly whelps, and they do me harm who have a wife and children, and wants to make an honest living. Damn'em. I wish I was a soldier." Whereat Uncle Sam's Troopers felt morally refreshed.[56]

On Saturday, July 7, the night following the fires at the Pan Handle yards, strikers stopped a Michigan Central train in Hammond and roughed up the engineer and fireman. Later, a large crowd stopped a Monon train and detached three Pullman sleepers. At the Michigan Central yards, vandals struck the switch inspector with a coupling pin, knocking him unconscious, while another mob drove a telegraph operator from the depot. By midnight, rioters had overturned cars and destroyed track. At three o'clock someone set fire to the three side-tracked Pullman cars. When reports of the vandalism reached federal authorities, they immediately dispatched troops to Hammond.[57]

The following morning, thirty-five soldiers arrived under the command of Captain Hartz. Mayor Reilly protested, insisting he had restored order. But Hartz ignored Reilly and stationed men about town, giving orders "to shoot to kill" anyone interfering with railroad property. The soldiers spent most of their time guarding men clearing the tracks of debris from the previous night. By afternoon, a crowd had gathered, consisting primarily of local residents curious about the troops and the events of the night before. The crowd also included newspaper men, including Remington, as well as a number of young toughs from Chicago drawn to the excitement.

The *Lake County News* reported all was quiet until four-thirty when the troops boarded a southbound train to clear the tracks for an incoming Monon. Once the troops were out of sight, a small crowd threw ropes around one of the burned Pullman cars to overturn the car and block the return of the troops.[58] Ray Stannard Baker was a young reporter for the *Chicago Record*. Later, he testified that the crowd was led by "a big rough-looking fellow, whom the people called Pat," one of the toughs who had arrived in Hammond the previous night. A large crowd gathered as Pat and a few others tried to overturn the Pullman. The soldiers raced back toward Hammond, riding on the running boards and fender of an engine. Without warning, they drew their rifles, aimed, and fired into the crowd. The townspeople scattered. Many were hemmed between rows of boxcars. When the shooting began, they were forced to run toward the troopers, who continued to fire.

Baker took cover by climbing a ladder behind a freight car. Believing himself safe, he caught his breath when a bullet shot through the car, passing an arm's length from his body.[59] The *Lake County News* claimed the troopers continued firing until they arrived at the burned Pullman cars. "Then three soldiers stepped from the engine and fired deliberately into the crowd of spectators. One [of the soldiers] stooped and aimed at some object over on the Erie Side of the track. His aim proved good and Charles Fleischer dropped."[60]

The death of Charles Fleischer made headlines across the country. Fleischer was a carpenter for the Hammond Company. He was not a member of the ARU and was not involved in overturning the Pullman car. Fleischer, his wife, and his children were spectators. When the soldiers fired, Fleischer's "child ran away from him towards the scene of trouble. Fleischer heeded not the protest of his wife but started in search of the child when he was shot down like a dog." Swaim called the shooting "cold blooded murder" and reported that the four others shot were also innocent spectators.[61]

After the shooting, "indignation ran at fever heat and had there been arms at hand a bloody riot would have followed." The local president of the ARU, Alex Shields, along with T. E. Bell, a local doctor, sent a telegram to Governor Matthews asking for protection from the federal troops. Matthews ordered state militia to Hammond. For the remainder of the day, Mayor Reilly and the police pleaded with citizens to stay away from the soldiers. Few listened. That evening, Reilly received word that "300 troops, each man with forty rounds of ammunition" were on their way to Hammond. The following day, 800 federal and state soldiers were stationed in the city, armed with two gatling guns, one positioned above a railroad station, the other at the intersection of State and Hohman Streets.[62]

On Sunday evening, July 7, Mayor Reilly called a mass meeting for citizens. With support from priests, ministers, and ARU men, Reilly asked residents to avoid confrontation with the troops. He announced that the city had issued a warrant for the arrest of the soldier who murdered Charles Fleischer. The following day, Chicago papers vilified Reilly claiming he acted treasonously in seeking the arrest of a U.S. soldier. That night, citizens gathered again in a mass meeting to protest the distortions and lies spread by Chicago newspapers. Led by a lawyer, a priest, a minister, and a merchant, the Citizens' Committee of Hammond passed resolutions expressing their views of the incident.

The meeting denounced "the sending of federal troops without first allowing civil and state authorities to exhaust their resources." They condemned the troops for shooting on "crowds of peaceable citizens, including women and children." Describing the military's actions as "reckless, uncalled for, and wanton," the meeting called on Congress to determine whether the shooting was criminal and whether Fleischer's widow should receive compensation. It concluded by endorsing the conduct of Mayor Reilly and Sheriff Friedreich as "wise, patriotic, and humane." They expressed "full confidence in [Reilly's and Friedreich's] integrity and patriotism, wisdom, prudence, and desire to comply with the law." Most residents believed the shooting would have been avoided if the troops had responded to Hammond officials. The *Lake County News* considered it a sign of good leadership that Hammond police had not arrested a single resident during the strike. The citizens' meeting ended with a proposal by Robert Gregory, a local lawyer, that Hammond endorse the protest of Governor Altgeld against the invasion of his state by the U.S. Army. This proposal received much discussion since it indicted the actions of the president of the United States, Grover Cleveland. Although many objected, a majority approved Gregory's resolution.[63]

Support for the ARU remained high following the meeting. On Thursday, July 12, five days after the trooper shot Fleischer, the Hammond Company received a large shipment of cattle and sheep. The company ordered employees to return to work, threatening to close the plant for a year if they did not. No one returned. Instead, managers and foremen slaughtered and packed the beef, much to the amusement of residents.[64] Local newspapers continued their support for the strikers by reporting misbehavior by the troops, such as the stealing of chickens. They also claimed that drunken soldiers verbally abused women on Hammond's streets. The *Lake County News* reported the guard of the gatling gun on State Street fell asleep on duty, only to awaken and find his hands and feet tied to the gun.[65]

On Friday, July 13, a small group of citizens formed the Law and Order League. They took exception to the resolutions that praised Reilly and Friedreich. Of the seventy-four men in attendance, most were American-born. They were led by Casius Griffin, a local attorney and son of a prominent Crown Point family, who often performed work for the railroads. The league denounced Reilly, blaming the mayor and sheriff for Fleischer's death. Fleischer died, the league argued, because Reilly did not arrest strikers the night before, a failure that demonstrated cowardice or sympathy for the ARU. The league also took exception to the resolutions passed by the Citizens' Committee. They considered the resolutions "evidence of the densest ignorance and grossest disrespect for the Constitution and laws of the United States."[66]

Three days later the Citizens' Committee met again. The Hohman Opera House was "too small to accommodate the laboring people and their friends." The committee denounced the Law and Order League and reaffirmed the earlier resolutions, with the exception of the endorsement for Governor Altgeld. They concluded "with three cheers for the flag, three more for Mayor Reilly, and three more for Sheriff Friedreich."[67] These actions were of no consequence. Two days later, on July 18, the Pullman company posted notice it would rehire workers. Within six weeks, 2,700 men were employed at the Pullman shops. Most had been employed by the company prior to the strike. They were, however, no longer members of the ARU.[68]

The Aftermath

In his autobiography, Ray Stannard Baker described the shooting of Charles Fleischer as the final incident of "one of the greatest industrial conflicts in American history." But he remembered the end of the strike as anticlimactic, for the "cowed and beaten workmen had crept back into the Pullman shops, the railroads were operating again, the evidence of fire and riot had been removed, nothing had been much changed. . . . Most people were just profoundly relieved to have the trouble ended."[69] The citizens of Hammond shared this sentiment. By the third week of July, the local ARU voted fifty-nine to twenty-two to end the boycott. Soon afterward, the militia withdrew, and Silas Swaim called for reconciliation: "After one month's military surveillance Hammond will again be without soldiers. During the recent troubles Hammond gained a reputation for lawlessness and mob acts. Let us now show to the world that our claim that these acts were not perpetrated by nor sanctioned by labor here was true. Any acts of violence or lawlessness will be taken by the outside world as the most positive evidence that from the first to the last the wanton deeds were committed by our citizens. Let Peace reign."[70]

Following the strike, class sentiments persisted. When Eugene Debs spoke in Hammond in the fall of 1896, he encountered a crowd so large no auditorium in the city could hold it. Debs went into the street and preached for two hours, denouncing the alliance between government and the corporations.[71] But Debs failed to unite labor. While he affected audiences emotionally, Debs never convinced "a majority of workers to jettison their traditional political loyalties."[72] As Richard Oestreicher argued, after 1896, labor simply had "nowhere to go politically" until the 1930s when the Democratic party appealed to "unmobilized pockets of class sentiment."[73]

Seven years after the Pullman strike, Hammond felt the sharp edge of corporate capitalism once again when fire destroyed the Hammond Company in October of 1901. Damages exceeded $500,000. Company officials announced plans to rebuild. It never happened. Instead, they sold the remaining property to National Packing, a trust controlled by Philip Armour. Armour chose not to rebuild, so Hammond lost 1,500 jobs.[74] The following year, the city's manufacturing output declined from $25 million a year to less than $8 million. To meet the crisis, Mayor Armanis Knotts created the Industrial Committee of Hammond, an organization of local business leaders responsible for attracting new industries.[75]

At the time of the strike, Knotts was a young lawyer who supported actively the cause of the ARU. He owned a Populist newspaper edited by his brother, Tom, who was arrested during the strike for encouraging ARU members to defy the injunction.[76] But in 1901, as mayor during an economic crisis, Knotts called for consensus so the city could overcome the loss of its largest employer. He appointed A.

Murray Turner to the Industrial Committee. Turner was Hammond's leading banker, the founder of the gas and electric company, and a large investor in local real estate. He had been a member of the Law and Order League that condemned Mayor Reilly's conduct during the strike.

In 1901 Knotts and Turner dismissed differences. Over the next year, they united with other leading citizens to persuade seven industries to locate in Hammond. To do so, they boasted that Hammond was "peculiarly a city of Homes." But home ownership no longer held its earlier political meaning, for the committee assured potential manufacturers that Hammond would "protect your interests first, last, and all the time." Another organization, the Business Men's Association, offered additional promises. They insisted that the Board of Metropolitan Police Commissioners would "preserve order in the strictest sense whenever there was any strike or other strained relations between employer and employee and at no time to permit outsiders to come into the city and agitate and create labor troubles among wage earners."[77]

According to the *Hammond Daily News*, the promise of industrial peace "placed Hammond on the list of desirable locations for factories."[78] City officials could not have done otherwise, for without such a promise they never would have attracted industries to replace the jobs lost with the destruction of the Hammond Company. Armanis Knotts expressed the conciliatory views of local leaders at a banquet celebrating the acquisition of the new industries:

> If Hammond is prospering, it is due to her experiences. We have outgrown our political differences and animosities which were a bad thing. We have quit pulling in different directions. Everybody wants to do something for Hammond. The newspapers have quit fighting each other and the people of Hammond are mastering the industrial and economic question. A united effort and determination for better citizenship must be made; the rights of employer and employee respected. The time has come when everybody in Hammond is willing to concede that each has rights to be respected. . . . Shun the knocker and the kicker. Work for the common good.[79]

Seven years earlier, Hammond had not shunned "the knocker and the kicker." In sympathy with Pullman workers, residents asserted local independence from corporate domination and acted powerfully in support of labor. In response, corporations and the federal government employed the power at their disposal to discipline Hammond. During the strike, important decisions were made by national figures with little concern for the welfare of those who lived in small industrial towns. Under these circumstances, local people could neither affect the outcome of the strike nor prevent an increase in the power of corporate capital. Following the strike, local leaders knew they must work within a system that favored the rights of corporations because growth depended on the goodwill of powerful outsiders. New jobs would be lost if outsiders perceived Hammond as a town friendly to labor. So the local middle class became brokers, referees in a contest weighted decisively in favor of capital. By the twentieth century, corporate power had disciplined industrial towns by eroding the sense of proprietorship that had aligned local capitalists with the working class.

The remaining chapters examine the period from the beginning of the twentieth century to the Great Depression. During this time, Hammond and other cities in the Calumet region attracted large numbers of new immigrants from eastern Europe. At best, these immigrants struggled for accommodation. They expressed little desire to oppose the economic system. Even if they had opposed it, no national political party or labor organization articulated a program capable of overcoming the ethnic and racial divisions of the American working class. Consequently, for a generation, corporations exercised enormous control over employment and the conditions of labor.

But new immigrants were not passive. Like the Germans who preceded them, they became a vital part of the local economy by purchasing houses and shaping the built environment to suit their needs. They also participated in local politics in a manner affecting their lives and the lives of their neighbors. So even after the Pullman strike, Hammond's working class enjoyed freedoms that George Pullman denied the residents of his model town. These freedoms allowed even poor immigrants like the Poles to create decent communities and develop a positive vision of urban, working-class life. As a result, despite the triumph of corporate capitalism, local markets remained socially and culturally significant. They continued to provide spaces largely free from the control of social and economic superiors. Consequently, they served as the primary location where new immigrants learned of the freedoms of American life.

PART THREE

NEW IMMIGRANTS, CITIZENSHIP, AND CHICAGO'S HOUSING MARKET

CHAPTER 4

Chicago Polonia and the Complex Market

At the turn of the century, with the emergence of corporate capitalism, native intellectuals warned that the rapid pace of social change threatened cherished notions of American democracy. They especially feared the continued immigration of southern and eastern Europeans. In 1907, the economist John R. Commons explained that "race differences are established in the very blood and physical constitution. They are most difficult to eradicate, and they yield only to the slow processes of the centuries." According to Commons, history already had reduced southern and eastern European Catholics to "an inferior race that favor despotism and oligarchy rather than democracy." Consequently, these immigrants felt "no sense of citizenly motives." Inevitably, they would fail as Americans because their "blood" differed from earlier immigrants, who had risen to the opportunities present in a free society.[1]

Southern and eastern Europeans were poorer and less skilled than previous immigrants. For more than a generation, a few of Chicago's Polish neighborhoods remained notorious for containing the largest concentrations of poverty in the city. But despite the poverty, Chicago's Polish community took advantage of opportunities resulting from the expansion of the city. Poles established churches and political organizations immediately upon settling in newer portions of metropolitan Chicago. They were able to do so because they belonged to a larger entity. New settlements were satellites of Chicago's established Polish community, whose centralized, institutional life was in place at the beginning of the century.

The creation of social, religious, and cultural institutions required enormous energy and produced intense debate among Poles over the proper form their communities should assume in the United States. Yet reformers, such as Commons, ignored these struggles. Reformers attributed conditions to factors external to the immigrant community, to low wages, to poor sanitation, and to an economic system prone to booms and busts. While neighborhoods were plagued with poverty, vice, crime, disease, juvenile delinquency, alcoholism, desertion, and infant mortality, these factors did not affect immigrant communities as pervasively as reformers suggested.

Chicago's Polish neighborhoods varied considerably. These variations increased as generational differences separated the earliest Polish immigrants and their children from later arrivals. Indeed, the high tide of immigration pushed the community in two directions. By 1920, Poles resided in outdated, deteriorating neighborhoods, as well as in a variety of newer neighborhoods, which offered greater amenities. A varied housing market allowed them to maintain the allegiance of both the poor and the more prosperous members of the community.

This chapter provides an overview of Polish settlement in Chicago from its origins to about 1940. It establishes the importance of Roman Catholicism for understanding the physical and social expansion of the community. For Poles, Catholicism provided a central, organizing principal that allowed them to disperse to various parishes throughout metropolitan Chicago and yet retain a common allegiance. Their actions were remarkably creative, part of what John T. McGreevy has described as "a specifically Catholic style of merging neighborhood and religious organized life" that was critical to the development of twentieth-century northern cities.[2] The process was never static or one-dimensional. It resulted from an evolving relationship among immigrants, the housing market, and an expanding and improving Catholic infrastructure. By examining various portions of metropolitan Chicago, this chapter establishes a larger pattern of immigrant resettlement, begun early in the twentieth century, which shows that Polish Catholics engaged in precisely those activities for which John Commons considered them racially unsuited.

Community Formation and Parish Life

In the United States, the Catholic hierarchy allowed immigrant groups to form parishes exclusively for their own use. These national parishes preserved the faith by allowing immigrants to maintain familiar traditions.[3] Among Poles, the national parish was especially important since 95 percent of Polish immigrants were practicing Catholics. National parishes developed solidarity in America, creating a larger identity by overcoming the differences engendered by attachments to villages and regions in Poland. Polish immigrants described this collective identity as "Polonia." In its broadest sense, Polonia stood for the great emigration, for the collective experience shared by those who left Poland to reside for a time in America.[4]

Membership in a parish linked individuals to a network of fraternal and religious institutions that supported the collective ideal. Most commonly, immigrants joined fraternal organizations to acquire insurance. But the benefits exceeded simple measures to protect oneself against misfortune. Polish Catholics developed a complete set of religious, social, and economic institutions that cared for members throughout their lives, from the cradle to the grave.[5] These institutions sustained individual members while promoting allegiance to the larger group, to Polonia. One priest expressed the attitude of most immigrants when he wrote, "The Polish Catholic who doesn't belong to any parish is homeless—without support, religious or national, he is a social bankrupt, a bandit on the open highway, and sooner or later he must perish because without support and help he will not be able to meet the test."[6]

The desire to form a church arose as soon as a few Poles settled in a city. The process was not orchestrated by the diocese or by the clergy. Invariably, a church began when a few immigrants organized a mutual benefit society for the purpose of establishing as quickly as possible a national parish where they could practice their faith. Once the society raised sufficient funds, it purchased land and petitioned the local bishop to send a priest. This pattern repeated wherever Poles resided in the United States, but especially in Chicago, Detroit, Milwaukee, and Buffalo. In each of these cities, Polish institutions grew phenomenally during the first generation of settlement.[7]

Even though Poles agreed on the importance of the national parish, they disagreed regarding the appropriate form of community life in America. Wherever Poles settled, intense conflicts arose over the ownership of church property and the role of laypeople in governing the parishes. These conflicts involved a struggle for power between those who supported authoritarian leaders—typically priests who wished to build large centrally controlled community institutions capable of uniting quickly an expanding immigrant population—and a lay opposition who recognized the need for unity but who challenged clerical leaders over the control of finances.[8] The division resulted from the priority of allegiances, over whether Poles in America should be Polish and Catholic, as the lay-controlled nationalist faction wished, or whether they should be Catholic and Polish, as the clerical faction wished. Neither faction was hostile to Catholicism or nationalism. The conflict concerned the degree to which an individual committed to each.[9]

In Chicago, the clerical faction was controlled by Vincent Barzynski, a Resurrectionist priest and the dominant figure in the early history of Poles in the United States.[10] For twenty-five years, Barzynski reigned as pastor of Saint Stanislaus Kostka, by far the largest Polish parish in the United States.[11] He influenced the religious character of Polish life in Chicago, as well as the social and geographical nature of the community.[12] During his tenure, Barzynski wielded power ruthlessly. Even fellow Resurrectionists described him as someone who "doesn't want to listen to any advice . . . [because] prudence and moderation are found in him rarely."[13]

The critical issues were not theological. Barzynski was not an inquisitor. He was a brick-and-mortar priest, a builder of churches and schools, concerned with construction, finance, and administration. Through his influence with the diocese, he determined whether Polish immigrants could establish parishes to serve new areas of the city.[14] Opposition to Barzynski was intense. In a number of instances, riots occurred when he used heavy-handed tactics to control the lives of Polish Catholics throughout the city.[15] Nevertheless, Barzynski presided over an enormous growth of the Polish community, both in numbers and institutions. When he died in 1899, his parish, Saint Stanislaus Kostka, claimed a membership of 40,000. Saint Stanislaus served as the centerpiece of an area known as the Polish Downtown, which contained a wealth of institutions both large and small. By comparison, Polish neighborhoods in other portions of the city were mere outposts with small populations.[16] (See table 10 and figs. 73 and 74.)

Chicago Polonia grew more rapidly following Barzynski's death, increasing from 60,000 in 1900 to 150,000 in 1910 to more than

Table 10 The Number of Priests, Teachers, and School Children for Polish Parishes in Chicago and Its Suburbs in 1900

Parish	Location	Clergy	Teachers	Children
St. Stanislaus Kostka	Polish Downtown	10	37	3,849
Holy Trinity	Polish Downtown	3	20	876
St. Adalbert	West side	3	12	1,240
Immaculate Conception	South Chicago	2	15	889
Sts. Cyril and Methodius	Lemont	1	3	322
St. Mary	Bridgeport	3	13	1,045
St. Josaphat	Lincoln Part	2	8	952
St. Joseph	Back of the Yards	2	9	694
St. Hedwig	Polish Downtown	2	9	985
St. Casmir	West side	1	6	360
St. Andrew	west Hammond	1	4	297
St. Michael	South Chicago	2	11	800
St. John Cantius	Polish Downtown	3	12	1,056
St. Hyacinth	Northwest side	1	3	230
Sts. Peter and Paul	Back of the Yards	1	2	79
Our Lady of Czestochowa	Cicero	1	1	75
St. Mary of Angels	Polish Downtown	2	3	447
St. Salomea	South side	1	...	...
Total	...	40	169	14,190

Source: *The Catholic Directory, Almanac, and Clergy List Quarterly for the Year of Our Lord 1900* (New York: P. J. Kennedy & Sons, 1900), 69–72.

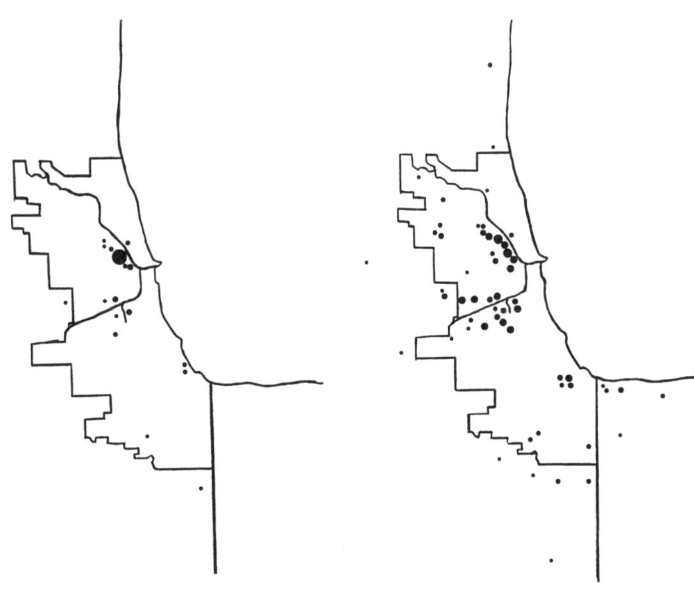

Figure 73 *(left)* Map showing the location of Polish parishes in metropolitan Chicago and the number of school children in parish schools in 1900. (Source: *The Catholic Directory, Almanac, and Clergy list Quarterly for the Year of Our Lord 1900* [New York: P. J. Kennedy & Sons, 1900], 69–72.)

Figure 74 *(right)* Map showing the location of Polish parishes in metropolitan Chicago and the number of school children in parish schools in 1930. (Source: *The Catholic Directory for the Year of Our Lord 1930* [New York: P. J. Kennedy & Sons, 1930], 44–56, 363–66.)

Table 11 The Number of Priests, Teachers, and School Children for Polish Parishes in Chicago and Its Suburbs in 1920

Parish	Location	Clergy	Teachers	Children
St. Stanishlaus Kostka	Polish Downtown	8	49	2,715
Holy Trinity	Polish Downtown	6	37	2,691
St. Adalbert	West side	5	45	2,571
Immaculate Conception	South Chicago	4	27	1,195
Sts. Cyril and Methodius	Lemont	1	5	170
St. Mary	Bridgeport	3	23	1,040
St. Josaphat	Lincoln Park	4	17	980
St. Joseph	Back of the Yards	2	23	1,300
St. Hedwig	Polish Downtown	6	39	2,259
St. Casmir	West side	5	20	985
St. Andrew	West Hammond	2	11	664
St. Michael	South Chicago	4	25	1,634
St. John Santius	Polish Downtown	6	33	2,350
St. Hyacinth	Northwest side	4	16	998
Sts. Peter and Paul	Back of the Yards	3	14	958
Our Lady of Czestochowa	Cicero	3	18	901
St. Mary of Angels	Polish Downtown	4	20	1,131
St. Salomea	South side	2	10	452
St. Stanislaus	Northwest side	2	12	719
St. Stanislaus	Posen	1	3	90
St. Isidore	Blue Island	1	4	184
Assumption	South side	2	9	427
St. Anne	West side	5	18	1,187
Holy Rosary	North Chicago	2	7	381
St. Florian	Hegewisch	1	8	395
Holy Innocents	Polish Downtown	5	30	2,113

400,000 by 1920.[17] Even an autocrat as skilled as Barzynski could not have controlled expansion during the high tide of immigration. From 1900 to 1930, the number of Polish parishes in Chicago and its suburbs increased from eighteen to fifty-nine (+275 percent); the number of priests from forty to 150 (+275 percent); school teachers from 169 to 1,107 (+555 percent); and the number of school children from 14,196 to 52,569 (+270 percent). Much of the expansion occurred outside the Polish Downtown. During the twenties, the number of school children in the huge Downtown parishes of Saint Stanislaus, Holy Trinity, and Saint John Cantius decreased by 21 percent, while school populations increased in other portions of the city (tables 11 and 12; fig. 74). By 1930, no parish equaled the size of Saint

Table 11 continued

Parish	Location	Clergy	Teachers	Children
St. Joseph	Chicago Heights	1	8	430
St. John of God	Back of Yards	5	24	1,511
Good Shepherd	West side	3	5	246
Five Holy Martyrs	Back of Yards	2	8	600
St. Francis	Northwest side	1	4	260
St. Barbara	Bridgeport	3	18	938
Sacred Heart	Back of the Yards	4	19	1,245
St. Mary Magdalene	South Chicago	2	14	728
Immaculate Heart	Northwest side	2	5	215
Transifiguration	Northwest side	1	4	200
St. Wenceslaus	Northwest side	2	8	372
Ascension	Evanston	1	2	125
St. Valentine	Cicero	1	4	182
St. Helen	Polish Downtown	2	5	230
St. Ladislaus	Northwest side	1	4	140
St. John the Baptist	Harvey	1	5	302
St. James	Northwest side	1	4	229
St. Constance	Northwest side	1	4	166
St. Adalbert	Whiting	2	6	310
St. John Cantius	Whiting	2	12	553
St. Stanislaus	East Chicago	3	17	966
St. Hedwig	Gary	2	12	675
St. Casmir	Hammond	2	9	442
Total	...	136	724	41,565

Source: *The Official Catholic Directory for the Year of Our Lord 1900* (New York: P. J. Kennedy & Sons, 1920), 43–56, 244–50.

Stanislaus at the time of Barzynski's death, when the school had an enrollment of 3,849, with one teacher for every 104 students. After 1920, most Polish children attended schools in the deconcentrated industrial areas of the south side or in the more comfortable residential areas of the far northwest side, where parishes were smaller.

Despite shifts in population, the Polish Downtown remained vital. Its strong institutions allowed Poles to disperse into fragmented city neighborhoods and still be members of centralized ethnic organizations that promoted unity. However, as Chicago's Polish population expanded, its membership became diverse. By 1920, it included a mature second generation more assimilated to American life. Yet most settlements still confronted problems result-

Table 12 The Number of Priests, Teachers, and School Children for Polish Parishes in Chicago and Its Suburbs in 1930

Parish	Location	Clergy	Teachers	Children
St. Stanislaus Kostka	Polish Downtown	5	42	1,954
Holy Trinity	Polish Downtown	7	43	2,505
St. Adalbert	West side	4	42	2,173
Immaculate Conception	South Chicago	3	27	1,175
Sts. Cyril and Methodius	Lemont	1	4	165
St. Mary	Bridgeport	3	37	1,737
St. Josaphat	Lincoln Park	5	16	982
St. Joseph	Back of the Yards	4	30	1,700
St Hedwig	Polish, Downtown	6	42	2,846
St. Casmir	West side	4	45	2,333
St. Andrew	West Hammond	3	15	873
St. Michael	South Chicago	3	35	2,096
St. John Cantius	Polish Downtown	4	30	1,634
St. Hyacinth	Northwest side	6	36	1,762
Sts. Peter and Paul	Back of the Yards	3	17	1,189
Our Lady of Czestochowa	Cicero	3	20	1,028
St. Mary of Angels	PolishDowntown	4	25	1,039
St. Salomea	South side	2	10	630
St. Stanislaus	Northwest side	2	24	1,385
St. Stanislaus	Posen	1	4	262
St. Isidore	Bllue Island	1	6	288
Assumption	South side	2	13	730
St. Anne	West side	5	45	1,380
Holy Rosary	North Chicago	2	12	580
St. Florian	Hegewisch	2	19	942
Holy Innocents	Polish Downtown	3	35	2,361
St. Joseph	Chicago Heights	1	11	500
St. John of God	Back of Yards	4	29	1,914
Good Shepherd	West side	1	9	479
Five Holy Martyrs	Back of Yards	4	29	1,820
St. Francis	Northwest side	1	6	461
St. Barbara	Bridgeport	3	17	1,197
Sacred Heart	Back of the Yards	3	22	1,200
St. Mary Magdalene	South Chicago	3	22	1,005
Immaculate Heart	Northwest side	1	9	310
Transfiguration	Northwest side	1	4	183
St. Wenceslaus	Northwest side	3	17	829
Ascension	Evanston	1	5	321
St. Valentine	Cicero	1	7	323

Table 12 continued

Parish	Location	Clergy	Teachers	Children
St. Helen	Polish Downtown	3	25	1,458
St. Ladislaus	Northwest side	2	9	600
St. John the Baptist	Harvey	1	9	582
St. James	Northwest side	2	17	884
St. Constance	Northwest side	2	17	652
St. Adalbert	Whiting	2	8	463
St. john Cantius	Whiting	3	17	795
St. Stanislaus	East Chicago	4	28	1,443
St. Hedwig	Gary	3	16	840
St. Casmir	Hammond	2	15	753
St. Bronislawa	South Chicago	3	10	512
St. Fidelis	Polish Downtown	2	9	650
St. Pancratius	Back of the Yards	2	20	970
St. Blaise	Argo	1	8	446
St. Bruno	Back of the Yards	1	11	603
St. Turbius	Back of the Yards	1	4	145
St. Thecla	Northwest side	1	8	214
St. Susana	Harvey	1	4	296
St. Roman	Back of the Yards	1	...	...
St. Camillus	Back of the Yards	1	10	350
St. Simeon	Bellwood	1	5	233
Total		153	1,147	59,180

Source: *The Catholic Directory for the Year of Our Lord 1930* (New York: P. J. Kennedy & Sons, 1930), 44–56, 363–66.

ing from a larger population of new arrivals. Philip Gleason has suggested that under these circumstances an immigrant group experienced "an identity crisis—a climatic turning point in its development that require[d] it to resolve the contradiction of being different from what it was in the past, and yet the same."[18] The housing market responded to these pressures by moving in two directions. The older neighborhoods became more crowded and foreign-born, while newer neighborhoods offered a more affluent second generation a greater share of the amenities associated with modern life.

The Nature of Chicago's Immigrant Housing Market

Immigrants did not disperse randomly upon arrival in the United States. The size of communities and their percentage of the total population varied from city to city. For example, the total populations of Chicago and Philadelphia were similar in 1900, yet Chicago was home to ten times as many Polish families (table 13). Philadelphia never developed a district like Chicago's Polish Downtown.[19] Some cities much smaller than Philadelphia had larger Polish communities with greater impact on local housing markets. In 1900, Milwaukee had 6,558 Polish families, who represented 11 percent of the city's population and 13 percent of all home owners. In contrast, Philadelphia's 2,052 Polish families were less than 1 percent of all families and a negligible percentage of home owners.

Rates of ownership also varied from city to city. Figure 75 compares home ownership in 1900 among native-born families, immigrant families, and Polish families in eight cities. Among the foreign-born, ownership ranged from as high as 63 percent of families in Milwaukee to as low as 22 percent in Philadelphia. Variations among just Poles were even greater. In Chicago, Buffalo, Pittsburgh, and Philadelphia, the percentages of Polish families owning houses were less than the percentages of native families and other foreign-born families. In Milwaukee and Cleveland, Poles were more likely than the native-born but less likely than the total foreign-born population to own houses. But Polish families in Detroit and Toledo had the highest rates of ownership. In Toledo, three of every five Polish families owned houses, compared with one in five in Chicago.[20]

By itself, a statistic such as the percentage of families owning homes has little value. Any study that compared ownership rates

Table 13 Residential Statistics for Cities with Large Polish Populations in 1990

		Residential	Families	Percentage of Buildings Occupied By		
City	Families	Dwellings	per Dwelling	One Family	Two Families	Three or More
Chicago	354,036	193,895	1.8	54	26	20
Philadelphia	263,093	241,589	1.1	93	05	2
Cleveland	82,014	63,205	1.3	80	16	4
Buffalo	72,436	49,914	1.5	69	22	9
Pittsburgh	62,922	51,024	1.2	81	15	4
Detroit	59,836	52,046	1.1	87	11	2
Milwaukee	58,889	45,809	1.3	75	21	4
Toledo	28,319	26,632	1.1	93	6	1
Total	979,565	724,114	1.4	77	15	8

Source: U.S. Bureau f the Census, *Twelfth Census of the United States, Populations*, pt. 2 (Washington, D.C.. U.S. Census Office, 1902), 614–15.

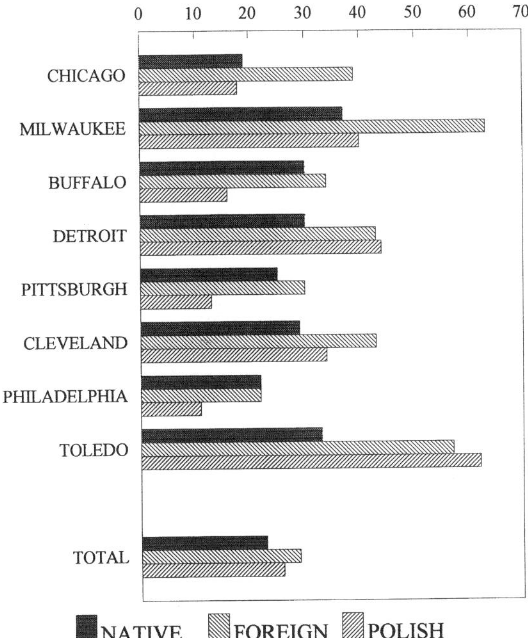

Figure 75
The percentages of native-born families, foreign-born families, and Polish families who were home owners in 1900. (Source: U.S. Bureau of the Census, *Twelfth Census of the United States, Population*, pt. 2 [Washington, D.C.: U.S. Census Office, 1902], 751–754.)

without additional considerations would mislead as much as it clarified. In 1900, Chicago was the great population center of the Midwest. Its housing market was so large that even though the percentage of families owning houses was low, the number of families owning in Chicago (86,435) was greater than the number in Milwaukee, Detroit, Cleveland, and Toledo combined. In addition, Chicago was distinguished from smaller Midwestern cities by a supply of residences housing three or more families (fig. 76).

The ratio of families per residential dwelling provides a convenient measure of the extent of multiple-family housing in a city. In 1900, Chicago averaged 1.8 families for every residential building, compared with a ratio of 1.1 families for every dwelling in Philadelphia. In other words, while there were eighteen families for every ten residential buildings in Chicago, in Philadelphia there were eleven. So even though Philadelphia had 90,943 (26 percent) fewer families, it had 47,694 (20 percent) more residential buildings (table 13).

Multiple-family residences affected tremendously the percentage of families whom census takers could record as home owners. A city with a separate residential building for every family (a ratio of one family per dwelling) had the potential for 100 percent home

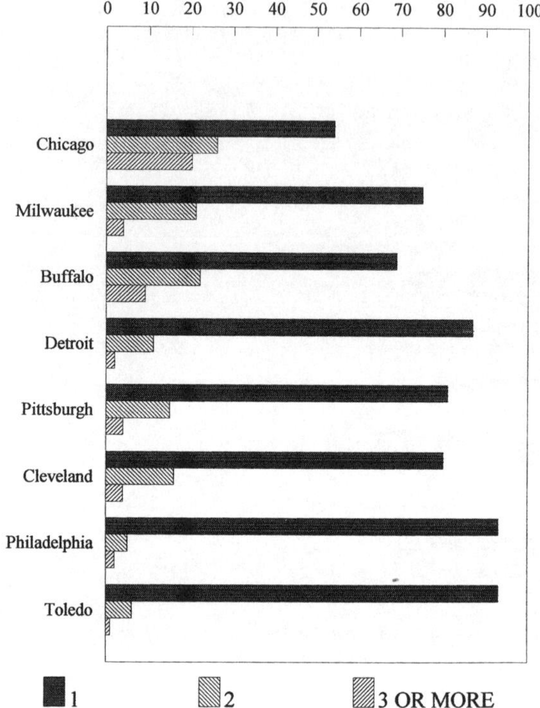

Figure 76 The percentages of residential buildings housing one, two, and three or more families for eight cities in 1900. (Source: U.S. Bureau of the Census, *Twelfth Census of the United States, Population*, pt. 2 [Washington, D.C.: U.S. Census Office, 1902], 621.)

ownership since every family living in that city theoretically could have owned the residence in which it lived. But a city with two families in every residential structure (a ratio of two families per dwelling) had the potential for only 50 percent home ownership since census takers could list only one family as home owner. The other family rented. Clearly, a large supply of multiple-family residences reduced substantially the percentage of Chicagoans who could be listed as home owners.

Another statistic, the percentage of residential buildings occupied by owner, is unaffected by multiple-family housing. All cities had the potential for 100 percent owner occupancy since every residential building could be occupied by an owner regardless of how many families lived in the structure. Buildings in Chicago were as likely to be owned by an occupant as buildings in cities with much higher rates of home ownership (fig. 77). In Chicago, Buffalo, Milwaukee, Detroit, Cleveland, and Toledo, slightly less than one-half of all residential buildings were owner-occupied. However, in Chicago, owners more often occupied buildings with multiple

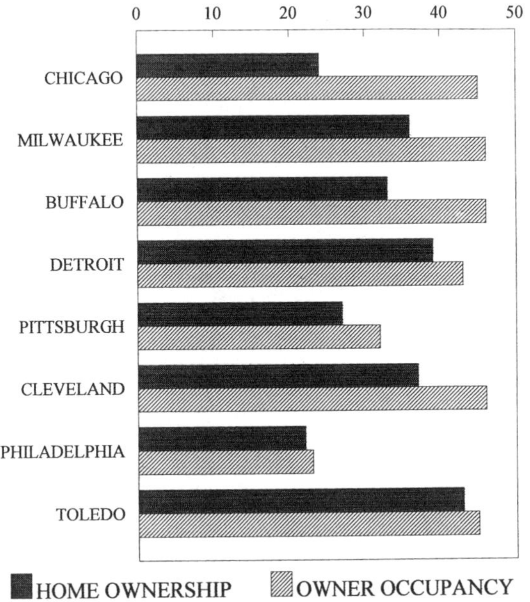

Figure 77 The percentages of families who were home owners and the percentage of buildings that were occupied by owners in 1900. (Source: U.S. Bureau of the Census, *Twelfth Census of the United States, Population*, pt. 2 [Washington, D.C.: U.S. Census Office, 1902], 640–659, 702–711.)

families. Polish neighborhoods, especially, consisted of home owners who were landlords. Among the Poles, a stable home-owning class profited from rents paid by a transient class of fellow immigrants. Consequently, most rent money remained in the community, supplementing the low wages earned by a largely unskilled working class.

Again, comparing Chicago with Philadelphia allows for a better understanding of the market. In 1890, the two cities were roughly equal in population, and both were divided into thirty-four wards. Figure 78 plots the average value of mortgaged houses in each ward for both cities, ranking the wards from the highest in average value to lowest. Two gaps are evident between lines A and B. One gap suggests that the value of housing in the more expensive wards of Chicago was greater than the value of housing in similar wards in Philadelphia. This fact has no significance for this study. But the second gap shows that a house in the lowest-valued wards of Chicago was less, on average, than a house in the lowest-valued wards of Philadelphia. However, the difference was even greater since the lower-valued wards in Chicago contained multiple-family housing. The Chicago wards had 1.5 families for every residential dwelling while the Philadelphia wards provided a separate residence for nearly every family (fig. 79).

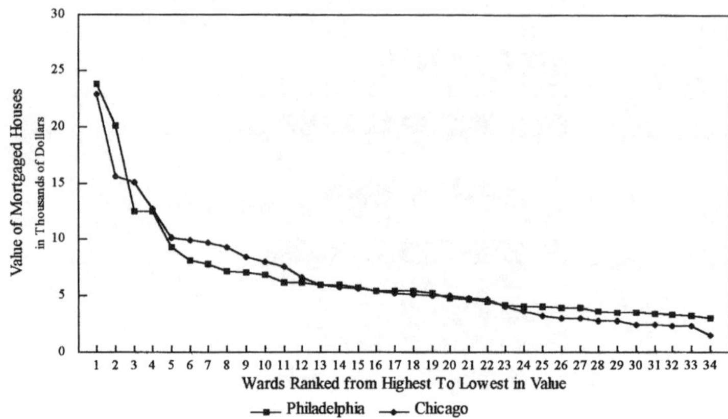

Figure 78
The average value of mortgaged homes by wards for Chicago and Philadelphia in 1890, with wards ranked from highest value to lowest. (Source: Department of the Interior, Census Office, *Compendium of the Eleventh Census: 1890*, pt. 1, *Population* [Washington, D.C.: Government Printing Office, 1892], 470, 472.)

These graphs suggest that multiple-family housing in the lower-valued wards of Chicago cost about as much as single-family housing in Philadelphia. Of course, the rough nature of the data makes generalizations precarious. But Philadelphia's single-family brick row housing probably was more expensive than frame cottages for one or two families. In eastern cities, brick row housing derived from eighteenth-century traditions, which encouraged the conservative development of real estate.[21] Midwestern cities were unbound by these traditions. They became important centers of population in a generation. To meet the demand for housing, Chicago, Detroit, Buffalo, Cleveland, Toledo, and Milwaukee built affordable one- and two-family frame cottages for the working class.

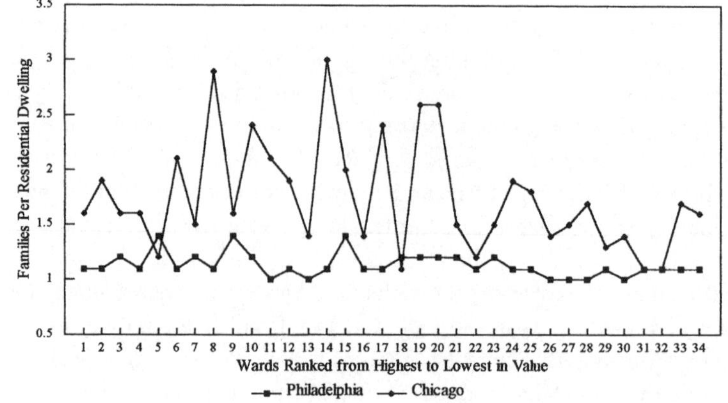

Figure 79
The ratio of families for every residential dwelling by wards for Chicago and for Philadelphia in 1890, with wards ranked from highest in value to lowest. (Source: Department of the Interior, Census Office, *Compendium of the Eleventh Census: 1890*, pt. 1, *Population* [Washington, D.C.: Government Printing Office, 1892].)

Figures 80 and 81 show that home ownership and owner occupancy were higher in the lower-valued wards of Chicago than in comparable wards in Philadelphia. In fact, Chicago's lower-valued wards had the highest rates of ownership. More than 40 percent of families in Chicago's eight lowest-valued wards owned houses, and 60 percent of the residential buildings were owner-occupied. In other Midwestern cities, the lowest-valued wards also had the highest rates of ownership. In Milwaukee, Ward 14 had a large Polish population. The average value of a mortgaged home was $1,400, a figure comparable to the cost of housing in Hammond. Ward 14 had the highest percentage of ownership in Milwaukee (57 percent), with nearly four of five residential buildings owner-occupied.[22] Detroit's, lowest-valued ward, 16, also had the highest rate of ownership. The average value of

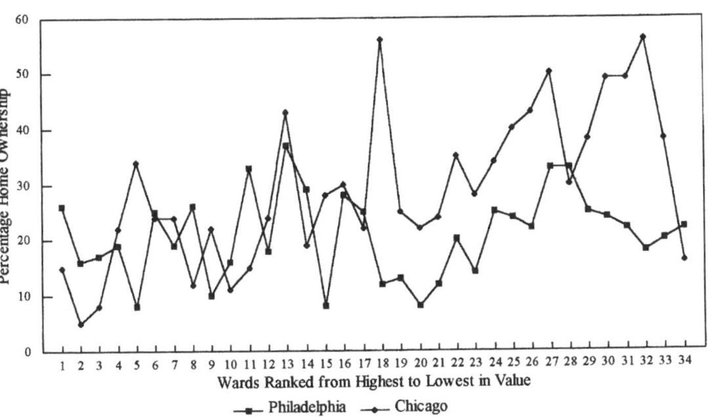

Figure 80
The percentages of families who were home owners for each ward in Chicago and Philadelphia in 1890, with wards ranked from highest to lowest in value. (Source: Department of the Interior, Census Office, *Compendium of the Eleventh Census: 1890*, pt. 1, *Population* [Washington, D.C.: Government Printing Office, 1892], 373, 377.)

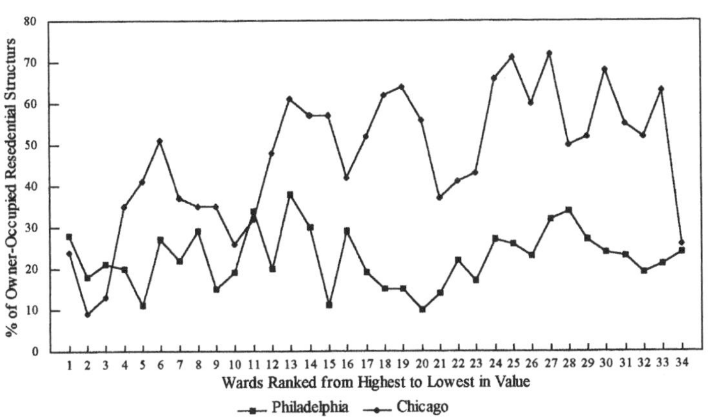

Figure 81
The percentage of buildings that were occupied by home owners for each ward in chicago and philadelphia in 1890 with wards ranked from highest to lowest in value. (Source: Department of the Interior, Census Office, *Compendium of the Eleventh Census: 1890*, pt. 1, *Population* [Washington, D.C.: Government Printing Office, 1892], 373, 377, 954, 955.)

a mortgaged home in Detroit was even less than in Milwaukee's Ward 14. In Cleveland, the highest rates occurred in Wards 25 and 40, where the average value of a mortgaged home was the same as in Milwaukee's Polish neighborhood.

High rates of ownership were common on the periphery of Midwestern cities.[23] Chicago had a large market for such housing. But it also contained inner-city neighborhoods, like the Polish Downtown, built on a vastly different scale than any neighborhood in Detroit, Milwaukee, or Cleveland.[24] Among Poles, inner-city neighborhoods grew because of decisions by powerful leaders like Vincent Barzynski, who committed resources to monumental parishes near the core of the city. But Polonia flourished because of a complex, varied market for housing, which included neighborhoods at both the core and the periphery of the city. The diversity of the market allowed Chicago's Poles to maintain close ties despite an increasing disparity between new arrivals and more assimilated members of the community.

Changing Neighborhoods and the Evolution of a Complex Market

By 1890, Chicago Poles had established five major areas of settlement: two on the west side and three on the south side.[25] Even the most general statistical evidence shows that neighborhoods differed from each other. As Chicago approached the high tide of immigration, the west side wards already were the most crowded in the city. A majority of the Polish population resided in Ward 16. In 1890, it had a ratio of three families for every residential dwelling (table 14). Many new residences were large brick structures housing numerous families (fig. 82). Thus the average value of a mortgaged home, $5,809, was nearly four times greater than in Milwaukee's Ward 14. Despite the cost, owners occupied three of every five residential buildings, as many Polish immigrants became landlords of expensive properties in the Polish Downtown.

On the lower west side, a majority of residential buildings still housed one or two families. But Wards 9 and 10 featured new brick construction like that near Saint Stanislaus Kostka. The average value of a mortgaged home was $3,876, still a relatively high sum compared with the cost of housing in less concentrated areas of the city. Nevertheless, ownership rates were among the highest in the city, with owners occupying seven of ten residential buildings. These rates suggest, once again, large numbers of immigrant landlords.

Table 14 Housing Statistics for Chicago Wards with Significant Polish Populations in 1890

	Polish Downtown	Lower West Side	South Chicago	Bridgeport	Back of the Yards	Total
Ward numbers	16	9, 10	33	6	29, 30	
Population	55,467	89,935	25,949	42,213	80,766	295,330
% native white	4	10	13	9	20	12
% native with foreign parents	39	43	36	45	39	40
% foreign-born	57	47	50	46	41	47
Residential dwellings	3,819	8,270	3,588	5,242	10,963	31,882
Families per dwelling	3.0	2.1	1.3	1.7	1.5	1.8
% of dwellings with:						
One family	24	45	77	61	66	56
Two families	24	27	16	24	24	24
Three families	18	12	4	8	6	9
Four or more families	34	16	3	7	4	11
Ownership:						
% of all families who own homes	19	32	38	38	38	33
% of structures occupied by owners	57	68	51	63	57	60
Average value of Encumbered homes ($)	5,809	3,876	2,777	2,306	2,950	

Source: U.S. Department of the Interior, Census Office, *Compendium of the Eleventh Census: 1890*, pt. 1, *Population* (Washington, D.C.: Government Printing Office, 1892), 373, 470, 527–28, 880, 954.

Figure 82
Tenement near Saint Stanislaus Kostka. (Source: author.)

South side wards were less crowded. In Bridgeport and Back of the Yards, 85 percent and 90 percent of residential structures, respectively, housed only one or two families, while near the steel mills of South Chicago, the figure was 93 percent. Within these districts, most structures were frame rather than brick, and the average value of mortgaged homes ranged from $2,306 to $2,950. But owner occupancy on the south side was no higher than in the Polish Downtown. In general, owners occupied three of every five residential buildings. These figures suggest that during the early Polish settlement of Chicago the concentration of population and the presence of multiple-family buildings affected the percentage of families who could own homes but not the percentage of structures that were owner-occupied. A majority of residential buildings in all Polish neighborhoods were owned by an occupant.

After 1890, the number of Polish immigrants rose dramatically in all the major settlements. But the effect was not uniform since population pressures affected older and newer areas of the city differently. Wards 11, 15, 16, and 17 on the west side became very crowded with an overwhelmingly foreign-born population (table 15). By 1920, owner-occupancy rates had declined in a few of the earliest areas of settlement, such as Saint Stanislaus Kostka, where owners occupied only one in three residential buildings. Ownership rates also declined in Bridgeport, which was burdened with the oldest housing on the south side. Elsewhere, ownership remained high, especially in newer areas of the south and northwest sides, where ratios of families to dwellings were lower and where rising portions of the adult population were Polish-Americans born in the United States. In a few south side wards, one-half of all families owned houses, and owners occupied seven of ten residential buildings (table 16). Similar conditions existed in industrial suburbs such as Cicero, where 52 percent of all families owned houses and where owners occupied 78 percent of all residential buildings.[26]

The great real estate boom of the twenties redefined the residential landscape of Chicago. Bungalows and modern, two-family apartment buildings became the common type of new construction instead of the cottages and brick tenements that had characterized construction during the earliest period of Polish immigration. By the end of the decade, one-fourth of Chicago's residential buildings were less than ten years old.[27] A 1939 Works Progress Administration (WPA) survey of Chicago housing provides by far the best account of the changes the boom produced in working-class neighborhoods. Like earlier surveys, the WPA provided information for large areas,

Table 15 The Percentage of Foreign-Born Males Twenty-One or Older for Wards in Chicago with Significant Polish Populations in 1920

	Percentage Males 21 and Older	Percentage Native-Born	Native with Foreign Parents	Percentage Foreign-Born	Percentage Poles among Foreign-Born
Polish Downtown:					
Ward 17	16,402	2	13	85	63
Ward 16	14,702	2	25	73	68
Ward 15	28,042	6	23	71	26
Ward 28	20,786	11	36	53	29
Ward 14	20,986	22	24	42	22
Total	100,918	9	25	57	40
Lower west side:					
Ward 11	16,937	4	22	74	42
Ward 12	18,787	5	29	64	24
Ward 34	29,043	6	31	60	6
Total	64,767	5	29	66	21
Northwest side:					
Ward 27	44,566	17	4142	15	
Ward 33	35,873	21	38	41	10
Total	49,833	14	25	61	26
South Chicago:					
Ward 8	29,193	13	27	60	40
Ward 9	25,640	14	24	62	13
Total	49,833	14	25	61	26
Back of the Yards/ Bridgeport:					
Ward 29	32,919	10	29	61	26
Ward 5	21,34310	28	62	35	
Ward 4	15,868	8	28	64	33
Ward 30	17,568	10	27	48	24
Total	87,698	10	28	59	29
Polish areas	383,497	11	29	56	28
All Chicago	874,239	20	29	46	17

Source: U.S. Department of Commerce, Bureau of the Census, *Fourteenth Census of the United States*, vol.2, *Population* (Washington, D.C.: Government Printing Office, 1922), 274–76.

dividing the city into seventy-five communities. But the WPA also published data for each of the thousands of city blocks that comprised the neighborhoods of Chicago. In combination, the general area and

Table 16 Housing Statistics for Wards in Chicago with Significant Polish Population in 1920

	Families	Dwellings	Families per Dwelling	% Home Owners	% Owner Occupied
Polish Downtown:					
Ward 17	12,277	4,661	2.6	12	33
Ward 16	11,540	4,660	2.5	19	46
Ward 15	11,141	8,850	2.4	22	52
Ward 28	16,737	8,940	1.9	28	52
Ward 14	15,389	8,573	1.8	20	35
Total	77,084	35,693	2.2	21	45
Lower west side:					
Ward 11	13,197	5,145	2.6	21	53
Ward 12	13,974	6,610	2.1	31	66
Ward 34	21,5.3	11,106	1.9	33	64
Total	48,674	22,861	2.1	29	62
Northwest side:					
Ward 27	35,883	24,138	1.5	46	69
Ward 33	28,169	18,722	1.5	43	65
Total	64,052	42,860	1.5	45	67
South Chicago:					
Ward 8	16,649	11,053	1.5	41	62
Ward 9	18,225	14,074	1.3	49	63
Total	34,874	25,127	1.4	45	63
Back of the Yards/ Bridgeport					
Ward 29	24,599	16,140	1.5	48	73
Ward 5	14,631	8,480	1.7	34	58
Ward 4	12,039	5,997	2.0	25	50
Ward 30	13,000	7,662	1.7	25	42
Total	64,269	38,279	1.7	36	60
Polish areas	289,053	164,820	1.8	34	59
All Chicago	623,912	346,767	1.8	27	49

Source: U.S. Department of Commerce, Bureau of the Census, *Fourteenth Census of the United States*, vol. 2, *Population* (Washington D.C.: Government Printing Office, 1922), 274–76.

specific block data offer an extraordinary record of the housing market.

In 1939, the older portions of the west side encompassed neighborhoods unaffected by new construction during the twenties.[28]

In the Polish Downtown, multiple-family structures built before 1894 were in poor condition (tables 17 and 18). West side neighborhoods with multiple-family structures built between 1895 and 1919 remained in better repair. But both districts contrasted sharply with the smaller Polish settlements on the far northwest side, where nearly all residences were modern structures built during the twenties (cf. figs. 83 and 82).

In some respects, the south side resembled the far northwest side since most structures housed one or two families. However, a majority of single-family houses on the south side were updated cottages, far less expensive than new homes on the northwest side. Cottages remained viable housing because areas surrounding the steel mills and stockyards never developed the intense crowding of districts like the Polish Downtown. Of course, in some south side areas, the older cottage housing deteriorated. But near the steel mills, housing was in much better condition than in the older areas of the west side. Forty-eight percent of South Chicago residences were in good condition in 1939, while 45 percent required only minor repair.

Figure 83
Bungalows and two-flats near Saint James Church. (Source: author.)

Table 17 The Types of Residential Buildings in Community Areas (CAs) of Chicago with Significant Polish Populations in 1939

	Structures	% One Family	% Two Family	% Three Family	% Four Family	% Apartment	% Business Dwelling	% Coverted Structures
Polish Downtown:								
CA 24	16,371	13	27	9	5	12	12	22
CA 22	12,394	22	35	7	2	6	8	20
CA 21	5,932	26	39	4	2	4	6	19
Total	24,697	18	32	7	3	9	10	21
Lower west side:								
CA 31	6,544	15	22	5	5	10	14	29
CA 29	8,319	16	36	11	1	14	7	18
CA 30	9,645	26	37	7	2	3	7	18
Total	24,508	20	33	8	2	8	9	20
Northwest side:								
CA 19	10,303	62	21	...	1	2	4	8
CAs 11, 15, 16	24,534	61	21	1	1	3	3	10
Total	34,837	61	21	1	1	3	4	9
South Chicago:								
CA 46	6,901	46	24	3	4	3	8	12
CAs 47, 50, 53, 55	7,639	63	18	1	2	1	7	10
Total	14,540	55	21	2	3	2	7	10
Back of the Yards/ Bridgeport:								
CA 61	10,055	27	33	3	5	2	10	20
CAs 58, 59	9,098	33	39	2	2	1	8	15
CA 60	6,280	29	28	5	6	4	12	16
CAs 56, 57, 62	3,289 69	31	...	...	...	5	14	
Total	28,722	34	31	3	4	2	9	17
All Chicago	377,854	43	25	4	2	6	6	14

Source: Chicago Plan Commission, *Residential Chicago*, vol.1 of *Report of the Chicago Land Use Survey* (Chicago: Chicago Plan Commission 1942), app., 4–5.

Despite the hardships of the Great Depression, ownership had increased since 1920 (table 19). As expected, seven of ten owners in older neighborhoods were landlords. But even in the newest areas of the south and northwest sides, between one-third and one-half of home owners were landlords. Overall, owners occupied 76 percent of

Table 18 The Age and Condition of Buildings in Community Areas (CAs) of Chicago with Significant Polish Population in 1939

	% Built before 1894	% Built between 1895 and 1919	% Built after 1920	% Good Condition	% Requires Minor Repair	% Poor or Unfit
Polish Downtown:						
CA 24	71	27	2	34	63	13
CA 22	45	49	6	24	69	7
CA 21	16	65	19	51	45	4
Total	52	42	6	24	63	13
Lower west side:						
CA 31	87	11	2	17	68	15
CA 29	18	73	9	24	67	9
CA 30	25	67	8	40	57	3
Total	39	54	7	29	63	8
Northwest side:						
CA 19	2	25	73	77	21	2
CAs 11, 15, 16	4	48	48	69	29	2
Total	3	41	56	71	27	2
South Chicago:						
CA 46	31	36	33	51	41	8
CAs 47, 50, 53, 55	28	48	24	46	49	5
Total	30	42	28	48	45	7
Back of the Yards/ Bridgeport:						
CA 61	54	41	5	27	63	10
CAs 58, 59	33	43	24	31	62	7
CA 60	86	10	4	17	70	13
CAs 56, 57, 62	3	41	56	46	47	7
Total	48	35	17	28	63	9
All Chicago	32	40	17	28	63	9

Source: Chicago Plan Commission, *Residential Chicago*, vol. 1 of *Report of the Chicago Land Use Survey* (Chicago: Chicago Plan Commission, 1942), app., 16, 25

single-family houses in districts with significant Polish populations, 69 percent in houses with two families, and 59 percent of structures with three families. In addition, owners occupied 65 percent of all converted structures (table 20). Converted structures were residences altered to provide a greater number of apartments. During the

Table 19 Home Ownership and Owner Occupancy Rates for Community Areas of (CAs) of Chicago with Significant Polish Populations in 1939

	Families	Families per Dwelling	% Home Ownership	% Owner Occupancy
Polish Downtown:				
CA 24	45,527	2.8	18	49
CA 22	31,303	2.5	25	63
CA 21	13,218	2.2	32	70
Total	90,048	2.6	22	58
Lower west side:				
CA 31	17,059	2.6	23	59
CA 29	25,190	3.0	19	57
CA 30	19,288	2.0	39	77
Total	61,537	2.5	26	66
Northwest side:				
CA 19	16,187	1.6	47	74
CAs 11, 15, 16	42,588	1.7	43	74
Total	58,775	1.7	43	74
South Chicago:				
CA 46	13,257	1.9	36	70
CAs 47, 50, 53, 55	10,719	1.4	48	68
Total	23,976	1.6	42	69
Back of the Yards/ Bridgeport:				
CA 61	20,427	2.0	33	67
CAs 58, 59	16,206	1.8	43	76
CA 60	13,109	2.1	31	65
CAs 56, 57, 62	4,161	1.3	38	71
Total	53,903	1.9	38	71
All Chicago	943,903	2.5	26	65

Source: Chicago Plan Commission, *Residential Chicago*, vol.1 of *Report of the Chicago Land Use Survey* (Chicago: Chicago Plan Commission, 1942), app., 10, 12, 14

Depression, financially strapped owners converted single-family houses in older portions of the city, often to provide space for relatives.[29] Conversions accounted for about one-fifth of all residential buildings on the west side, in Bridgeport, and in the more crowded areas of the Back of the Yards. In nearly all of these areas, in every

Table 20 The Percentages of the Types of Buildings That Were Occupied by Owners for Community Areas (CAs) with Significant Polish Populations in 1939

	% One Family	% Two Family	% Three Family	% Four Family	% Apartment	% Business Dwelling	% Converted Structures
Polish Downtown:							
CA 24	52	53	49	49	42	34	55
CA 22	74	67	59	53	35	37	65
CA 21	80	74	59	48	27	44	64
Total	68	63	53	50	39	36	67
Lower west side:							
CA 31	54	59	65	57	63	51	65
CA 29	73	66	45	52	30	37	59
CA 30	84	80	78	63	56	60	75
Total	75	71	61	59	44	50	67
Northwest side:							
CA 19	78	73	65	55	32	48	88
CAs 11, 15, 16	81	71	70	43	19	38	75
Total	80	71	69	46	23	42	78
Sourth Chicago:							
CA 46	78	70	70	27	35	52	66
CAs 47, 50, 53, 55	73	61	72	14	51	50	68
Total	75	66	70	23	38	51	67
Back of the Yards/ Bridgeport:							
CA 61	70	70	72	54	51	52	70
CAs 58, 59	79	78	76	61	28	60	82
CA 60	69	65	65	56	51	55	74
CAs 56, 57, 62 80	79	50	. . .	29	70	62	
Total	75	73	70	61	48	56	73
All Chicago	77	68	51	49	30	39	60

Source: Chicago Plan Commission, *Residential Chicago*, vol. 1 of *Report of the Chicago Land Use Survey* (Chicago: Chicago Plan Commission, 1942), app., 4–5

type of building, rates of owner occupancy in areas with Polish populations compared favorably with rates for all of Chicago.

The data for city blocks confirm the impressions derived from the general information for community areas. By 1939, Poles lived in new and old portions of the city, in neighborhoods that varied considerably in average rents, families per dwelling, and rates of ownership (table 21). While neighborhoods varied, the blocks within specific neighborhoods were similar, as may be seen in figures 84–91, which describe the neighborhoods surrounding fifteen Chicago Polish churches. The clearest distinctions existed between an old, crowded district, such as Saint Stanislaus Kostka, and a new, prosperous parish, such as Saint Ladislaus. The residential buildings surrounding Saint Stanislaus had been built before 1900, and many required major repair. Nearly all of the structures housed multiple families. They offered some of the lowest rents in the city. In 1939, these blocks were among the few Polish areas where owner occupancy was less than 50 percent. Under these circumstances, fewer than one in every ten families in the district owned a house.

In contrast, rents near Saint Ladislaus were three times higher. Nearly all houses were built after 1920, and only a few in the

Table 21 Cumulative Data for the Block Data of Fifteen Polish Parishes in 1939

	Structures	Families	Owners	Average Rent($)	% Home Ownership	% Owner Occupancy	Families per Dwelling
Northwest side:							
1. Stanislaus Kostka	1,155	3,769	506	13	13	44	3.3
2. Mary of Angels	719	1,708	446	16	26	62	2.4
3. Hyacinth	646	1,718	506	29	29	78	2.7
4. Stanislaus Bishop and Martyr	428	802	307	26	38	72	1.9
5. Wenceslaus	856	2,043	630	31	31	74	2.4
6. James	823	1,052	535	35	54	65	1.3
7. Ladislaus	640	1,110	506	41	46	79	1.7
South side:							
8. Joseph	425	1,043	353	16	24	59	2.5
9. Michael	1,030	2,107	703	23	33	68	2.0
10/11. Pancratius/Five Holy Martyrs	2,026	3,876	1,647	25	42	81	1.9
12. Bruno	249	407	220	25	54	88	1.6
13 Mary Magdalene	1,218	1,869	1,011	31	54	83	1.5
West side:							
14. Casmir	675	1,695	467	18	28	69	2.5
15. Good Shepherd	612	1,050	485	23	46	79	1.7

Source: Chicago Plan Commission, *Residential Chicago*, vol. 1 of *Report of the Chicago Land Use Survey* (Chicago: Chicago Plan Commission, 1942), 190, 198, and *Land Use in Chicago*, vol. 2 of *Report of the Chicago Land Use Survey*, 89, 93, 107, 113, 127, 135, 153, 155, 211, 215, 247, 267, 271, 367, 369.

Note: The numbers for parishes relate to figure 84.

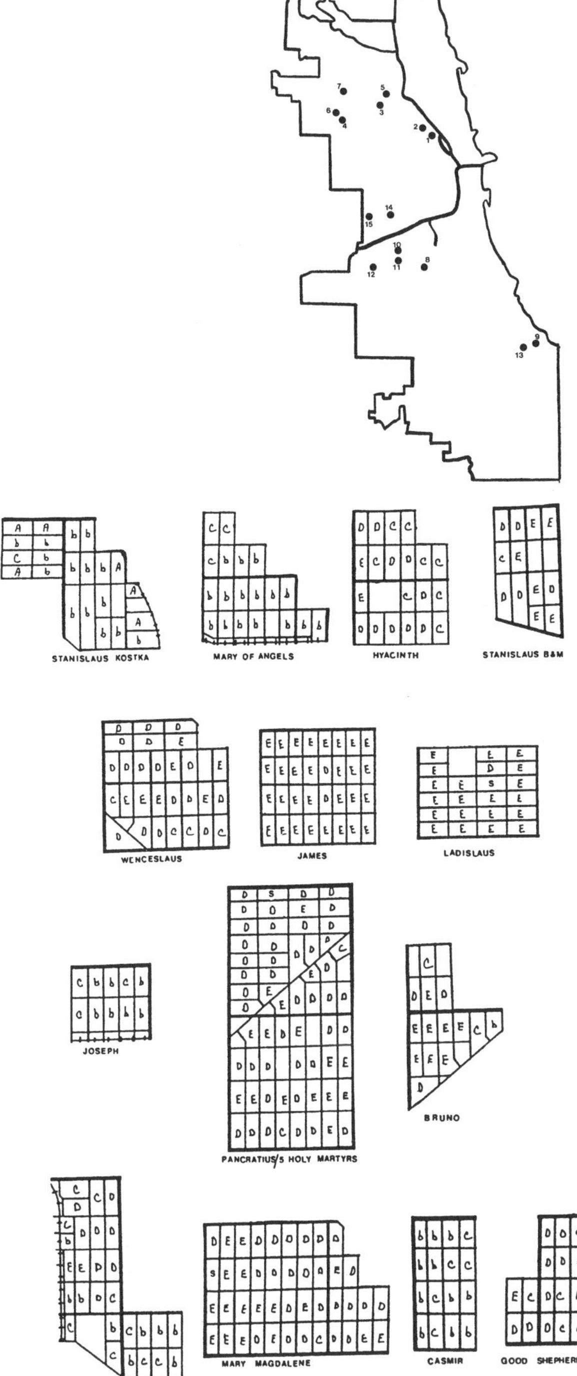

Figure 84
The location of fifteen Polish parishes in 1939. The numbers on the map are keyed to the parish names in table 21. (Source: author.)

Figure 85
The median year built for residential structures by block. Median year built: *A* = 1884 or before; *b* = 1885–1894; *C* = 1894–1904; *D* = 1905–1919; *E* = 1920–1930. (Source: Chicago Plan Commission, *Residential Chicago*, vol. 1 of *Report of the Chicago Land Use Survey* [Chicago: Chicago Plan Commission, 1942].)

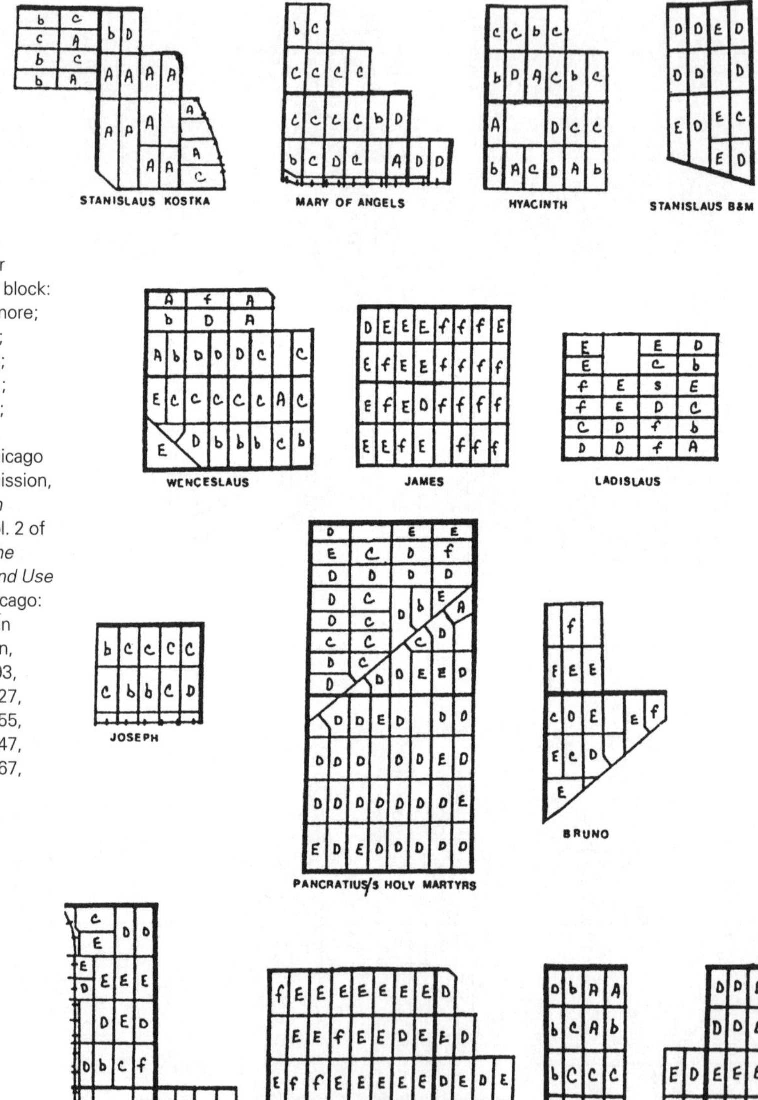

Figure 86
Families per dwelling by block: *A* = 3.0 or more; *b* = 2.6–2.9; *C* = 2.2–2.5; *D* = 2.8–2.1; *E* = 1.4–1.7; *f* = 1.0–1.3. (Source: Chicago Plan Commission, *Land Use in Chicago*, vol. 2 of *Report of the Chicago Land Use Survey* [Chicago: Chicago Plan Commission, 1942], 89, 93, 107, 113, 127, 135, 153, 155, 211, 215, 247, 267, 271, 367, 369.)

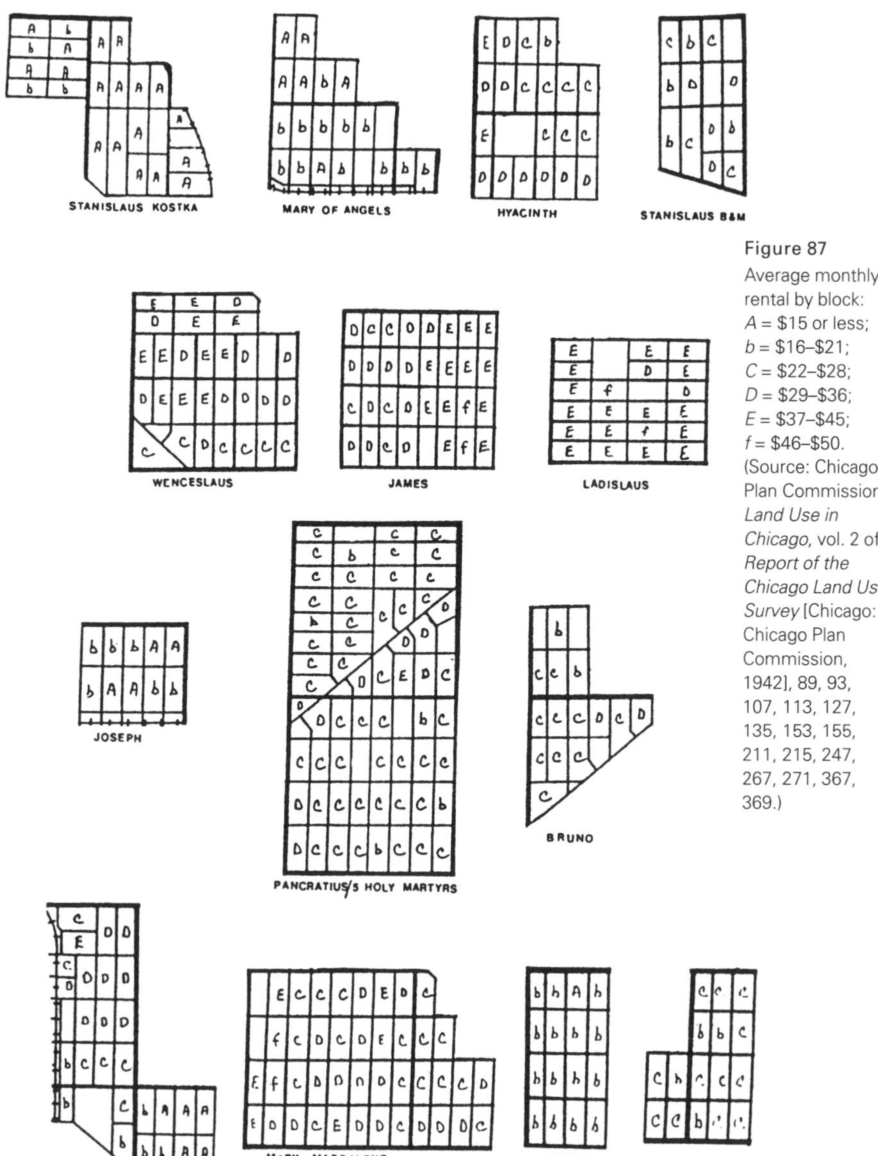

Figure 87
Average monthly rental by block: *A* = $15 or less; *b* = $16–$21; *C* = $22–$28; *D* = $29–$36; *E* = $37–$45; *f* = $46–$50. (Source: Chicago Plan Commission, *Land Use in Chicago*, vol. 2 of *Report of the Chicago Land Use Survey* [Chicago: Chicago Plan Commission, 1942], 89, 93, 107, 113, 127, 135, 153, 155, 211, 215, 247, 267, 271, 367, 369.)

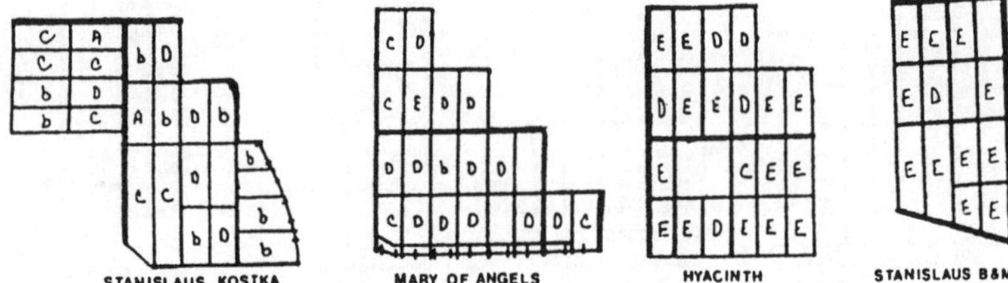

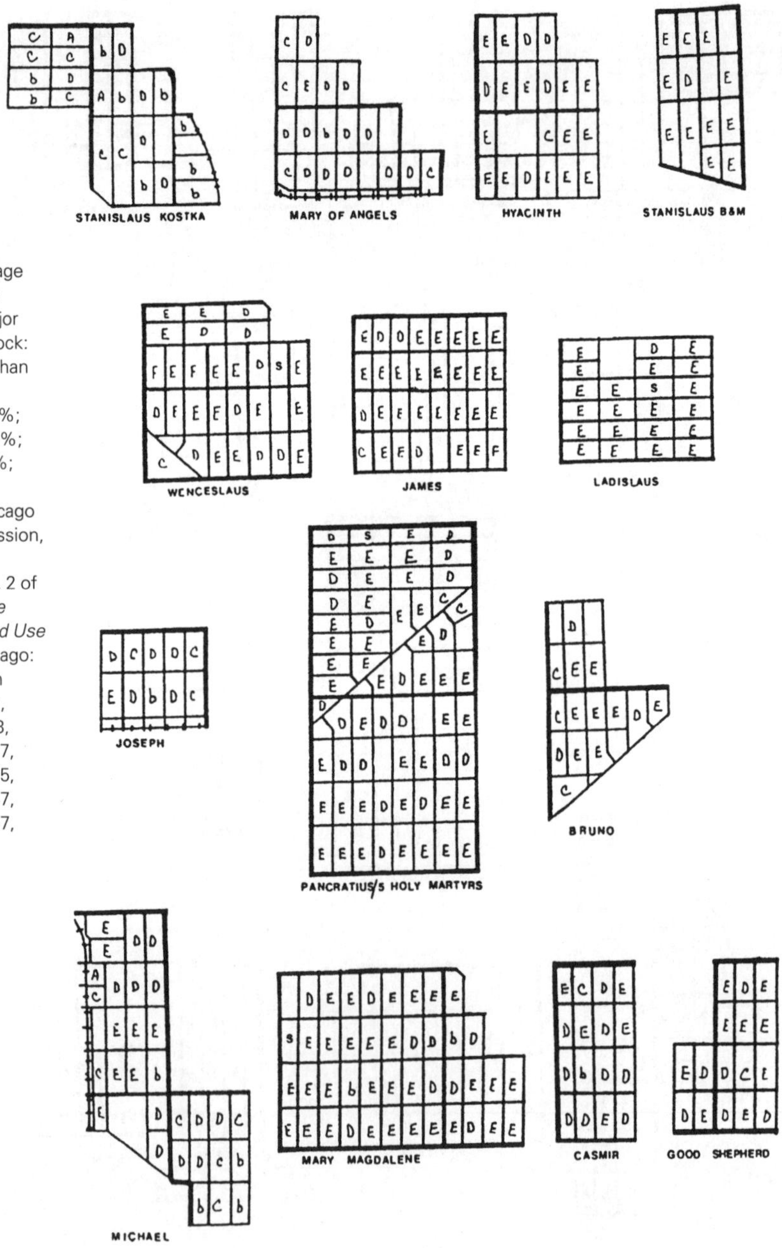

Figure 88

The percentage of structures requiring major repairs by block: *A* = greater than 50%; *b* = 21%–50%; *C* = 11%–20%; *D* = 1%–10%; *E* = none. (Source: Chicago Plan Commission, *Land Use in Chicago*, vol. 2 of *Report of the Chicago Land Use Survey* [Chicago: Chicago Plan Commission, 1942], 89, 93, 107, 113, 127, 135, 153, 155, 211, 215, 247, 267, 271, 367, 369.)

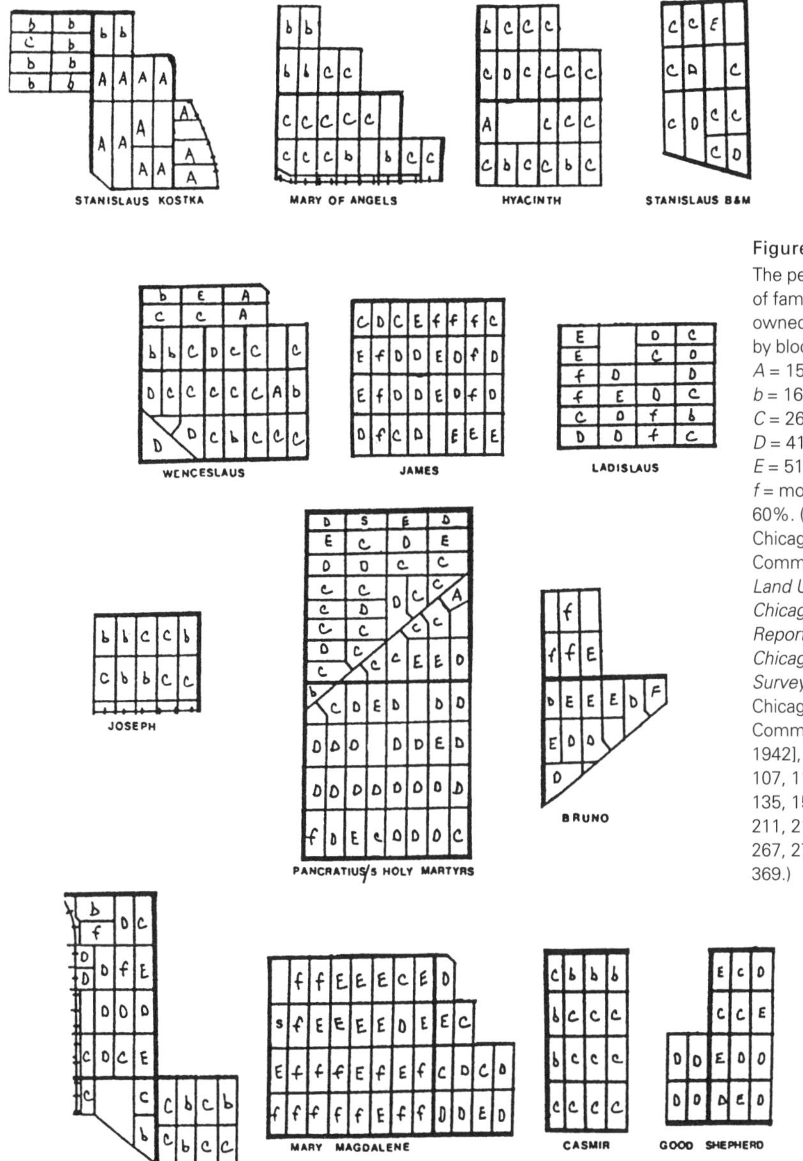

Figure 89
The percentage of families who owned homes by block: *A* = 15% or less; *b* = 16%–25%; *C* = 26%–40%; *D* = 41%–50%; *E* = 51%–60%; *f* = more than 60%. (Source: Chicago Plan Commission, *Land Use in Chicago*, vol. 2 of *Report of the Chicago Land Use Survey* [Chicago: Chicago Plan Commission, 1942], 89, 93, 107, 113, 127, 135, 153, 155, 211, 215, 247, 267, 271, 367, 369.)

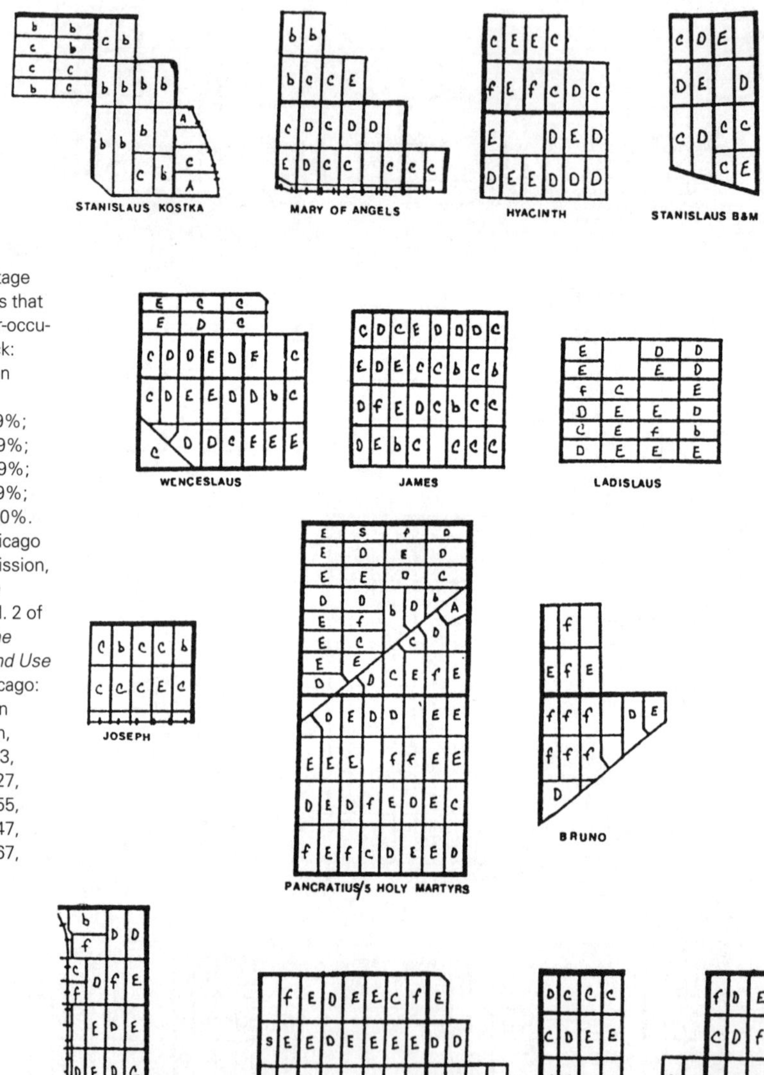

Figure 90
The percentage of structures that were owner-occupied by block: *A* = less than 30%; *b* = 30%–49%; *C* = 50%–69%; *D* = 70%–79%; *E* = 80%–89%; *f* = 90%–100%. (Source: Chicago Plan Commission, *Land Use in Chicago*, vol. 2 of *Report of the Chicago Land Use Survey* [Chicago: Chicago Plan Commission, 1942], 89, 93, 107, 113, 127, 135, 153, 155, 211, 215, 247, 267, 271, 367, 369.)

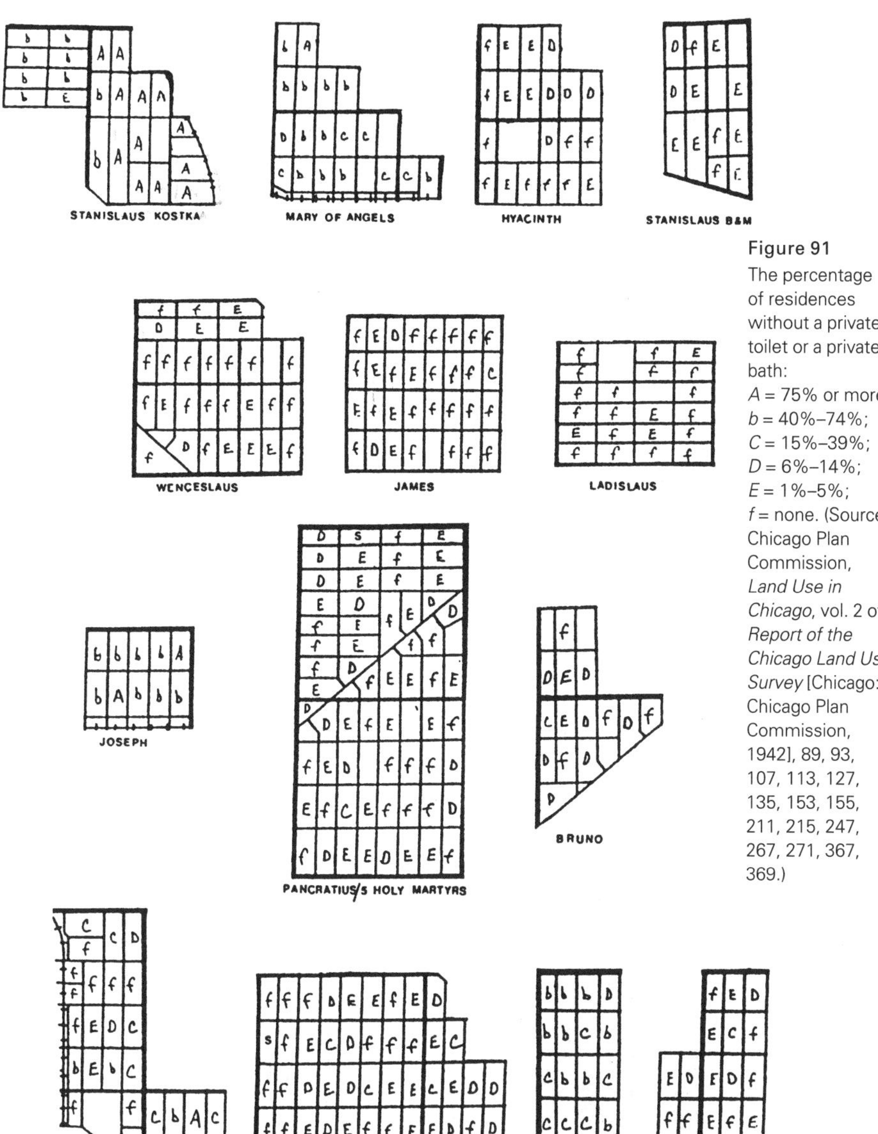

Figure 91
The percentage of residences without a private toilet or a private bath: *A* = 75% or more; *b* = 40%–74%; *C* = 15%–39%; *D* = 6%–14%; *E* = 1%–5%; *f* = none. (Source: Chicago Plan Commission, *Land Use in Chicago*, vol. 2 of *Report of the Chicago Land Use Survey* [Chicago: Chicago Plan Commission, 1942], 89, 93, 107, 113, 127, 135, 153, 155, 211, 215, 247, 267, 271, 367, 369.)

district required significant repair. While the Saint Ladislaus neighborhood contained multiple-family buildings, they were stylish and of modern construction (fig. 92). In most Polish neighborhoods, rents ranged between twenty-five dollars and thirty-six dollars per month. Although less fashionable than Saint Ladislaus, neighborhoods surrounding Saints Pancratius, Bruno, Mary Magdalene, and Five Holy Martyrs were similarly modern. In these newer areas, roughly half the families owned houses, and owners occupied four of every five structures.

The presence or absence of amenities distinguished Polish neighborhoods more than did rates of ownership. According to the WPA, nearly every residence in Chicago was electrified and contained a modern gas stove by 1939. However, methods of refrigeration varied. A majority of middle-class houses had electric refrigerators. But most of the working class still used ice boxes, while roughly 10 percent had no refrigeration. These statistics held whether families rented or owned (tables 22 and 23). Similarly, while three-fourths of residences in Chicago were centrally heated, the figure was smaller for areas with large Polish settlements. Only 23 percent of the residences near Saint Stanislaus Kostka, 8 percent on the lower west side, and 16 percent in Bridgeport had central heating, although figures were higher for buildings occupied by owners.

Statistics for plumbing demonstrate a radical distinction between the oldest and newer neighborhoods. By 1939, 85 percent of Chicago's residences had at least one private toilet and bathtub, 7 percent had a private toilet but no bathtub, and 8 percent did not

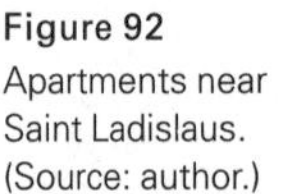

Figure 92
Apartments near Saint Ladislaus. (Source: author.)

Table 22 Heating, Refrigeration, and Plumbing Amenities for All Occupied Dwellings in Community Areas (CAs) of Chicago with Signification Polish Populations in 1939

	Occupied Dwellings	% Central Heating	% Refrigeration			% Toilet and Bath	% Toilet No Bath	% Shared Toilet
			Electric	Ice	None			
Polish Downtown:								
CA 24	45,527	23	17	71	11	63	25	12
CA 22	31,303	50	47	48	4	88	10	2
CA 21	13,218	56	49	45	3	96	3	1
Total	90,048	37	33	59	8	76	16	7
Lower west side:								
CA 31	17,061	8	13	75	12	37	35	26
CA 29	25,190	78	59	40	1	97	2	1
CA 30	19,288	22	34	62	4	85	11	4
Total	61,539	57	44	48	8	83	14	2
Northwest side:								
CA 19	16,188	82	60	36	2	97	2	1
CAs 11, 15, 16	42,589	86	73	25	1	99	1	...
Total	23,977	57	44	48	8	83	147	3
Back of the Yards/ Bridgeport:								
CA 61	20,429	29	25	60	15	63	29	7
CAs 58, 59	16,206	34	29	64	7	88	10	2
CAs 56, 57, 62	4,161	55	33	57	9	90	7	3
Total	53,904	27	36	62	12	71	23	5
Polish areas	288,245	47	43	52	5	80	14	5
All Chicago	943,174	70	58	37	5	85	7	8

Source: Chicago Plan Commission, *Residential Chicago*, vol. 1 of *Report of the Chicago Land Use Survey* (Chicago: Chicago Plan Commission, 1942), app., 4–5.

have a bathtub or private toilet. Home owners were more likely to have both amenities. But again, the figures were much lower in areas like those adjacent to Saints Stanislaus, Michael, Joseph, and Mary of Angels (fig. 91). In the most crowded areas near Saint Stanislaus, only one in ten families had a private toilet and bathtub. Their absence explains declining rates of ownership. Large, antiquated, multiple-family residences could not be adapted easily to accommodate modern plumbing or central heating. It was easier and much less

Table 23 Heating, Refrigeration, and Plumbing Amenities for Owner-Occupied Dwellings in Community Areas (CAs) of Chicago with Significant Polish Populations in 1939

	Occupied Dwellings	% Central Heating	% Refrigeration			% Toilet and Bath	% Toilet No Bath	% Shared Toilet
			Electric	Ice	None			
Polish Downtown:								
CA 24	8,074	30	22	69	8	75	19	5
CA 22	7,803	57	42	51	5	91	8	1
CA 21	4,169	65	45	48	4	97	2	1
Total	20,046	48	34	58	6	86	12	2
Lower west side:								
CA 31	3,892	16	21	72	7	58	31	11
CA 29	4,705	71	58	40	2	98	2	...
CA 30	7,474	32	36	61	3	91	7	2
Total	16,071	40	39	57	4	85	11	4
Northwest side:								
CA 19	7,647	86	57	39	2	98	2	...
CAs 11, 15, 16	18,277	91	70	26	2	99	1	...
Total	25,934	89	66	30	2	99	1	...
South Chicago:								
CA 46	4,832	68	65	41	4	90	9	1
CAs 47, 50, 53, 55	5,177	76	43	47	8	93	4	1
Total	10,009	72	48	44	6	92	7	1
Back of the Yards/ Bridgeport:								
CA 61	6,747	36	30	59	10	78	20	2
CAs 58, 59	6,944	48	29	64	7	91	8	1
CA 60	4,086	30	25	64	10	71	25	3
CAs 56, 57, 62	2,597	63	31	59	9	83	15	2
Total	20,374	42	29	62	9	83	15	2
Polish areas	92,424	59	44	49	5	89	9	2
All Chicago	247,103	75	61	36	3	94	5	1

Source: Chicago Plan Commission, *Residential Chicago*, vol. 1 of *Report of the Chicago Land Use Survey* (Chicago: Chicago Plan Commission, 1942), app., 4–5.

expensive to update smaller cottages such as those found throughout the south side. Nevertheless, by the 1930s, most Poles had embraced a new conception of home ownership that valued the amenities associated with modern housing.

Conclusion

During six decades of Polish immigration, Chicago's housing market was never static or one-dimensional. From 1870 to 1900, Poles established their own downtown with large inner-city parishes and a wealth of services and institutions. The church promoted unity among recently arrived immigrants. But the largest parishes also produced crowded neighborhoods of three- and four-story brick buildings. In Chicago, these districts were far more extensive than those of other Midwestern cities with large Polish populations.

After 1900, the high tide of immigration placed enormous pressures on inner-city neighborhoods. In response, established immigrants dispersed to rapidly growing parishes on the periphery, which offered a range of accommodations. These neighborhoods contained large numbers of one- and two-family houses. Under these conditions, roughly half the Polish families became home owners in neighborhoods where owners occupied from 70 to 90 percent of residential buildings.

The continually high rates of owner occupancy for two- and three-family buildings suggests that housing was an important investment for immigrants. For two generations, money from rents remained in the community, the hard-earned profit of a great many ethnic landlords. Undoubtedly, these funds helped finance the second generation's move to more comfortable accommodations, as distinctions between old and new Polish neighborhoods became striking. Some of the oldest inner-city neighborhoods deteriorated because buildings could not be plumbed and heated to modern standards. The Poles in these neighborhoods remained among the poorest residents of the city, a position that had characterized members of these communities during six decades of Polish residence in Chicago.

Concentrating on severe poverty misses a greater story, however. Most neighborhoods did not deteriorate as a result of Polish immigration to the city. Regardless of obstacles, a larger portion of Poles gained access to comfortable accommodations in a residential landscape that offered a range of amenities. As Poles struggled to improve their neighborhoods, they fought among the most significant cultural battles of the twentieth century. By becoming respectable, they challenged the severe racial and economic assumptions of persons such as John R. Commons, who believed that southern and eastern Europeans would destroy a traditionally high American standard of living. Part 4, which follows, examines very closely the experiences of two generations of Polish residents in West Hammond in order to understand intimately the process by which immigrants and their children expanded notions of citizenship in America.

PART FOUR

POLISH COMMUNITY LIFE AND THE DEVELOPMENT OF WEST HAMMOND

CHAPTER 5

Polish Settlement in West Hammond

When Chicago's first Polish community expanded, its members entered a booming real estate market. The city was preparing for the World's Columbian Exposition, an event that attracted 27 million visitors to the lakefront.[1] Prior to the exposition, speculators subdivided outlying lands for sale as "cheap lots," affordable to nearly everyone.[2] The developers then employed aggressive strategies to promote sales. Chicago's most prominent developer, Samuel Eberly Gross, printed thousands of brochures in various languages espousing home ownership as a reward for honest labor. He offered prospective buyers free rail passes for promotional events that included band concerts, picnics, fireworks, and bicycle races. The promotions attracted thousands encouraged by an "easy payment system" that allegedly made ownership cheaper than renting. In the course of a decade, Gross sold 40,000 lots and built 7,000 houses.[3]

Unfortunately, prior to the exposition, the nation entered an economic depression, and the real estate market collapsed. A generation later, during an even more severe depression, the economist

Homer Hoyt attributed the collapse to "prosperous times" when "full employment . . . placed small accumulations of capital in the hands of thousands of persons" who were then induced "by the boom psychology of the period and the persuasive tactics of subdividers to buy a lot on easy payments."[4] Hoyt described outrageous swindles when subdividers earned profits of 600 percent on land flooded for most of the year. He considered immigrants especially helpless before unscrupulous real estate agents whose efforts brought "disillusionment and despair to the great masses of people in Chicago." Indeed, Hoyt claimed the most significant role for immigrants was to lower property values. He even ranked ethnic groups according to their negative impact on real estate.[5]

When Hoyt described real estate agents, he drew on a standard literary convention rather than a careful examination of the market. The convention received notable expression in Upton Sinclair's novel The *Jungle*, the story of Jurgis Rudkis, a Lithuanian immigrant, who believed he would prosper because he was strong and willing to work.[6] After finding employment in the Chicago stockyards, Jurgis purchased a home for his wife and their extended family. The idea came when he saw a colorful advertisement that described a cottage as an appropriate reward for every workingman. Jurgis could afford the down payment and monthly installments so long as all members of the family worked steadily. Still, he hesitated until persuaded by an immigrant employed as a real estate agent. He was "a smooth and florid personage, elegantly dressed: who spoke Lithuanian." Jurgis did not question the agent. "To press the matter would have seemed to be doubting his word and never in their lives had any one of them ever spoken to a person of this class called 'gentleman' except with deference and humility."[7]

Of course, Jurgis was swindled. The house was in poor condition, and the contract was deceptive. When Jurgis was injured, he lost his job, so the family could not make the payments. The purchase of a house marked the turning point in The *Jungle*. It began the process of decline and ruin in one of this century's most often read melodramas. To this day, many regard the book as a sympathetic portrayal of immigrant life. But Jurgis was not simply ignorant of American ways. He was a fool, an imbecile, dim-witted to the point of absurdity. At one point, the family decided to look at other homes before making a purchase. But "they did not know where any were, and they did not know any way of finding out."[8] The suggestion was preposterous. But it was acceptable to middle-class readers who shared a prejudice regarding the intelligence of eastern Europeans.

For all its detail, The *Jungle* was a book of omissions, the product of a sometimes well-meaning outsider. Upton Sinclair portrayed Jurgis as an individual who did not have the protection offered by the church, fraternal organizations, and trusted friends. If historians wish to understand working-class home ownership, they must move beyond the melodrama of The *Jungle*. Proper analysis requires examination of the actual people, houses, neighborhoods, and communities that served as the basis for Sinclair's fiction. The following chapters describe the experiences of two generations of Polish residents in West Hammond, Illinois. These chapters analyze in detail the significant changes that occurred within one Polish community during the transition from cottages to bungalows.

The Syndicate

The strengths of the immigrant community were apparent when Poles settled in West Hammond. The settlement originated in September of 1890 when a syndicate of investors—managed by a Protestant Chicago realtor, Oliver Brooks—purchased 320 acres of land one mile south of the G. H. Hammond Slaughterhouse for $160,000. The syndicate cleared the land and platted a subdivision, raising the investment to $200,000, or $625 an acre.[9] By January of 1891, the subdivision consisted of thirty-six blocks with each block divided into forty-eight lots, for a total of 1,728 lots. The number was remarkable since Hammond's population was only 8,000. Local investors had never developed so large a property.

But during the boom that preceded the Columbian Exposition, many syndicates purchased large sections of undeveloped land near outlying industrial districts. Most land syndicates were risky, short-term investments organized to develop a single property. They profited if business concluded within five years. After that time, property taxes eliminated profits.[10] Consequently, successful syndicates required a strategy for selling lots as quickly as possible. In November of 1890, the *Building and Real Estate Journal* announced that the West Hammond syndicate intended to sell exclusively to Polish immigrants because it recognized "the sentiment on the part of these people to obtain homes at a minimum cost and at the same time to cultivate an acquaintance as far as possible among their own race by establishing churches and schools compatible with their own desire."[11]

Homer Hoyt denounced land syndicates. He assumed the evils of speculation outweighed the advantages of providing affordable housing.[12] But a contemporary, Helen Corbin Monchow, saw benefits to a speculative market. Monchow argued that syndicates met Chicago's immediate needs by selling lots on terms workers could afford. Prior to syndicates, the sale of a lot required a down payment of one-fourth the value of the property, followed by three annual payments at 6 percent interest to cover the balance of the debt. Syndicates distributed the risk among investors, so they required a down payment of only ten dollars on a lot costing $200. The balance was paid in monthly installments of ten dollars. This "easy payment system" widened appreciably the market for working-class housing, allowing for the rapid development of industrial districts in Chicago Heights, West Pullman, Harvey, Waukegan, and Stickney.[13]

Monchow knew syndicates often failed. Occasionally, a syndicate lacked capital and would mortgage property soon after its purchase in order to pay for improvements to that property. If sales were slow, the syndicate could not retire its debt and deliver clear title to lots even after purchasers completed their installments. More often, problems resulted when working-class families acquired land without sufficient cash reserve. When towns installed streets, sidewalks, sewers, water pipes, and gas lines, the buyers could not pay the assessments for the services, leading the municipality to confiscate property.

Monchow suggested that most land owners found a way to pay these costs or to sell the land and save at least some of their investment.[14] Unfortunately, she did not provide detailed analysis of any syndicates, so she did not speak with authority regarding rates of success and failure. Subsequent historians have written with even less authority, for they have relied on housing reformers, on Hoyt, or on literary sources such as *The Jungle* rather than on detailed analysis of how land was developed and sold to the immigrant working class.[15] While swindles occurred, many syndicates developed successful communities. The success of a syndicate depended on the strategy chosen to attract potential buyers to its property rather than to other subdivisions offering cheap lots for the working class.

Once the West Hammond syndicate chose to sell land to Poles, Oliver Brooks hired Adam Stachowicz, a thirty-six-year-old Polish teamster, as an agent for the syndicate. Stachowicz emigrated from the German partition of Poland to the United States with his parents in 1871 when he was sixteen.[16] The family resided near Saint Stanislaus Kostka. So Stachowicz knew that construction of a Polish church required the approval of Vincent Barzynski. In all likelihood, Stachowicz orchestrated an agreement with Barzynski that allowed for a church in West Hammond.[17]

The first advertisement for the subdivision appeared on February 7, 1891, in Chicago's leading Polish language newspaper, *Dziennik Chicagoski*. By this time, Stachowicz had been elected president of the Society of Saint Andrew. The society formed in January for the purpose of establishing a Catholic church in West Hammond.[18] The syndicate agreed to donate one city block as a site for the church and to contribute five dollars from the sale of each lot for its construction. Stachowicz also required each family who purchased a lot to contribute five dollars toward the building. In other respects, the advertisement was typical of those boosting the sale of land in outlying industrial districts. It boasted that Hammond was a modern city destined to be "the great American Birmingham," where employment was certain for all laborers. Like most syndicates, the West Hammond group sold lots on the "easy payment system," suggesting that ownership was cheaper than renting.[19]

Free transportation served as the means to assure potential buyers that claims were true and promises would be met. Any Polish family wishing to see the subdivision visited Adam Stachowicz at his home to receive rail tickets for trains that departed Chicago for Hammond early on Sunday mornings. Within a year, the syndicate was employing sixteen agents in various Polish neighborhoods throughout Chicago to provide free transportation to the subdivision. Among these men, only Stachowicz and one or two others settled in West Hammond.

For three years, the society promoted the sale of land and the establishment of a church. On April 25, 1891, Stachowicz announced in *Dziennik Chicagoski* that a meeting of the society would occur in West Hammond to discuss important business. The syndicate provided free transportation for those who had purchased land as well as for those who were interested in buying a lot. The society fined members who failed to attend fifty cents, a sum equivalent to one-third of a day's pay for an unskilled laborer.[20] A few weeks later on May 10, members of the society gathered in West Hammond and celebrated as Adam Stachowicz read aloud the Constitution of the Society of Saint Andrew.[21]

Two months later, during a similar celebration, the syndicate presented Stachowicz with the deed to the church property and with a contribution of five dollars for each of the 500 lots sold. Soon after, the society gathered and voted to rename the subdivision Sobieski Park in honor of the valiant Polish king. They also voted to rename the streets: two in honor of Polish kings, Sobieski and Poniatowski; two in honor of saints, Andrew and Stanislaus, and two in honor of Poles who fought in the American Revolution, Pulaski and Kosciuszko.[22] These names represented a balance, respecting equally Polish nationalism, American patriotism, and Roman Catholicism.

Once construction of the church began in September of 1891, advertisements encouraged landowners and their guests to visit each Sunday and see the progress in Sobieski Park. On September 20, the parish celebrated the laying of the cornerstone. The occasion attracted religious and patriotic societies from Hammond and Chicago, all of whom contributed to the church fund while enjoying a day of parades, music, and dancing (fig. 93). In late March of 1892, the first pastor, Francis Wojtalewicz, invited all the Polish people of Chicago, especially those owning land in Sobieski Park, to attend the first mass, celebrated on Easter Sunday, 1892. Free transportation made these events attractive to immigrants, who participated in various activities that provided additional revenue for the parish.

In appeals for financial support, Wojtalewicz combined religion, nationalism, and home-spun economics:

Figure 93 Advertisements for Sobieski Park. (Source: *Dziennik Chicagoski*, June 29, 1891 and September, 15, 1891.)

WIELKI POLSKI

BASKET PIC-NIC

W HAMMOND

ODBĘDZIE SIĘ DNIA 4-go LIPCA 1891.

Zabierzcie ze sobą pożywienia w koszyk i wraz z familią opuście miasto na ten dzień, w którym można się ucieszyć do syta.

DOBRA MUZYKA I TAŃCE.

Przybądźcie i zobaczcie piękne miejsce pod nowy Polski kościół; przybądźcie zobaczyć Hammond, miejsce, które w niedalekiej przyszłości będzie obfitować w największej fabryk całego świata; przybądźcie zobaczyć loty w West Hammond, okolicy w której majątku się można dorobić.

Pociąg odejdzie z dworca przy Polk ulicy, prosto w Dearbourn ulice o 7.30 albo o 10 godzinie rano. Przybądźcie lepiej rychlej ażeby uniknąć natłoku i gorączki. Jazda tam i napowrót darmo dla Polaków.

Po bliższe informacye zgłosić się do niżej wymienionych agentów, którzy przy odjeździe na dypot będą za wami czekać.

O. H. Brooks & Co., Tacoma Building, Chicago.

J. R. Niemczewski, 31st blisko Main str.
Adam Stachowicz, 45 Sloan str.
A. Majewski, 664 Noble Str.
Frank Stauber, 724 Milwaukee Ave.
L. Groszkiewicz, 143 W. Division Str.
Józef Napieralski, 681 W. 17. Str.
B. Pruminski, 813 Wood Str.
John Rozynek, South Chicago.
Max Barański, } 525 Noble Street.
Jan Adamowski, }

> Dear Countrymen:
>
> With the permission of Archbishop P. A. Feehan and the Grace of God, we have signed the contract for the building of the Polish Catholic church in Sobieski Park. It will be built of wood, and when finished, will be new and beautiful evidence of the great devotion and generosity of the Polish people, who always strive first for the kingdom of God; that is, for God's greater Glory and honor on earth. The church, proper, without the lots (which were donated), and all the particulars necessary for a church will cost near $12,000.
>
> The foundation is already paid for, but the additional $10,000 we must pay for with a collection of offerings from parishioners and benefactors.
>
> Noticing that everyone buying a lot in Sobieski Park promised to pay $5.00 for the building of the church, we have faith in God and the promise of our future parishioners that when after Easter we begin to collect the promised money, we will gather a sufficient sum that it will not be necessary to borrow from a bank and pay high interest rates. Consider this, dear brothers, when the church is completed, the debt will be paid off.[23]

As progress continued, Wojtalewicz invited all of Polish Chicago to Sobieski Park again in October of 1892 for the blessing of the bells and in May of 1893 for the consecration of the church, which was attended by Bishop Feehan and the city's Polish clergy. Each event provided opportunities to offer financial support for the new parish. At the consecration, the parish received $230 in gifts from Polish societies and from other parishes.[24] On another occasion, the Polish Democratic Marching Club sponsored a trip to Sobieski Park charging passengers twenty-five cents, the proceeds going to the parish.[25] It is likely that each week the parish sold beer and provided games of chance to those who visited Sobieski Park.

Clearly, Poles were never as ignorant and easily swindled as the fictional character Jurgis Rudkis. Polish settlements were orchestrated movements of people. Immigrants visited West Hammond. They saw the land and the progress of construction. They participated in the creation of the community. But it is wrong to suggest all went smoothly. A tornado destroyed the new church two months after the first mass. The parish salvaged lumber to build a rectory for Wojtalewicz and then built a new brick church.[26] By April of 1893, the syndicate no longer advertised Sobieski Park, and many families experienced difficulty meeting payments.

In November of 1893, Oliver Brooks published a letter in Dziennik Chicagoski to those in arrears:

> READ THIS CAREFULLY!
>
> To all who have joined with us, the following is of interest: we wish to inform you that from now on Mr. Julian Piotrowski is our collector. Mr. Piotrowski lives at 3117 Laurel Street near Thirty-first Street and has full authority to collect the money for lots that were purchased in Hammond, Illinois. We also give him the right to cancel any of our contracts. We ask all who are in arrears with their payments not to delay but with the assignment of Mr. Julian Piotrowski we ask that they pay as much as they can afford.
>
> Do not lose your lots or whatever you have paid in because the cost of lots in Hammond will rise and as a result the value of your lots will rise.[27]

The depression prevented most families who wished to settle in West Hammond from doing so. From April of 1891 until June of 1895, the *Building and Real Estate Journal* listed 307 Poles who purchased lots in Sobieski Park. Of these, 106 were residents in 1900. Of the remaining 201 families, only twenty-two moved to West Hammond by 1910. In all, 128 (42 percent) of the 307 settled in West Hammond.[28] This statistic is sobering. The depression must have tempered enthusiasm toward the purchase of land. However, the parish expanded regardless of individual setbacks. In 1896, the community built a one-room school, attended by eighty students the following September. At first, a laywoman served as teacher. Within a year, the parish supported three German nuns as teachers. That same year, the church purchased an organ for the extravagant sum of $1,600, a price higher than the value of most homes in Sobieski Park.[29] But Polish hymns were an integral part of community worship, and the parish did not forgo this extravagance even during a period of economic hardship.

The Settlers

Manuscripts for the 1900 and 1910 federal censuses provide the best source for understanding the people who purchased land and settled Sobieski Park. Studies of home ownership have avoided detailed analysis of census manuscripts and have relied heavily on computers and aggregate data for entire cities, leaving out the specific contexts that give substance to numbers. To understand neighborhoods, historians must heed the advise of Lawrence Stone "to work with smaller samples and to use a hand calculator" rather than a computer and the complex statistical packages created for the social sciences.[30] A detailed, highly personal study reveals the motivations for creating a place like Sobieski Park.

In 1900, nine years after the syndicate began selling land to Polish immigrants, Sobieski Park consisted of 234 families and a population of 1,400. Nearly all the heads of families had emigrated from the German partition of Poland, in sharp contrast to the new Polish community in East Chicago, Indiana, where residents came from the Austrian partition. Polish origins mattered and so did a period of residence and adjustment in Chicago. Among the heads of families in West Hammond, 80 percent had resided in the United States for at least ten years. Most residents were among the early wave of Polish immigrants to Chicago. Very few came directly to West Hammond from Poland.

In 1900, nearly all heads of families were male and were married. Most were young. Roughly, 40 percent were in their thirties, and 35 percent were in their forties. Only 15 percent were over fifty. Despite relative youth, about seven of every ten heads of families had been married for ten or more years. In addition, the community was almost entirely working class. About 70 percent of the heads of families were unskilled laborers, while another 20 percent were semiskilled or skilled. Almost three of every five heads of family worked for the G. H. Hammond Company, while fewer than one of every ten owned a small business.[31]

As one might expect, home ownership rates were high. In 1900, 69 percent of families owned their houses, 121 (74 percent) with mortgages and forty-seven (26 percent) free of encumbrance. The percentage of houses with mortgages was much higher in West Hammond than was common in the established Polish neighborhoods of Chicago, where fewer than one-half of all home owners held mortgaged property. Like the easy payment system for land, building and loan associations expanded considerably the population who could purchase houses after 1880. In West Hammond, Poles created the King John Sobieski Building and Loan to promote ownership.[32]

More than other factors, age distinguished those who owned houses from those who did not. Fewer than one-third of heads of households under thirty were home owners, while three-fourths of those over thirty owned a house. The families who rented were more recently immigrated and more recently married persons with fewer children. One-half of the heads of families who rented were under thirty-five, and 43 percent had lived in the United States for fewer than ten years.

Children accounted for 62 percent of the population. Twenty-five percent of all residents were children under age six, who remained at home with their mothers. At age six or seven, they entered school, where they remained for six or seven years. By age fourteen, nearly all had entered the workforce as unskilled laborers. Sixty percent of the boys found work at the slaughterhouse, while 62 percent of the girls worked as bookbinders at the W. B. Conkey plant. Children lived with their parents until their early twenties, when most left home, presumably to begin families of their own. In all, each child provided the family with six or seven years of wages that helped pay for the house. However, since West Hammond families were so young in 1900, only 15 percent of children were employed and contributing income to their families. The families who owned houses without mortgages had the highest percentage of children who had entered the workforce.

Ten years later, the Polish population in West Hammond had nearly doubled. The 1910 census reported 489 Polish families with a population of 2,642. But growth was not steady. More than half the community lost their jobs in 1901 when fire destroyed the Hammond Company. The local economy did not recover until 1907, when Standard Steel Car established a car works that employed 2,000 workers. Despite the crisis, 73 percent of home owners in 1900 (122 of 168) remained in 1910 in contrast to 30 percent (22 of 74) of renters. About one in four heads of families who remained improved their jobs. But gains were very modest, usually a slight upgrade in skill. The overwhelming majority continued to work as unskilled or at best semi-skilled laborers. Clearly, as the Calumet region boomed, employment became widely available, but it offered Poles only limited chances for occupational mobility.

In most respects, heads of households in 1910 were like those in 1900. They were all foreign-born; a second generation had not quite come of age. As in 1900, home owners were overwhelmingly Poles born in the German partition. They had been married longer, had larger families, and had resided in the United States for a longer period than the families who rented. Children remained the largest segment of the population, accounting for 60 percent of all residents. But in 1910, one-third of the children were old enough to enter the workforce, a percentage more than twice as high as in 1900, a result of the fact that home owners from 1900 were now older.

Overall, home ownership rates declined from 71 percent of all families in 1900 to 63 percent in 1910. The decline resulted from a larger percentage of young families in the population, for age remained the critical factor distinguishing owners from renters. Ownership was common for heads of households over thirty. In 1910, 24 percent of heads of households under thirty owned houses, compared with 63 percent between thirty and forty-nine, and 80 percent of those over fifty.

Like other Midwestern industrial cities, West Hammond had a significant percentage of owner-occupied, multiple-family structures. These structures accommodated the younger population who rented. Of the 390 residential buildings in 1910, roughly 70 percent housed one family, 20 percent two, and 10 percent three or more families. As in Chicago, about 70 percent of structures were owner-occupied, with multiple-family residences as likely to be owned by an occupant as single-family houses. Opportunities to become a landlord affected the economic structure of immigrant communities such as West Hammond. Historians have argued that purchasing a house was, in general, a bad idea for poor immigrant families since it did not offer a return on the money invested.[33] But the evidence shows that ownership often was an investment for landlords who derived income and shelter from the purchase of a house.

Once again, the built environment provides compelling testimony regarding the nature of ownership. In West Hammond, the first arrivals built small, very simple, inexpensive, frame cottages like the one owned by Martin and Rose Kunkel (fig. 70).[34] A site like West Hammond offered Chicago Poles greater opportunities for ownership of very inexpensive houses since unimproved suburban lots were much cheaper. Original owners did not pay the cost for installing streets, sidewalks, or water, electric, and gas services. After 1900, increases in the numbers of single males and young married families led to greater demands for residential space. Cottage housing responded to these demands in a remarkably flexible manner.

To profit from rents, many families modified their original cottages by raising them on brick foundations (fig. 94). The new space provided a second apartment. In this way, an owner could profit from rents during periods of high employment when the number of residents increased. But he or she could reconvert the building into a larger, single-family house later if the extra income no longer proved

Figure 94
West Hammond raised cottages. (Source: author.)

necessary or attractive. Less frequently, owners built small houses at the rear of their lots (fig. 95). While these buildings avoided the problems of living with a second family in the same building, the new construction sacrificed the backyard, which was a significant amenity for the residents of less concentrated urban areas.

An equal number of families invested in more substantial multiple-family structures, most often two-flats or four-flats. The least

Figure 95
West Hammond rear houses. (Source: author.)

expensive choice was a two-story, frame cottage with separate apartments on each floor (fig. 96). Many two-story cottages contained businesses on the first floor and apartments above. By 1911, West Hammond Poles began to build larger brick apartment buildings, some representing a considerable cost (fig. 97). In doing so, Poles introduced features of Chicago's more densely crowded environment into the Calumet region. The more prosperous German community of Hammond seldom converted cottages or built larger, multiple-story brick "tenements." But for the Poles, ownership of a multiple-family home offered the prospect of economic mobility at a time when formal education was limited, when most employment was for laborers, when many families were young and recently immigrated, and when immigrant communities contained large numbers of transients who moved about as employment opportunities changed.

At the same time, boarders provided income predominantly to families who rented rather than to those who owned houses. A majority of owners in West Hammond lived with large families in small,

Figure 96 *(left)* West Hammond two-story cottage and business. (Source: author.)

Figure 97 *(bottom left & right)* West Hammond brick "tenements." (Source: author.)

inexpensive cottages. While not uncommon, having boarders among these families was never typical. Eighty-nine percent of Poles who owned residences free of encumbrance and 79 percent of those with mortgages housed only parents and their children. Families who rented were younger, with few if any children. One-third of these households contained boarders, often more than one. Of the families who rented and took in boarders, twenty-nine of the fifty-one (57 percent) housed two or more boarders. Boarders were most common in the large, inner-city Polish neighborhoods, where families were young and where land values were much higher.

Conclusion

In West Hammond, the cottage housing market served a diverse immigrant population that received low wages and required additional income. Most houses were small, inexpensive cottages owned by families of unskilled laborers whose children went to work at an early age to help pay the cost of the house. Immigrants also purchased multiple-family residences and earned steady incomes from the rent they charged others, usually younger immigrant families. In turn, these same young families often took in boarders to supplement their incomes. When combined, the various sources of income allowed Poles to enter the housing market at an early age despite limited resources and irregular employment. At times, families sacrificed comfort to acquire savings. When taken to extremes, severe economies led to high rates of mortality and disease.[35]

But ownership provided social and cultural rewards that exceeded economic considerations. Establishing an ethnically and religiously centered community like Sobieski Park was a creative enterprise. It required cooperation among families, friends, and fellow countrymen. Adam Stachowicz and others in the Society of Saint Andrew made a place for themselves and for their children where none had previously existed. They were the founding families of a community that provided sustenance to generations of Poles. The satisfactions cannot be measured only in dollars and cents. Home ownership led to spirited local politics that encouraged Poles to recognize the interests they shared with persons outside the ethnic community.

CHAPTER 6

First-Generation Politics and Reform in West Hammond

The success of the West Hammond syndicate depended on maintaining exclusiveness. Poles desired residential separation from others. But segregation had limits. The residents of Sobieski Park depended on local industries for jobs and on Hammond for basic services. To improve access to these services, Poles formed the Village of West Hammond in January of 1893, joining Sobieski Park with an older settlement one mile to the north (fig. 98). The north side contained about 300 families. Two-thirds were German Protestants who established Saint John Evangelical Lutheran Church in 1888, three years prior to the formation of the Society of Saint Andrew. One-third were a mixture of Irish, Scandinavian, and American-born residents.[1]

The north side resembled other working-class neighborhoods in Hammond. A majority of houses were single-family cottages owned by occupants. However, a vice district flourished to the northeast of Saint John's. Beginning at the Illinois state line and extending west for a few hundred yards along Plummer Street, the district harbored six or

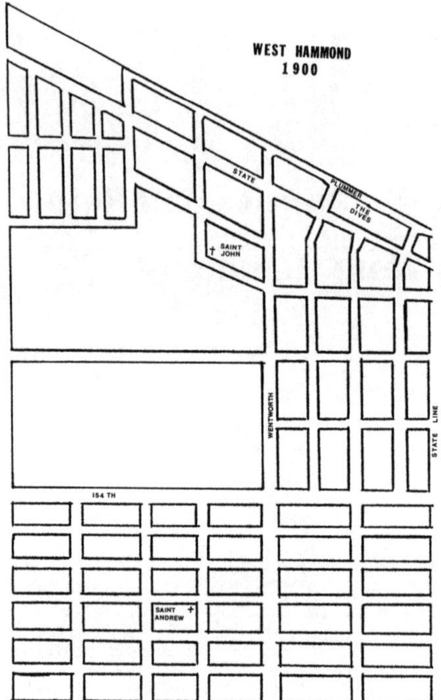

Figure 98
West Hammond, 1900. (Source: author.)

seven saloons offering gambling and prostitution. During Hammond's lawless days, the saloons operated "wide open." They continued to do so following Hammond's incorporation since Indiana authorities could not prosecute a district located across the state line. With the incorporation of West Hammond, "the dives" became subject to the taxing and policing powers of local government.

West Hammond officials, however, did not seek to eradicate gambling and prostitution. Unlike other cities in the region, West Hammond never attracted industries to provide revenue for local government.[2] Aside from property taxes, saloons were the most important source of revenue. If the new village wished to provide services at a low cost, it depended on license fees paid by the saloons. So, despite notoriety, the dives were allowed to operate. Most residents did not object because the district was segregated. Poles expressed the least concern since they lived a mile from the district. Polish residents encountered the dives only if they sought them out.

Initially, Germans controlled the village government. In the first election in 1893, they won the races for president, clerk, and treasurer, as well as four of six positions as trustees. The following year, Adam Stachowicz organized a political party to oppose the Germans. But only three of seven candidates on his People's Party ticket were Poles, and no Polish candidate won election. Stachowicz ran for village president again in 1896 and 1898. Each time he lost because voters cast ballots along ethnic lines, and Poles were the minority.[3] Consequently, the village hall, the jail, and the public school were built on the north side.[4] These first elections began two decades of political conflict. To no one's surprise, yearly elections remained partisan as the north side Germans opposed the south side Poles.

Throughout the Midwest, the creation of working-class neighborhoods and towns led to countless battles to establish respectable and efficient local governments. Urban journalists seldom reported the commonplace events critical to these struggles. During the first decades of the century, journalists provided stories of the tawdry elements of urban life. Novels, such as Theordore Dreiser's *Sister Carrie*, further developed a literature where heroes encountered the dark side of life. Ambitious but poor, Carrie Meeber desired a pleasurable life in Chicago. Desire led her to prostitute herself. In doing so, Carrie left behind the world of her sister Minne, the wife of an American-born Swede who worked in the stockyards. Minne lived a dull but honest life in a small, third-floor apartment on West Van Buren. But she and her husband saved to build a house "on two lots far out on the West Side." According to Dreiser, they possessed "narrower conceptions of pleasure."[5] Throughout the literature of urban realism, characters like Minne served as foils. The dullness of her life allowed readers to accept Carrie's decision to abandon convention.

Historians confront a more difficult problem than do novelists. Regardless of the literary record, it remains rather obvious that dull but honest persons greatly outnumbered the Sister Carrie's of Chicago. Fairness requires historians to tell Minne's story in an interesting manner. The silence of working-class communities complicates the problem. The Minnes of the world seldom left accounts describing the satisfactions derived from establishing a home on the west side. Statistical records help overcome the problem by telling something of the lives of modest property owners. Unfortunately, a reliance on quantitative sources often produces history more boring than the lives themselves. Thankfully, in the case of West Hammond, local newspapers recorded the political activities of the local Polish community. These accounts make it possible to breathe life into the story and overcome the corpse-cold qualities of statistical analysis.

This chapter and the one following show how Polish leaders acted in imaginative, surprising, and sometimes powerful ways to overcome the disadvantages inherent in working-class towns. Never simply the victims of corporate capitalism, they served as agents in a dynamic local economy. This chapter shows how members of the first generation, such as Adam Stachowicz, established a voice for Polish home owners in local affairs. Once they acquired power, Polish leaders struggled to create an efficient and capable local government. The next chapter shows how the second generation built on these efforts. In a manner no less dynamic, they fought to increase opportunities for a comfortable life while gaining a measure of respectability for themselves and their community. By doing so, they encouraged fellow citizens to overcome the parochialism that divided neighborhoods.

First-Generation Politics

In 1899, the Poles formed a coalition with the village's small Irish Catholic population. The coalition replaced Adam Stachowicz at the head of the People's Party ticket with Patrick Kennedy and ran Irish candidates for police magistrate and trustee. Although Kennedy lost the race for village president, Poles won the races for village treasurer, village constable, and one trusteeship. However, the north side Germans retained control of the village board since they held the presidency and a majority of the trusteeships.[6] Following the election, the board contracted for a new sewer system that did not provide service for Sobieski Park. Reverend Francis Brygier, the pastor of Saint Andrew's, filed an injunction to halt construction of the new sewers. The motion was defeated just prior to the 1900 village election.

Outraged, Brygier encouraged parishioners to defeat the Germans by supporting Irish candidates on a coalition ticket. Altogether, 487 voters turned out, an increase of 16 percent over 1898. The coalition received 54 percent of the vote, electing eight of nine candidates. Irishmen became president and clerk. But Poles won the treasurer's office, the constable's office, and three trusteeships. Adam Stachowicz was the only loser among the Polish candidates. He lost the race for police magistrate to an Irish candidate by eight votes.[7]

Although successful, the coalition proved difficult to maintain. In 1902, Poles again ran as candidates for president and clerk. Without Irish candidates at the top of the ticket, they received 47 percent of the total vote and lost the election. One year later, the coalition intact, the People's Party received 56 percent of the vote, and four Poles won election. In 1904, Poles made up the entire ticket. But the election did not include a race for village president since the term had been extended to two years. In this election, Martin Finneran, a young, ambitious Irish resident, ran a third party slate that did not include a Pole. Polish candidates won every office with 47 percent of the total vote, to 34 percent for the German-controlled Citizens Party and 19 percent for Finneran's ticket. Two years later, Finneran altered his strategy and won election as village clerk. He included four Poles on his ticket. With the Polish vote divided, Finneran received 198 votes to 190 for Stachowicz and 168 for the German candidate John Brehm.[8]

By 1907, Poles had participated in fourteen local elections. They achieved significant victories, but only when Irish candidates headed their ticket or when a third party split the north side vote. Increases in the south side population led Poles to believe they could defeat the Germans without Irish assistance.[9] So in the People's Party primary, the south side nominated an entire slate of Poles, including Jacob Czaszewicz for village president. The Germans responded with concerted effort. But on election day, 616 voters provided Czaszewicz a huge margin of victory, electing him the first Polish village president. Czaszewicz defeated Henry Lindner 385 (63 percent) to 231 (37 percent). Eighty-three percent of voters cast straight party tickets for either the German or Polish candidates.[10]

Poles won again the following year. As a consequence, the village president and all six trustees were Polish immigrants. In 1909 when Czaszewicz ran for reelection, the local newspaper predicted Poles would sweep the election since the south side had the a majority of voters.[11] Everyone imagined that a majority Polish population insured election for the People's Party. To the surprise of "winners as well as losers," the North Side Citizens Party received 56 percent of the vote in a heavy turnout. Czaszewicz lost the presidency to John Hessler, 349 votes (56 percent) to 278 (44 percent). Many Poles voted against Polish candidates. After the election, the *Lake County Times*, or simply the *Times*, as it was known locally, reported that Polish politicians had initiated "too many costly improvements on the South Side against the wishes of property owners."[12]

During the previous three years, politicians had promoted measures to pave the streets, construct sidewalks, and install sewers. Many south siders believed the new construction benefitted a few owners of large sections of real estate. These investors included Village Clerk Martin Finneran, Village Attorney Samuel Markam, and Reverend Bronislaw Nowakowski, the pastor of Saint Andrew's. Markam was the most controversial figure. Jewish and a lawyer, Markam served as village attorney but did not live in West

Hammond. However, he owned a great deal of undeveloped property there.[13] In 1906, when village leaders proposed a sewer to drain marshes on the south side, Markam wrote a contract calling for a twenty-inch tile sewer to cost $155,000. South side property owners, who would be assessed the cost of the sewer, defeated the plan in a special election.

Following the defeat, Markam presented a second plan for a sewer to cost $108,000. But engineers informed village officials that a twenty-inch sewer was too small. So Markam devised a third contract, earning a third legal fee. This plan called for construction of a thirty-inch brick sewer. "Think of that!" the *Lake County Times* wrote,

> A 30-inch brick sewer to cost $33,000 less than the schemers had first attempted to foist on the village a 20-inch tile sewer. Hammond's wide experience in graft and boodle pales into insignificance in comparison with this. Then, too, it was arranged that the village attorney was to get 5 per cent of the total contract and the engineer 6 per cent. Thrifty officials surely. Then to make the burden on the property owner still greater the Michigan Central [Railroad] is to be relieved of any assessment as is also Stein Hirsch Co., Burnham subdivision and Schlitz Brewing company property. This will mean a cost of $60 to $75 per lot to property owners for the sewer.[14]

Because of the controversy, Poles denied their candidates reelection in 1909. The vote demonstrated that group loyalty did not insure Polish control of local government. As was the case among Hammond's Germans a decade earlier, taxes and the cost of improvements were vital concerns for working-class property owners. In Hammond, voters ousted prolabor politicians because the German home owners, like the Poles, demanded good services at a reasonable cost.[15] Voting incumbents out of office was the best means for showing displeasure with the politics of graft and boodle.[16] If Polish officials could not provide services at a reasonable cost, Polish voters were prepared to elect outsiders who might.

Following the defeat, the People's Party reorganized in order to restore the Polish south side to power. In the 1910 primary, eleven of thirteen candidates were Polish, and Poles won all four positions on the ticket, including village clerk. In this race, a young Polish candidate, Ignatius Mankowski, defeated incumbent clerk Martin Finneran. Mankowski and three other Poles then won the general election.[17] However, Poles remained a minority on the village board since a year remained in the terms of Village President John Hessler and the three German trustees, who had won victories in the surprising election of 1909. Unfortunately, the north side politicians proved unworthy of the voters' trust.

Local Politics and Reform

The problems began the following summer when President Hessler announced that West Hammond had grown too large to be governed as a village and, therefore, should adopt a city form of government. The village board authorized Samuel Markam to prepare for a special election. In presenting the plan, Markam argued that as a city West Hammond could annex land to the south and west that was owned by the railroads. Currently, these areas paid taxes to the county. Markam claimed the new taxes would double the village's revenue and reduce the tax burden of current property owners by 30 or 40 percent.[18]

The power to annex appealed to persons like Finneran and Markam who held large interests in West Hammond real estate. If the city annexed property, it could then expand streets and services, raising the value of undeveloped lands. Of course, Hessler and the incumbent north side politicians would benefit as well. If West Hammond remained a village, the north side would lose all political offices in the next election since Poles now represented a clear majority of voters and trustees were elected by a general vote. However, a city form allowed for aldermen elected by specific wards. With a city government, the Germans would maintain some power as representatives of the north side.

The incumbent politicians expected residents to approve the measure to make West Hammond a city. But to their great surprise, the election was "Thwarted by a Girl." Two months earlier, twenty-year-old Virginia Brooks and her mother moved to the Polish section of West Hammond. Brooks was the daughter of Oliver Brooks, the Chicago realtor who had organized the West Hammond syndicate. After her father's death, Virginia Brooks discovered that West Hammond officials levied $20,000 in special assessments against her father's property. Learning of the plan to make the village a city, she moved to West Hammond and began a house-to-house canvas, telling Polish residents that a city form of government would increase taxes.[19]

The day before the special election, she organized a mass meeting for voters. About 150 residents gathered in White Eagle Hall, as Miss Brooks, according to newspapers, found herself the only woman in a smoke-filled hall of Polish men. Climbing a table, she urged voters to "clean up the village of West Hammond, first, before you attempt to saddle a city government managed by the old political clique onto this shamefully mistreated community."[20] The following day Virginia Brooks became a celebrity. Chicago papers ran headlines describing the young Protestant reformer's brave mission among the Poles. She became the "Joan of Arc of West Hammond" (fig. 99).

The Chicago papers failed to mention that Poles had participated in many elections without the aid of a Protestant Joan of Arc. Instead, they suggested that Poles were brutish and ignorant and that any woman brave enough to enter a room filled with such men must be heroic and remarkably pure. But Virginia Brooks did not turn out a large vote for the special election. In 1910, West Hammond had about 800 eligible voters. Typically, 80 percent voted in local elections. Only 342, slightly more than 40 percent, voted in the special election, 161 to make West Hammond a city, 181 against.[21]

The controversy continued when the village board declared the first election invalid and scheduled a second special election for the following month. Brooks organized another mass meeting. Again, the papers reported her crusade against the poor quality of public improvements, against confiscatory assessments, and against attempts to make the village a city. Brooks claimed these efforts constituted only a small portion of her "program of opposition against the powers that be." To publicize these efforts, she established a newspaper, the *Searchlight*, which she promised to "turn on" prominent officials, especially Finneran and Markam.[22]

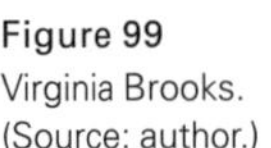

Figure 99
Virginia Brooks. (Source: author.)

A Chicago paper financed her efforts.[23] But Chicago reporters seldom traveled to West Hammond. Polish home owners were never interviewed even though most spoke English. Valiant and pure, Virginia Brooks was the story. Residents were her "loyal Polish following" who treated her "with deference and respect."[24] Among the dramatic incidents, newspapers reported her protest over a special assessment levied to improve 155th Place, a street running through the center of the Polish south side. To pay for a sewer, drain, water pipe, brick street paving, and repair of the cinder sidewalks, the village assessed the owner of each lot $185. Brooks claimed the assessment was horribly inflated. When appeal failed, she and twenty Polish women armed with mops, brooms, and rolling pins marched to the site, "bearing no uncertain evidence that they mean business." Upon arriving, the women sat on the brick piles to halt construction. When police arrived, they arrested the protestors for disturbing the peace. When a Polish officer placed his hand on Brooks's shoulder, she slapped him and was taken to jail. Despite Brooks's removal, the crowd increased, stopping work for the day.[25]

The story of mobs and riots proved sufficiently popular for the Hearst paper to finance legal proceedings to reduce the assessment. Victory came the following summer with a reduction of $16.10 on each assessed lot, 9 percent less than the original assessment.[26] Again, Virginia Brooks gained attention as the protector of helpless immigrants. However, many Poles disagreed with her continued opposition to the city form of government and with her statements regarding the extent of corruption in West Hammond. One hundred members of the West Hammond Taxpayers Association, an organization of Poles established two years before Brooks arrived, presented villagers with a report favoring a city form just prior to the second special election.[27]

A few days later, 227 residents voted in favor of the city form and 196 against. It seemed West Hammond would become a city. But Markam had not understood the laws regarding special elections. To pass, votes in favor had to exceed one-half of the number of votes cast in the previous village election. Since the turnout was small, the 227 votes in favor fell thirty-one short of a majority.[28] Six months later, the village failed to pass the measure for the same reason even though 71 percent voted for the city form of government.[29] The measure passed a fourth special election held on December 27, 1911. After one year of political mix-ups, West Hammond became a city due principally to the efforts of young Polish reformers.[30]

Confusion following the second special election delayed their efforts. Village officials had appealed the defeat in the courts. However, the courts failed to rule in time for the spring election. The People's and Citizens parties chose to conduct the election as if West Hammond were a city, anticipating a ruling validating the majority vote in the second special election. The parties divided West Hammond into four wards, the first and fourth on the north side, the second and third on the south. The primaries selected candidates for mayor, clerk, treasurer, and an alderman in each of the four wards.[31]

As expected, Poles swept the elections, winning the races for mayor, clerk, and treasurer and for aldermen in the second and third wards. The new mayor and clerk, Konstantine Woczszynski and Ignatius Mankowski, were younger than previously elected Polish politicians.[32] By 1911, Adam Stachowicz, Joseph Goyke, and Jacob Czaszewicz were in their fifties, tainted by associations with Finneran and Markam. Woczszynski, Mankowski, and alderman Paul Kamradt were in their thirties. Wosczynski's career resembled those of previously elected officials. He had emigrated with his parents from Poland to Chicago in 1889 when he was seventeen. He found work in a bicycle factory where he remained for six years until he married and moved to West Hammond. For eight years, Wosczynski worked in Hammond factories, eventually becoming a foreman. Then he managed a movie theater in East Chicago for four years. In 1907, he both opened a saloon in West Hammond and began his political career.

Mankowski and Kamradt were members of a second generation, the children of immigrant parents who settled in West Hammond and prospered. Mankowski's family arrived in 1894. His father became a successful building contractor. After a brief education at Saint Andrew's, Ignatius worked as an apprentice butcher at G. H. Hammond. After fire destroyed the plant, he joined his father, learning the mason's trade and becoming a contractor. Both Woczszynski and Mankowski served as officials in the King John Sobieski Building and Loan Association. Woczszynski established the association and became president, while Mankowski served as chief financial officer of this institution, which had property valued at $110,000 in 1910.[33]

After their elections, Woczszynski and Mankowski did not assume office, because the courts ruled West Hammond a village, invalidating the election of city officials. As a consequence, the old village board remained in office until West Hammond sorted out its problems. The decision extended the terms of four north side residents who had won office in the surprising election of 1909. If the city election had been valid, Poles would have been a majority of the new city council. Instead, Village President John Hessler and the north side trustees retained control. Despite a dubious hold on the presidency, Hessler arranged a meeting of the board without informing the Polish trustees. At this meeting, the board transferred the village's electrical service to another company at a cost of $18,000. The board then voted to adjourn until October, with provision their salaries be paid in advance of their two-month vacation. They made no plans for a new election.[34]

Virginia Brooks denounced the "old gang" of politicians and published testimony from a local man who overheard Hessler and others in a saloon discussing the bribe that led to the switch in electric companies.[35] Of greater importance, Konstantine Woczszynski organized a mass meeting to protest the actions of the board. At the meeting, Mankowski announced he would not sign pay vouchers for the vacationing board members.[36] In October when the board finally met, the village hall overflowed. Immediately, the Polish trustees introduced a petition calling for an election. Hessler tabled the motion and proceeded to transfer electrical service. He dismissed protests by hammering his gavel and swearing "Shut up, G—d damn you, shut up."[37]

Two months later, the controversy remained unsettled. The *Times* wrote, "In no city in the United States is there such brazen defiance of the wishes of the people as there is in West Hammond."[38] When the village held a legal city election in the spring of 1912, the decent element united in opposition to the old gang. The actions of the village board destroyed the Citizens Party, on whose ticket Hessler had run in 1909. So attention focused on the People's Party primary. Woczszynski and Mankowski organized a slate of reformers, including two German candidates for aldermen in the north side wards. The reformers received 60 percent of the primary vote. One month later, they ran unopposed in the general election.[39]

Virginia Brooks supported the reformers but did not play a role in the campaign. After the election, the *Times* praised Brooks as "the creator of a new spirit in West Hammond" that would not have succeeded without the work of Woczszynski, Mankowski, and Kamradt.[40] The reform campaign of 1912 marked a dramatic change in the attitude of the *Times* toward Polish politicians. For the first time, the paper praised their conduct. But Chicago papers expressed no interest in local leaders. Virginia Brooks remained the story as the election brought attention from papers and magazines across the country, including the *National Municipal Review*, *Literary Digest*, and the *Pictorial Review*.[41]

Brooks supplied every request for information, describing herself as a young, attractive, heroic, and pure Christian woman who had acted selflessly and saved the helpless Poles from grafting politicians. Such self-praise was harmless. However, a few months before the 1912 primary, she began a crusade to clean up the village dives. As always, her methods were sensational. In one instance, she published the names of prominent Hammond men who owned the buildings that housed these saloons. When she addressed the Hammond Women's Club, she appealed to the wives of these men, providing horrifying details of their husbands' affairs. When the wives expressed ignorance, Brooks asked the members to join her crusade by expelling any woman whose husband profited from gambling and prostitution.[42]

Brooks provided Chicago papers with stories of white slavery and parties where men and women swam naked. Her exposures contributed to tales of sex, drugs, and decadence that served as standards in the popular literature of Progressive reform. The most memorable effort came in a rainstorm in September of 1912 when Brooks led a parade of 5,000 men, women, and children, including long columns of Boy Scouts, Campfire Girls, bible students, and members of the Women's Christian Temperance Union, in a long march through Chicago's notorious levee district as bands played and marchers sang "Onward Christian Soldiers."[43]

As Brooks became famous, West Hammond became infamous, bringing shame especially to the Polish community. Virginia Brooks claimed that Polish children learned to shoot craps and drink whiskey in unsavory saloons and that children were born blind because their fathers contracted venereal disease from prostitutes. Local official Paul Muschelewicz responded that there were no blind children in West Hammond.[44] Yet Brooks continued, telling an Indianapolis audience: "The Polish people in West Hammond were earning on the average about $10 a week. Most of them were supporting five or six children, and paying out their money on every conceivable form of taxation. They started in living on potato soup. They were soon forced to come down to bread and coffee, and before the epidemic of graft was over, hundreds of children went to Hammond daily, where they stole three meals a day out of garbage cans."[45]

Local Reform and the Vice District

Mayor Woczszynski's reform programs were less spectacular than Virginia Brooks's claims of depravity. Prior to the exposure prompted by Brooks, local papers regarded prostitution in West Hammond as a misfortune common to industrial districts. Nevertheless, the first reform campaign began in 1907 with the election of Jacob Czaszewicz, the first Pole to serve as village president. Under Czaszewicz, the village board refused to renew the liquor licenses of fifteen saloons notorious for sheltering prostitutes, and once their licenses had expired, the police raided them, charging the operators with selling liquor without a license. Czaszewicz also threatened to prosecute the prominent Hammond citizens who owned the properties that housed the dives.

Prostitution was difficult to eliminate, however. The business was so profitable that fines were of little use. In one instance, a dive owner remained in business even after conviction by county prosecutors and a penalty of $1,000. When raids were too frequent, dives moved their operations, scattering into residential districts. Still, the *Times* praised Czaszewicz for cleaning up West Hammond. Prostitution and gambling continued, but not brazenly. The dives operated quietly in an isolated district along Plummer Street where a few favored houses remained open under management as reputable as possible given the nature of the business.[46]

In 1909, new Village President John Hessler allowed the dives to run wide open once again. Czaszewicz had banished the most notorious dive owner, Con Moor, from West Hammond. Moor returned when Hessler assumed office and soon was arrested for harboring an eighteen-year-old against her will.[47] The *Times* reported in the spring that scantily clad prostitutes once again displayed themselves from windows, smoking cigarettes and calling to passersby. Citizens complained to the Illinois state's attorney.[48] It was at this time that Virginia Brooks arrived in Hammond and began her crusade.

Upon assuming office in 1912, Mayor Woczszynski and the reform council acted quickly against disreputable establishments. First, they passed an ordinance that required West Hammond residents to be responsible financially for the character of the city's saloons. Previously, large breweries signed the bonds West Hammond saloons presented as guarantees of orderly conduct. The breweries showed no concern as to whether or not a saloon operated in an orderly manner so long as beer sales remained profitable. When West Hammond prosecuted a disorderly saloon, the breweries provided lawyers who initiated legal actions that West Hammond could not afford to pursue. The new city ordinance required a resident property owner to sign the bond. The city could prosecute a resident more easily than a brewery, especially if it threatened to confiscate property.[49]

The mayor also sent the police on raids to arrest patrons as well as prostitutes. When the Polish police chief proved ineffective, he was replaced.[50] Then in August of 1912, Woczszynski revoked the licenses of four dives in a council meeting that attracted 400 residents. In retaliation, the dive owners informed outside authorities of gambling in Polish neighborhood saloons. Detectives then raided fourteen south side saloons, arresting their owners for possessing slot machines. Three days later, Woczszynski ordered a raid of the vice district in which police destroyed twenty-one slot machines valued at $50–$200 each. The *Times* called this "reform in dead earnest."[51]

Successful reform required repeated actions and a commitment by citizens to rid the city of prostitution. To gain support from voters, Woczszynski did not expose outrageous and immoral behavior. Repeated exposures harmed the city's reputation. Instead, he appealed to home owners by arguing that a reputation for vice lowered property values throughout the city.[52] The test of Woczszynski's policies came in March of 1913 as the city prepared for primary elections. Before the primary, the *Times* wrote that decent citizens were united behind the mayor and his slate of candidates, a slate that included Ignatius Mankowski for clerk, former reform president Jacob Czaszewicz for treasurer, and Adam Stachowicz for police magistrate. The candidates represented the older and younger generations of Polish politicians, all of whom identified with reform. They encountered two sources of opposition. First, the old gang ran Henry Peters for mayor and Frank Green for police magistrate. Second, Saint Andrew's pastor Bronislaw Nowakowski supported Polish candidates opposed to the mayor. Pastor for more than a decade, Nowakowski was involved in real estate dealings with Martin Finneran and others associated with the old gang. The *Times* suggested that Nowakowski intended to split the Polish vote in order to elect Peters and Green.[53]

The reformers won a decisive victory. Woczszynski received 58 percent of the vote, 60 percent from the Polish wards and 53 percent from the north side. Ignatius Mankowski won a more impressive victory, with 72 percent of the vote on both sides of town.[54] The Polish politicians had transcended ethnic divisions by uniting citizens in defense of their community's reputation. Following the election, city officials criticized Virginia Brooks. Though she no longer lived in West Hammond, she still provided newspapers with sensational stories. Woczszynski said she went "too far with her spectacular methods" because "the notoriety she gains continually keeps the old bad record of the city before the public eye" even though West Hammond had become "a quiet, orderly, and decent place."[55]

Soon after the 1913 election, Brooks married Charles Washburne, a Chicago reporter. Within weeks, a Chicago paper published exposés, which Brooks claimed to have written. The articles became a play and then a novel. But Virginia Brooks never wrote these works. Another Chicago reporter wrote the articles, and a play doctor turned them into melodrama. *Little Lost Sister* made a small fortune.[56] Five theater companies performed the play throughout the country for two years. Critics denounced it as "irresponsible," an effort to "draw warm applause from the grovelers in cheap sentiment." An Indianapolis critic believed that "if Virginia Brooks wrote, as it is alleged, 'Little Lost Sister,' . . . she should be ashamed of herself."[57] Brooks traveled with the play, exposing vice in whatever city she visited, encouraging box office by insuring local opposition to "the dirty play furor."[58]

Following the success of the plays and books that bore her name, Virginia Brooks led an anticlimactic life. She divorced Washburne after less than two years of marriage and moved to Montana with her nine-month-old child. She died sixteen years later at age thirty-nine.[59] Her brief moments of fame are remembered for their comic quality, a modest contribution to the popular culture of the Progressive era. Despite her lambasting of local officials and business owners and her colorful demonstrations, Brooks was never actually responsible for reforms in West Hammond. She was the product of an implausible, fanciful literature, a reform fiction that employed stereotypes of immigrants as foils to the heroism of an educated, Protestant middle class. The true source of reform was internal to the Polish community, a consequence of the improving fortunes of second-generation Polish Americans.

CHAPTER 7

The New Civic Culture

In the spring of 1914, while Mayor Woczszynski fought the infamous saloons, he also worked to improve West Hammond's finances and encourage the construction of better houses. The city required a forward-looking plan since a great rebuilding was transforming the quality of Chicago's housing. To attract modern buyers, Woczszynski insisted West Hammond establish a business administration as quickly as possible. The term did not imply a fondness for an emerging corporate culture. A business administration meant a properly managed, fiscally responsible city government that provided affordable services and amenities of high quality. The struggle to achieve these goals produced compromises that middle-class reformers would have considered distasteful. Nevertheless, the policies of second-generation leaders promoted a broader civic vision that produced a shift from a Polish to a Polish-American culture.

Rebuilding West Hammond

Second-generation Polish-Americans came of age

during the high tide of immigration when their neighborhoods experienced levels of poverty and crowding uncommon among Germans and other more prosperous immigrants. Previous chapters have shown that the built environment responded to these pressures in two ways. Poles converted cottages into multiple-family residences and built larger frame and brick tenements to house rapidly expanding populations of poor newcomers. But they also established new neighborhoods that offered greater amenities and comforts. Distinctions between older and newer neighborhoods were never simple and clear since older neighborhoods retained prosperous residents, many of whom profited from ownership of properties that provided considerable incomes. In general, however, after 1915, new construction provided the upwardly mobile with bungalows and modern two-flats.

In West Hammond, the first Poles to purchase bungalows and two-flats were the prosperous members of the second generation, including prominent local politicians (figs. 100 and 101). They did not build modern houses in the oldest areas among converted cottages and tenements. Poles built bungalows at the undeveloped edges of their neighborhood or nearby in new subdivisions composed entirely of modern structures. These new districts contained a variety of

Figure 100 (*top & bottom*) Mayor Paul Kamradt's and City Clerk Andrew Stachowicz's bungalows. (Source: author.)

Figure 101
Modern two-flats, West Hammond. (Source: author.)

restrictions, calling especially for larger lots with frontages of at least thirty-five feet. Prior to 1920, restricted subdivisions in Hammond were exclusively middle class (fig. 102). But the twenties' boom created restricted neighborhoods for a much larger segment of the population. The residential portions of these subdivisions did not contain saloons or the various small stores associated with the old ethnic culture. In addition, builders installed sewers, streets, and services before the construction of houses. So residents never engaged in battles over special assessments and services. Modern subdivisions possessed a standard level of amenities from the first days of settlement.

Frank Wachewicz was West Hammond's most significant promoter of modern subdivisions. Raised in West Hammond, Wachewicz was a second-generation Pole committed to an Americanized vision of urban life.[1] In 1912, he persuaded a Chicago businessman to finance the development of land located between the south and north sides. Since he intended to build "better homes," Wachewicz supported Mayor Wosczszynski's measures to establish a business administration. Wachewicz considered a reputation for fiscal responsibility essential if the city wished lenders to provide mortgages to buyers interested in West Hammond.[2]

Prior to 1916, Wachewicz combined an insurance and real estate business. He built a few small, modern brick houses for Poles. But they were more cottages than bungalows (fig. 103). In most cases, he served merely as a middle man between buyers and sellers of existing houses. Then, in 1916, Wachewicz built sixty-three single-family houses in West Hammond at an average cost of $2,800 each.[3] These structures included houses for Paul Kamradt and Andrew Stachowicz (fig. 100). By this time, Wachewicz was dividing properties into three categories: cottages, modern homes, and investment properties. The distinctions revealed a great deal about the evolving housing market.

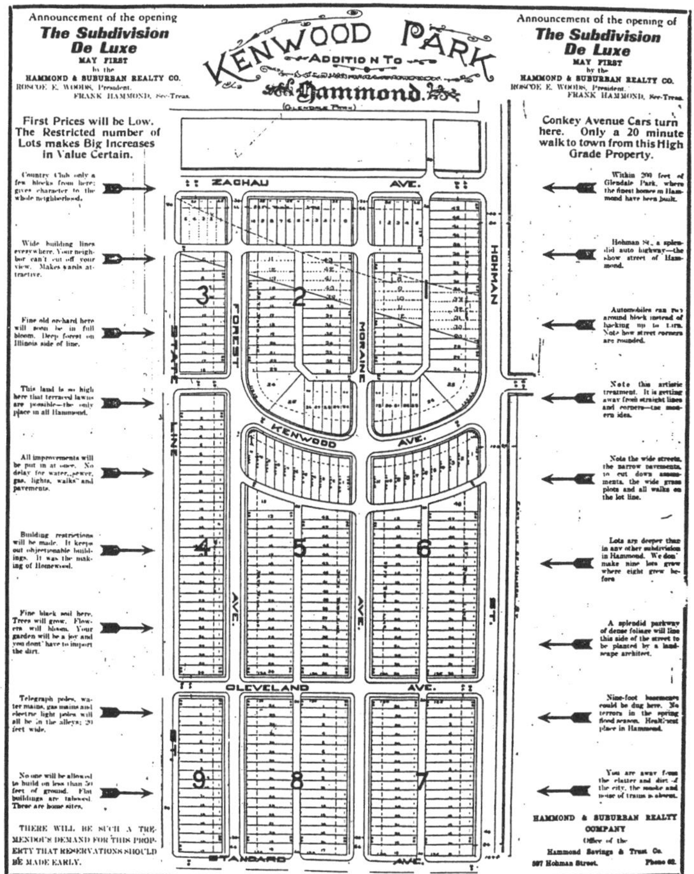

Figure 102
Kenwood Park, Hammond. (Source: Lake County Times, April 10, 1913.)

Figure 103
Modern brick cottage built by Wachewicz. (Source: author.)

Between 1917 and 1918, Wachewicz offered forty-eight cottages for sale. All contained plumbing and electricity, but only a few had central heating. Most contained five or six rooms. More than half were on lots larger than the standard twenty-five by 125 foot lot. Typically, larger lots were either fifty or thirty-seven-and-one-half feet wide.[4] The average price for a smaller cottage was $1,900, while larger cottages with amenities cost as much as $2,500.

Wachewicz identified slightly more than half the homes he sold in 1917 and 1918 as modern. In most cases, they were bungalows, all with at least six rooms, some with seven or eight. The bungalows contained modern conveniences and central heating. The least expensive cost $3,000, but most sold for between $3,500 and $3,800, with a few costing as much as $5,500. In addition, Wachewicz offered thirty investment properties, mostly residential buildings with two apartments. The older type were two-story cottages, common in Hammond since the first days of settlement. Like most cottages, they had modern plumbing and electricity but no central heating. The newer investment properties were brick buildings with flat roofs of a type that became common throughout Chicago (fig. 101). Like the bungalows, these structures offered all the amenities, including central heating. They varied significantly in cost, from nearly $5,000 to as much as $10,000.[5]

After World War I, Wachewicz expanded his business as a subdivider and builder. He specialized in affordable bungalows as did most builders in the region, some of whom were from Chicago.[6] Like Marcus Towle, S. E. Gross, and Oliver Brooks a generation before, Wachewicz advertised small down payments and low monthly mortgage installments. His slogan was "Easy to Pay the Wachewicz Way." Buyers purchased a modest new bungalow for $1,000 down with payments of $30–$40 a month. The mortgage payments approached the highest end of the rental market for apartments in Polish neighborhoods. His houses were affordable but only to a new class of more affluent buyers.

From 1918 to 1924, Wachewicz built 210 modern homes: 120 in West Hammond, thirty-seven in Hammond, and the remainder scattered throughout the Calumet region. Only thirty-four houses in West Hammond were built for Poles. City directories allowed identification of the occupations of 112 of the 149 buyers in Hammond and West Hammond. Of the 112, forty-six (41 percent) were professionals, businessmen, managers, or clerks. Forty-seven (42 percent) were foremen or skilled workers, and only nineteen (17 percent) were semi-skilled or unskilled laborers.

After 1919, most of Wachewicz's clients were not Polish, and none were poor. As his business expanded, he appealed to wider audiences with increasingly sophisticated advertisements (fig. 104 and 105). In addition, Wachewicz moved to larger offices in Hammond

Figure 104 Wachewicz advertisement, Park View Gardens. (Source: *Lake County Times*, May 12, 1922.)

Figure 105 Wachewicz advertisement: realtor, builder, subdivider. (Source: *Lake County Times*, September 13, 1924.)

and established a sales staff, which included a general manager, an insurance manager, salesmen, and clerical workers. Only the general manager, John Nowicki, was Polish, and Nowicki left soon after to establish his own office. By 1925, Wachewicz's associates were named Boyers, Maxwell, McGarry, and O'Connor. Only a few of the excavators, plasterers, carpenters, masons, electricians, and painters he employed were Polish.[7] As a businessman, Frank Wachewicz looked beyond the Polish community.[8] Poles simply could not provide sufficient numbers of house buyers of the type Wachewicz desired.

When Wachewicz and Woczszynski spoke of attracting a better class of residents, they knew a majority would be neither Polish nor immigrants. New forms of housing changed not only the physical appearance of West Hammond, but its social character as well, especially in the newly created Fifth Ward, which contained the city's best housing.[9] In 1915, ambitious members of the second generation balanced two worlds. They recognized the continuing problems of massive immigration and the increasing desire for social and cultural mobility. In confronting the events surrounding Prohibition, World War I, and the booming twenties, they articulated the forward nature of their vision.

Prohibition and the Business Administration

West Hammond faced a major obstacle in achieving a business administration. During the previous decade, the city incurred considerable debt issuing municipal bonds for streets, sewers, sidewalks, and other improvements. Repayment required revenue from taxes and assessments on property owners. But property owners often stopped paying taxes on lots in undeveloped portions of the city. During a brief boom, investors purchased land that was underwater for much of the year. When developments failed, the owners abandoned the properties. Consequently, West Hammond could not retire the debt contracted in expectation of funds, and the city developed a poor credit rating. Contractors routinely inflated bids for work in West Hammond, anticipating the city would not fulfill its obligations.[10]

Once in office, Woczszynski sought to determine the extent of the city's indebtedness. Unfortunately, the failure to pay its debts involved the city in unresolved legal actions. Frustrated, the mayor ordered the city attorney to accept reasonable judgments against West Hammond. When totaled, the debt amounted to $25,000. In May of 1914, Woczszynski proposed "one big sweeping assessment" of $52,000 to pay the debt and establish a modern fire department.

Since West Hammond lacked industry and a commercial district, property taxes and saloon license fees were the main sources of revenue. The city raised both, tripling the property tax from $1.82 for every $100 in assessed value to $5.55, while increasing the saloon license fee from $150 to $500 a year.[11]

Citizens were shocked. The mayor insisted high taxes were a temporary measure to meet a crisis. To persuade residents, Woczszynski requested support from the West Hammond Club, an organization of local businessmen from the German north side. The most prominent member was George Hannauer, the general manager of the Indiana Harbor Belt Line Railroad. Respected by all as honest and nonpartisan, Hannauer told reporters the city council was "above reproach," but so drastic an increase required a detailed examination of the problem. The *Times* considered the increase inevitable since it addressed "the real issue, whether or not the city can pay its debts and become a thriving corporation."[12] But the Calumet Terminal Transfer Railroad took West Hammond to court. The city won the first ruling but lost an appeal when the Illinois Supreme Court ruled the increase illegal. The ruling forced West Hammond to return its tax levy to the original rate.[13]

As debate continued, West Hammond faced a second crisis in March of 1914 when the township voted on an option prohibiting the sale of alcoholic beverages. The prospect of a dry township threatened the revenue from saloon license fees. If Thornton Township voted for Prohibition, West Hammond would lose $18,000, an amount equal to the annual revenue from property taxes.[14] Residents feared the vote because a new Illinois law enfranchised women, and the Women's Christian Temperance Union (WCTU) was strong in Harvey, Thornton Township's largest city. Campaigning in West Hammond, the WCTU called on women to vote dry to protect their homes from the evils of the saloon.[15]

West Hammond leaders held mass meetings for women on both the north and south sides.[16] At Saint Andrew's, 400 Polish women heard Adam Stachowicz explain the procedure for completing a "wet" ballot.[17] On election day, 1,372 West Hammond residents cast ballots, with women accounting for 47 percent of all voters. Ninety-one percent of the men and 97 percent of the women voted against Prohibition, defeating the measure in Thornton Township.[18] Residents knew that solvency depended on revenue from saloons. The vote also recognized the importance of women voters. After 1914, Poles knew they would remain dominant in local politics only if Polish women, as well as men, voted.

The victory did not lessen the financial crisis. When Mayor Woczszynski announced he would seek a third term, he faced opposition from Paul Kamradt and Henry Peters. Kamradt was a second-generation Pole with a reputation for honesty. Peters was a saloon owner associated with prostitution and the old gang. He hoped Woczszynski and Kamradt would split the Polish vote. During the campaign, the candidates pledged to run business administrations. Woczszynski boasted he had cleaned up the vice district and attracted seventy-six new homes of high quality to West Hammond.[19] He criticized officials in Gary, Indiana, who allowed a segregated vice district to operate. If West Hammond followed this policy, Woczszynski argued, prostitution would flourish, and "a town whose principal product is prostitution is not the kind of town in which respectable people come to live."

Kamradt avoided controversy. He promised to attract new industry and reduce the tax burden on home owners.[20] Kamradt won the primary by 128 votes in an election attracting 1,256 voters, nearly one-half of whom were women. He owed nomination to Polish voters who gave him 68 percent of their vote.[21] Following the primary, Martin Finneran reentered politics, organizing a slate that included Andrew Stachowicz and Richard Zimmerman as candidates for clerk and treasurer, respectively. The campaign was fierce. Finneran denounced Kamradt as the "loud-mouthed blatant champion of the gas company" and called the People's Party slate "putrid and foul smelling." Finneran denied associations with dive owners, claiming he was a reform candidate favoring a business administration. But Finneran vowed never to raise taxes or concede claims against the city, actions he described as "shamelessly extravagant." Instead, he promised to pay debts without creating hardships by cutting the cost of government.[22]

Unable to avoid controversy, Kamradt bravely defended Woczszynski. He argued that West Hammond must pay its debts "even if they were contracted by the irresponsibles of the old gang." Kamradt admitted higher taxes were necessary. But he promised to spend tax dollars wisely, reminding voters that Finneran and other "gray wolves [had] preyed on the humble and courageous workingman, nearly ruining the city financially."[23] Kamradt won by twenty-three votes in an election where 1,670 residents cast ballots. Again, he owed victory to the Polish Second Ward, where he received 62 percent of the vote. However, Second Ward voters split their ballots, voting for Kamradt but against Ignatius Mankowski, the incumbent clerk identified with Woczszynski.[24]

The new administration was dominated by Americanized Poles more comfortable with the larger culture (figs. 106 and 107). Once elected, Kamradt praised Woczszynski and pledged to continue his policies and achieve a business administration.[25] Indeed, during their terms, Woczszynski and Mankowski had acted courageously. They reformed the vice district and called for higher taxes. But the election taught the new mayor that he must devise a means to repay the debt without overburdening property owners.

World War I, Prosperity, and the New Civic Culture

Problems arose when the railroads won a reduction in the property tax. Prior to the ruling, Mayor Kamradt budgeted $24,000 toward

Figure 106 Mayor Paul Kamradt and the city council. (Source: E. Palma Beaudette-Neil, *Thornton Township, Cook County, Illinois: A Brief Sketch of the Township's Prominent Men and Industrial Establishments* [Hammond, Ind.: Neil Publishing, 1920], 65.)

Figure 107 The Kamradt Colts baseball team. (Source: Saint Andrew the Apostle Church, *Diamond Jubilee, 1892–1967, November 5, 1967, Saint Andrew the Apostle Church, Calumet City, Illinois* [Calumet, Ill.: Saint Andrew the Apostle Church, 1968].)

retiring the debt. Afterward, the city reduced the debt by $1,500.[26] A few months later, the Indiana legislature debated state-wide Prohibition. The debate led frightened Hammond saloonkeepers to look for sites across the state line. But Woczszynski's reform council had passed an ordinance limiting the number of saloons to thirty-four. If an Indiana saloonkeeper wished to operate in West Hammond, he needed one of the thirty-four licenses. The value of the licenses skyrocketed as Prohibition in Indiana became likely.[27]

West Hammond residents feared resurrection of the vice district. The *Times* warned, "If one-tenth of the big things proposed for West Hammond . . . materialize, the city over the state line will surely be a hummer."[28] Frank Wachewicz was optimistic that West Hammond no longer wished to be "the dumping ground for the undesirable saloon element."

> Two or three factors are decidedly in our favor. In the first place, the law already limits the number of saloons in Illinois territory, and secondly West Hammond is essentially a city of home owners who control their government. There is too a continual growth of the West Hammond spirit, which causes the inhabitants of the city to take pride in their city and its good reputation. We always had some fine people, and we are daily getting more desirable families. All this has a tendency to check and drive out the undesirable element.[29]

The city council debated license restrictions two weeks prior to the 1917 election. Mayor Kamradt estimated West Hammond required $48,000 in revenue each year to retire the debt and still provide the services necessary to attract new home owners. This figure represented an increase of $12,000 over Woczszynski's budget of 1914. But no one wished to raise property taxes at a time when West Hammond was populated by many immigrant owners with low incomes and little savings. A few council members favored revoking the ordinance that limited the number of saloons in order to raise revenue from license fees. Kamradt opposed "a more the merrier attitude" that threatened to "make West Hammond the greatest saloon town in the United States." Kamradt won the argument and reelection.[30]

For one year, the council remained opposed to more saloons despite rumors of a slush fund to bribe council members. When Indiana law closed Hammond saloons on April 2, 1918, the number of West Hammond saloons remained at thirty-four, each paying a

$500 license fee. At the next council meeting, forty-eight applicants petitioned for new licenses, and the council revoked the ordinance limiting saloons. Kamradt vetoed the measure. However, the council overrode the veto seven to one.

The council then renewed thirty licenses, refusing four "on the grounds that saloon keepers had not conducted business properly." Next, they raised the yearly license from $500 to $700, after which they granted twenty-seven new licenses. Before concluding, the council passed an ordinance limiting the number of saloons to fifty-two, the number of licenses it granted that day.[31] In one evening, West Hammond appeared to solve the financial crisis that had vexed reform mayors for five years. The fifty-two saloons paid the city $36,000 annually for licenses. Consequently, property taxes remained at the level that existed when Woczszynski took office, and the city still received $50,000 in annual revenue. In addition, Indiana Prohibition proved a windfall for the courts. In 1918, the city earned $13,000 in fines, the vast majority from arrests for public drunkenness.[32]

West Hammond faced a difficult problem. The city desired revenue from saloons but not the reputation as a saloon town. To prevent the return of undesirables, north side residents formed a Law and Order League. The league monitored conduct in north side saloons. Their reports led the city council to revoke the license of Henry Peters, the former candidate for mayor, for running a house of prostitution. When Peters's saloon reopened with a new owner but a similar clientele, the city passed an ordinance prohibiting the reopening of any saloon for one year following the revocation of its license.[33]

West Hammond's financial windfall ended in January of 1920 when the Volstead Act required the nation to go dry. City Clerk Andrew Stachowicz called a mass meeting in July to explain the effects of Prohibition. The city began 1920 with seventeen dollars in the treasury, $2,500 in unpaid bills, and $7,936 in old debt. Some residents criticized officials for the city government's persistent debt. But the record showed that West Hammond had reduced its debt by two-thirds during six years of reform administrations. On the south side, citizens were resigned to higher taxes. The *Times* advised residents to unite once again to solve their financial problems.[34]

Higher property taxes proved unnecessary. West Hammond resolved the crisis by disregarding the Volstead Act. The city allowed "soft drink parlors" to operate in the same manner as saloons before Prohibition. In 1921, the city directory listed forty-four soft drink parlors in West Hammond. In 1923, there were fifty-three, one less than the number of saloons before Prohibition.[35] West Hammond police did not interfere.[36] The city's gamble paid huge dividends since it did not slow development of the bungalow district. The soft drink parlors were located close to the state line, in the vice district and in the older portion of Sobieski Park (fig. 108). They did not affect the residential character of better neighborhoods.

By August of 1921, West Hammond had repaid its debt and deposited $11,000 in its treasury, achieving a solvent administration by ignoring federal law. Because property taxes remained low, one-third Hammond's rate, West Hammond experienced a housing boom that lasted the remainder of the decade.[37] The boom was not prevented by the violation of federal law because the city used its resources to develop a new, forward-looking civic identity.

The first sign of these new attitudes appeared during World War I. Historians have described the war as a period of xenophobia, when the federal government repressed radical labor movements and compelled immigrant workers to accept Americanization without question.[38] However, in the Calumet region, groups such as the Poles expressed patriotism without coercion. In April of 1918, Poles throughout the region participated in Polish Day. The celebration included a huge parade, with each marcher carrying an American flag. During the event, organizers sold $15,000 in Liberty Bonds.[39] Inspired, City Clerk Andrew Stachowicz and Alderman John Jaranowski

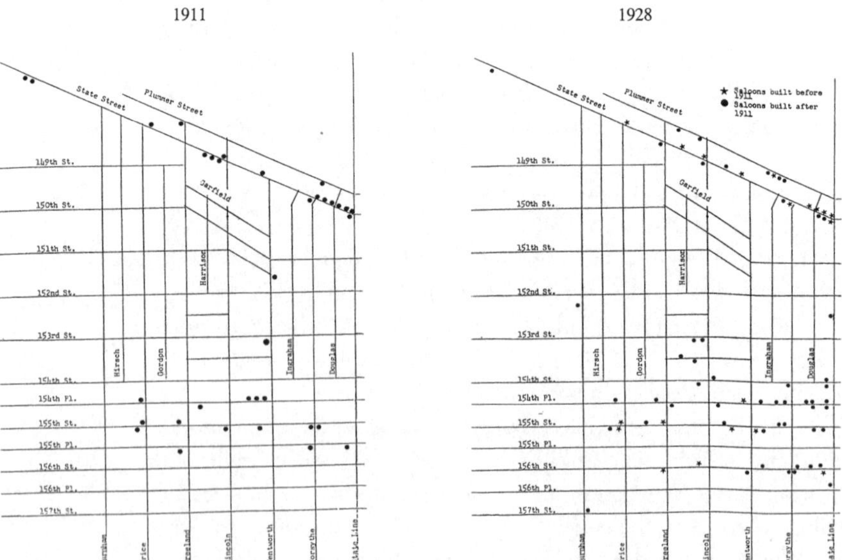

Figure 108 Location of West Hammond saloons in 1911 (left) and in 1928 (right). (Source: author.)

visited the homes and work places of West Hammond residents. Their solicitation enabled the city to become the second town in Cook County to "go over the top" and exceed its quota of war bond sales.[40]

Expressions of wartime patriotism set in motion a series of events that altered the social and physical character of West Hammond. Following the war, Hammond and West Hammond celebrated Armistice Day jointly (fig. 109). Twelve hundred ex-servicemen participated in events that included a parade, fireworks, and a series of patriotic addresses. Never before, the *Times* commented, had the region expressed so united a spirit "because nothing could be attempted which could be expected to appeal to such a vast proportion of the people."[41] Twenty-one months later, a more somber commemoration occurred when the remains of Joseph Lietzan returned from France. Lietzan died thirty miles outside Paris when a shell exploded as he attempted to rescue wounded comrades. The *Times* wrote, "More than any other deed, the heroism of Joseph Lietzan spurred the people of Hammond and West Hammond to united devotion in the war."

To West Hammond Service Men!

The Home Coming Celebration Tomorrow includes Our West Hammond Boys

All West Hammond Soldiers Sailors, Marines & Citizens

desiring to Parade will assemble at the West Hammond City Hall 12:45 P. M. Tuesday

Our column will leave there at 1:15 p. m. sharp proceed to Wentworth Avenue to 155th Street to State Line Street and join the main parade on Rimbach Avenue

Let's have a turnout that will keep up the proud war record of our city.

Service men are especially urged to join in the parade and to wear their uniforms

Paul M. Kamradt
Mayor

Figure 109 Welcome home celebration. (Source: *Lake County Times*, November 10, 1919.)

The family held the funeral at Saint Andrew's and buried the body in the Polish cemetery on the city's southern border. Two thousand people attended the funeral, including the mayors of Hammond and West Hammond. Anthony Halgas, the pastor of Saint Andrew's, preached the sermon in Polish, and Polish school children sang the requiem. Seventy-five automobiles followed the hearse to the cemetery.[42]

Prosperity and a new patriotism led West Hammond to honor its veterans by establishing a public park located between the German and Polish sections of town. A committee of sixty-two residents from the north and south sides created the plan. After visiting parks in Chicago, they concluded that $60,000 could provide "a good sized community building and a playground equipped with swimming and wading pools." To finance the plan, they promoted a bond issue with a rally attended by 400 veterans. Following the rally, residents approved the bond by a four to one margin.[43]

Memorial Park opened in the summer of 1922. The park boasted the first public swimming pool in the Calumet region (figs. 110 and 111). The day the pool opened "cool weather and threats of rain meant nothing" to fifty men and boys who swam. The following day with warmer weather, 560 people had "a high old time" while crowds "lined the fence and watched the fun." Pool Director Paul Lisenfeldt expressed the spirit of the occasion when he announced that West Hammond did not limit use of the pool to its residents. "We don't bar anyone, it is free to the public of the United States."[44]

The city organized an elaborate ceremony to dedicate the new fieldhouse on Armistice Day, 1922. Once again, West Hammond

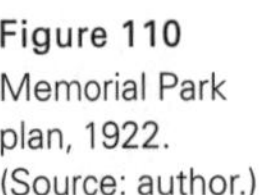
Figure 110
Memorial Park plan, 1922. (Source: author.)

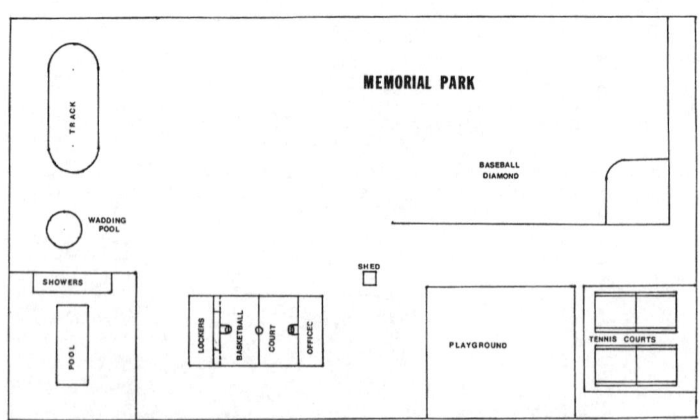

Figure 111
Swimming pool and fieldhouse. (Source: author.)

celebrated the holiday jointly with Hammond, but the celebration was "one-sided." West Hammond "furnished the greater part of the parade, the crowd, and the public spirit in what was supposed to be a twin-city celebration." Following the parade, 5,000 persons gathered to dedicate Memorial Fieldhouse. After the ceremony, an "orchestra furnished music and dancing which lasted until late in the evening." The *Times* praised the park board for exceptional service and concluded that Memorial Park "stands as a monument to the energy and civic interest which West Hammond has been displaying so effectively in recent years."[45] Clearly, the war and its commemoration presented the city with a remarkable opportunity to create a new civic culture that transcended the old divisions between Germans and Poles.

Expanding the New Civic Culture

Memorial Park became the centerpiece of a new community life that transcended the boundaries of the ethnic neighborhood. Citizens gathered in the park on the Fourth of July, which was celebrated each year with fireworks. The city also hired Ed Fedosky as director of athletics. Throughout the year, Fedosky organized programs for children, making good use of the track, swimming pool, basketball court, tennis courts, and baseball diamond. In addition, West Hammond hired a city nurse, Faith Bailey, who in 1923 established a clinic in the fieldhouse. Every Tuesday a dentist provided free care for children, while on Wednesdays a doctor provided free check-ups. Once a month, the city arranged for a specialist to test children for tuberculosis. Again, West Hammond provided services without restriction. The clinic was available to all without charge whether or not they resided in West Hammond. "Our aim," Faith Bailey told the newspaper, "is making it possible for every child to have a body free from any handicaps, physical or mental."[46]

By 1924, patriotism, disregard for Prohibition, and a booming economy had transformed life in West Hammond. In July, city officials announced plans for a new $75,000 municipal building that would have offices, a council chamber, a jail, and better facilities for Faith Bailey (fig. 112). West Hammond possessed sufficient reserves to pay for the building without a tax on property owners.[47] That same year, new residents in the city's north side bungalow district established a Catholic church and school. Saint Victor's was a territorial parish not dominated by one nationality.[48] Two months later, residents of the south side bungalow district took control of the public school that Polish residents had neglected for decades. Immediately, they changed its name from Sobieski to Lincoln, announcing plans to improve the faculty and build a modern school, which they completed in March of 1925.[49]

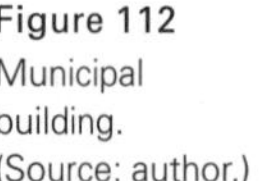
Figure 112
Municipal building.
(Source: author.)

The crowning achievement of 1924 occurred when the township unveiled plans to build a $300,000 public high school in West Hammond (fig. 113).[50] In 1920, 55 percent of fourteen- and fifteen-year-olds attended school. Ten years later, following construction of the local high school, the figure rose to 90 percent.[51] The school mixed students from German, Polish, and American backgrounds and encouraged a wide range of activities (fig. 114). By 1938, the most popular girls included Genevieve "Gena" Jablonski who "beamed with pep" and Dorothy "Dot" Bonkowski, the "swankiest" dresser, who resembled Kay Francis. Among the boys, Walter Waskelo was the school's "own Fred Astaire," while 147-pound Walter "Champ" Pawlowski was captain of the conference-champion football team, rushing for five touchdowns in a thirty-nine to seven victory over Bloom.[52] Pawlowski advanced to Michigan State, where in his moment of glory he outrushed Michigan's Tom Harmon in a head to head battle.

Figure 113 (*left*) Thornton Fractional North High School. (Source: author.)

Figure 114 (*bottom left & right*) Sports and clubs at Thornton Fractional North. (Source: Students of Thornton Fractional North, *Chronoscope 1938* [Calumet City, Ill.: Thornton Fractional Township High School, 1938].)

Like the park, the high school provided a new public turf where children experienced a larger culture separate from the ethnic community. Few high school teachers were Polish, and neither were most of the new residents who purchased bungalows. Prosperity transformed the city. From 1920 to 1930, the population increased 64 percent, from 7,492 to 12,298, while the number of residential structures increased 74 percent, from 1,316 to 2,295. In 1930 immigrants remained a majority of home owners, though the median value of their houses was significantly less ($5,396) than the value of houses owned by the American-born ($6,646). However, for the first time, immigrants were no longer a majority of the voting population. In 1930, 32 percent of potential voters were immigrants, while 37 percent were second generation, and 31 percent were American-born of American-born parents.[53]

The Emergence of Polish-American Culture

More than a generation ago, Oscar Handlin described the process that allowed immigrant children to enter the larger society. Handlin suggested that among the older generation the children's success offered a "sad satisfaction" since new opportunities threatened traditional allegiances. Handlin expressed this view eloquently when he wrote "that every step forward was a step away from home."[54] Undoubtedly, a decided preference for American habits and the English language saddened parents. But the rift between parent and child can be greatly exaggerated. Assimilated children did not forsake old allegiances because modest social and economic advances did not compel individuals to break ties with ethnic neighborhoods.

By 1920, Chicago's Polish communities had evolved. They offered a range of housing that accommodated both immigrant parents and their acculturated children.[55] In West Hammond, the range of housing options allowed even the most prosperous second-generation Poles to remain members of Saint Andrew's parish. In fact, they expanded and rebuilt the parish at the same time they worked to attract a new and more diverse population to the city. The rebuilding began in 1912 when the parish built a $60,000 school, a $35,000 rectory, and a $20,000 convent (figs. 115–17).[56] The convent and school solidified the church's educational mission. Their completion provided cause for a celebration that attracted Polish priests and fraternal organizations from Chicago as well as German Catholics from Saint Joseph's parish in Hammond. The *Times* reported that "flags decorated scores of homes, the Polish Falcons and the Polish

Figure 115
Saint Andrew's School. (Source: author.)

Figure 116
Saint Andrew's Convent. (Source: author.)

Figure 117
Saint Andrew's Rectory. (Source: author.)

National Alliance marched in uniform to the tune of martial music, and a thousand members of the congregation and children fell in line in the afternoon for a parade that marched through the streets of the city."[57]

Unfortunately, five years later, fire destroyed the church at a time when a large debt remained from the rectory, convent, and school.[58] The congregation worshiped in the school basement for thirteen years under conditions less than satisfactory for weddings, funerals, and holy days. Finally, in October of 1931, the parish consecrated a new church, valued at $300,000, with Italian marble altars and statuary (figs. 118 and 119).[59] The church compared favorably

Figure 118
Saint Andrew's Church. (source: author.)

Figure 119
Main altar, Saint Andrew's Church. (Source: author.)

with the best new Polish churches in Chicago. These churches became features common to the landscape of Midwestern industrial cities, providing dignity to Polish-American neighborhoods. They also announced to outsiders that Poles were a permanent and substantial people.

Refinements affected both the religious and secular dimensions of Polish-American life. First communion photographs of a mother and of her child suggest a movement toward a more fashionable and stylish life (fig. 120). The children of the second generation embraced a tailored look, with shined shoes and pressed pants. Certainly, they were no longer the stereotyped images of Ellis Island. Yet continuity existed because Poles incorporated fashion into traditional occasions that were celebrated across the generations. The more prosperous second generation may have lived in bungalows and provided their children with more fashionable clothes and better educations, but they still worshiped and celebrated with their immigrant parents.

Certainly, glimpses of an affluent society changed the attitudes of the prosperous second generation. Local stores, such as Kaufman and Wolf, employed new methods of advertising, seductively promising that "Everybody Can Have It" because prices were low, values were high, and installments were easy (fig. 121). Some historians have seen in such claims the influence of a hegemonic middle-class culture disseminating downward. But the relationship was more nuanced, a fact often missed by those who focus on national

Figure 120
First Communion photographs, mother (left) and son (right), circa 1905 and 1933. (Source: author.)

Figure 121
Complete four-room outfit. (Source: *Lake County Times*, May 18, 1926.)

advertising campaigns aimed at the middle class. Seductive advertising did not overwhelm local cultures.[60] In fact, a history that relies entirely on national, middle-class campaigns distorts the process by which ordinary people acquired amenities. Certainly, an innovation like modern plumbing first occurred in wealthy residences.[61] But the United States did not become the best plumbed nation by selling elaborate goods to the wealthy. The American standard was simple sanitary ware sold at low cost, with uniform dimensions, and threaded pipe connections.[62] Modern plumbing resulted from a confluence of middle-class notions of cleanliness and manufacturing innovations prompted by a huge market of working-class home owners.[63] No matter how seductive the images in national magazines, the working class acquired plumbing because of improvements they witnessed in local markets (fig. 122).

Poverty prevented a majority of Poles from acquiring the wide variety of goods that resulted from mass production. Yet, by 1930, most Polish-Americans shared some portion of the benefits of a

Figure 122 Advertisement: Hammond Heating and Plumbing, (Source: *Lake County Times*, March 7, 1924.)

more affluent society. The majority attended better parochial schools, learning to read, write, and pray in a tradition that was now Polish and American Catholic. In church, they experienced baptism, communion, confirmation, marriage and burial in more elaborate environments. At the same time, children went to the public park, played with more assimilated friends, listened to the radio, and graduated from the public high school, where recreations were secular and where Americanization was paramount.

In her account of the Polish response to the Americanization of Catholicism, Lizabeth Cohen errs when she argues that resistance to the Americanization programs of Cardinal Mundelein strengthened and unified a defensive Polish community.[64] Certainly, powerful Polish priests did not wish to relinquish authority over schools, cemeteries, and younger clergy to the archdiocese. Many acted like feudal barons. But the Polish language newspapers and religious correspondence that supported such views were vehicles for older priests and not for the younger and more affluent second generation. Priests faced competition for the hearts and minds of Polish-Americans from members of the second generation who advanced in a secular world. While assimilated Poles did not forsake the ethnic church, neither did they wish it to remain an immigrant, foreign-language institution. Most Poles who prospered did not wish to live next to their poorest fellow countrymen. They used terms like "greenhorn" or the more derogatory "hunky" with greater regularity than nativists.[65]

By 1930, unity among Poles resulted not from defensiveness and resistance to the dominant culture but from the ability to alter the physical and social qualities that defined Polish neighborhoods throughout Chicago. These neighborhoods provided a wide range of options capable of holding both newcomers and the assimilated. Certainly, Poles remained religiously, socially, and, to a lesser extent, geographically separated from others. But practical needs always limited segregation. Everyone needed work, and the community did not control employment. Ethnic politicians and entrepreneurs recognized that more money could be made and more favors gained by making connections outside the community. So men like Frank Wachewicz and Paul Kamradt crossed and recrossed the line dividing Poles from the larger culture. In doing so, the second generation introduced changes felt throughout the community. Consequently, a new immigrant arriving in 1910 did not experience the same world as those who had arrived in 1880. Even the children of the poorer new arrivals played in the parks and went to high school, a prospect difficult to imagine a generation before.

Conclusion

In West Hammond, prosperity derived from the coming of age of second-generation leaders and from the revenue gained by disobeying the Volstead Act. Unfortunately, when West Hammond chose to ignore federal Prohibition laws, the city bargained with the devil. At first, mobsters from Chicago Heights provided the soft drink parlors with beer and liquor. However, in 1923, Al Capone initiated a gang war. Capone was savage. He won because he murdered those who opposed him. A number of his henchmen lived in West Hammond so they could accompany the trucks that distributed the beer. Corruption increased because violation of the law involved great sums of money. By 1930, the city was home to more than a hundred licensed soft drink parlors. Whenever officials attempted to reduce the number, unlicensed saloons opened in residential neighborhoods.[66]

Repeal of Prohibition did not eliminate the problem. Organized crime established financial interests in the old vice district. When beer sales no longer profited criminals, they introduced gambling and striptease shows, along with prostitution. In January of 1924, the city council voted unanimously to change West Hammond's name to Calumet City. They desired an identity separate from Hammond, and they wished to rid themselves of the notoriety gained during the Virginia Brooks crusade.[67] Unfortunately, the name Calumet City became even more notorious.[68] In a 1941 pictorial, *Life* magazine told America that Calumet City was "the Barbary Coast of the booming Midwest," where seven nights a week scores of workers drank "their way westward, zigzagging from club to club, . . . ogling half-a-dozen strip teasers," until at five in the morning they found themselves "weary, bleary, and broke."[69]

Local residents resented this portrayal. The *Times* admitted "the existence of a wild night life," but questioned whether it was fair "to show only the weaknesses of an American community, . . . which has, despite many obstacles, begun to produce the new American Civilization, the everyday working Americans who stem from a half a hundred different nationalities." The point was valid. In fifty years, the Calumet region was transformed from dunes and swamp into one of the most productive regions of the world. The *Times* boasted that the Calumet area was the "Workshop of America."[70] Too often, the spectacular problems engendered by massive immigration, poverty, and urban growth overshadow the achievements of this "new American Civilization." West Hammond's story involved more than a bargain with the devil. An open market for housing and the rise of middle-class culture allowed ordinary people to create respectable lives for themselves and their children. In doing so, they, and so many others like them, expanded greatly notions of who might become a proper American citizen.

CONCLUSION

The Search for Order

A generation ago, in a masterful analysis, Robert Wiebe described the vast consequences resulting from the rise of corporate capitalism. Prior to 1880, America was "a nation of loosely connected islands," of small towns where individuals judged "the world as they would their neighbors." Thirty years later, the nation was governed by large organizations, with order imposed from the top down. This shift reconfigured social relationships, creating a managed society whose "complex arrangements nothing short of a revolution could destroy."[1]

In the twentieth century, affluent suburbs became hallmarks of the new social order, the reward for those who navigated successfully the ranks of management. The distinctive qualities of these suburbs governed the images of consumer culture published by the most popular journals and magazines. As comfort spread generally through society, the lower ranks embraced these images. To most, it appeared the values of the new corporate culture trickled downward, the consequence of the talented few who manipulated images on a grand, national scale.

But the concept of an organizational revolution should not serve as the Rosetta stone for interpreting the development of great cities such as Chicago. Long after the triumph of organizational society, loosely connected and inadequately controlled housing markets continued to thrive. These markets derived from a separate dynamic, from a local market for inexpensive, adaptable cottage housing. The market for cottages produced another signature element of the landscape: ethnic, working-class neighborhoods with high rates of home ownership. These neighborhoods bred a competing ethic, an alternative form of capitalism, which generated a wealth equal to that of the most expertly managed corporations.[2]

Ethnic neighborhoods flourished because they provided a range of accommodations. They housed the poorest newcomers, as well as the more assimilated second generation. By the 1920s, improvements in Chicago's housing market allowed for construction of bungalows and two-flats, stylish modern residences with central heating, plumbing, and electrical services. The bungalow and the two-flat blurred distinctions between working-class and middle-class houses. The simplest bungalows were little more than updated, nineteenth-century cottages, clear evidence of the continuity of house forms (fig. 123). But new bungalow neighborhoods encouraged divisions by class, separating the members of ethnic groups into those who could and those who could not afford modern housing. Bungalow neighborhoods especially enticed a younger generation, testing their commitment to traditional religious and ethnic communities.

Most of the second generation retained their allegiance to ethnic communities. But greater prosperity allowed for a vision of citizenship broader than their immigrant predecessors. The second generation bridged the division between immigrant communities and educated, middle-class reformers. Both groups desired healthier, more refined environments. However, the latter group insisted on orderly, managed reform, while the former favored greater opportunity and freedom of choice. Among groups such as the Poles, second-generation leaders adopted reforms according to the needs of working-class constituents. While less comprehensive than the schemes espoused by reformers, their efforts provided immigrants with a measure of control as they adjusted to American life.

By the 1920s, ethnic communities participated in traditional activities within their neighborhoods as well as in the new public culture of parks and schools. The process evolved in fits and starts, due to inadequate income and the boom and bust cycles of the economy. The Depression and World War II halted the creation of

Figure 123
Bungalows and cottages in the Polish areas of West Hammond and East Chicago. (Source: author.)

new neighborhoods. But development resumed with a vengeance following the war, expanding in an unprecedented manner the process set in motion when the poor first gained access to affordable housing.

After the war, Chicago's working class improved on old forms, but more often accepted newer styles of housing that spread across enormous sections of the metropolitan landscape (figs. 124 and 125). The social changes resulting from this rebuilding of the city lies

Figure 124
The bungalow, 1970. (Source: author.)

Figure 125
Ranch housing, 1960. (Source: the author.)

beyond the scope of this study. But once again, countless modest gains refashioned the qualities of everyday life, increasing the privileges enjoyed by groups who, at the beginning of the century, were considered beyond redemption.

Improvements in Chicago's ethnic, working-class neighborhoods challenged the assumptions of Progressive reformers. Confronting enormous social change, the Progressives developed sophisticated methods for researching and presenting information about the built environment. While intellectually courageous, their efforts were seriously flawed since most reformers shared common prejudices regarding the inferiority of southern and eastern Europeans. More significant, they were too confident in their diagnosis of the causes of social problems. After 1910, they seldom went into the field with open minds to confront the built environment. Instead, they became predictable, relying on old assumptions that showed little respect for the modest gains that altered substantially the character of modern society.

Local markets remain contested territory. Their successes and failures affect social attitudes because most Americans still judge the world as they would their neighbors. Conventional wisdom suggests that current divisions in society represent a racism more virulent than the forms present at the beginning of the century. Evocative and unsettling images support this view. But once again, the prevailing images fail to capture a diversity of condition, especially as Chicago experiences population movements and a surge of building as significant as any in its history. When the research for this book began, few

Figure 126
An African-American suburban community, 1996. (Source: author.)

would have imagined that a young, educated, urban population would spend enormous amounts of money to live in the old Polish Downtown, reclaiming buildings once described as the city's greatest social evil. Current movements among the city's African-American population into the southern suburbs also defy simple explanations (fig. 126). But then ordinary landscapes surprise those who confront them directly, for they represent a more subtle and complex expression than the social theories with which we attempt to make our world easily comprehensible.

NOTES

PREFACE

1. See Carl Smith, *Urban Disorder and the Shape of Belief* (Chicago: University of Chicago Press, 1995); James Gilbert, *Perfect Cities: Chicago's Utopias of 1893* (Chicago: University of Chicago Press, 1991); Karen Sawislak, *Smoldering City: Chicagoans and the Great Fire, 1871–1874* (Chicago: University of Chicago Press, 1995); and Daniel Bluestone, *Constructing Chicago* (New Haven, Conn.: Yale University Press, 1991).

2. Smith, *Urban Disorder and the Shape of Belief*, 271.

3. For an excellent example of detailed, artifactual analysis of a modern building type, see John A. Jakle and Keith A. Sculle, *The Gas Station in America* (Baltimore: Johns Hopkins University Press, 1994.) I stated my preference for this type of scholarship in a review essay; see Joseph C. Bigott, "Comprehending the Landscape: Gas Stations, Grass, Great Streets, and Grand Avenues," *Journal of Urban History* 25, no. 1 (November 1998): 103–9.

4. Cary Carson, "Material Culture History: The Scholarship Nobody Knows" in *American Material Culture: The Shape of the Field*, ed. Ann Smart Martin and J. Ritchie Garrison (Knoxville: University of Tennessee Press, 1997), 401–5. A historian and advocate for material culture studies, Carson presented a devastating critique of the field. According to Carson, the field has never influenced mainstream American history because it has not produced a work combining sophisticated analysis of artifacts and a broad new interpretation of history based on that analysis. I share his desire for a study that brings material culture studies into the mainstream of American history.

For this to occur, Carson argued that material culture studies must do "painstaking and unglamourous" (411) research in written records in order to fulfill the standards of modern social history. Carson suggested that even the finest works in material history have avoided such work. Instead, they have imported ideas from the grand theoretical works of Claude Lévi-Strauss, Michel Foucault, and Karl Marx rather than learn "from close study of the men and women who left behind the artifacts" (Carson, "Material Culture History," 409).

To overcome the problem, Carson calls for well-chosen case studies that address the most significant questions of mainstream history:

> Only by thoroughly understanding the mechanisms that drove historical change in one locality can we hope to create an analytical tool—a working hypothesis—that can then be used to test its efficacy elsewhere and thereby possibly to extend its

> explanatory reach farther afield. The goal is always to discover the larger forces at work in history, including those that shaped material life. Solid success will come incrementally by raising bigger and bigger ideas on a well-built foundation of local research that demonstrates, not just asserts, the links between people's everyday experience and the production of their material culture. (Carson, "Material Culture History," 413)

5. Some scholars have dismissed the examination of residential landscapes as "subjective," "irrelevant," and "ahistorical." They have suggested that sophisticated analysis requires historians to "move beyond what style and appearance could reveal" and to accept a "more theoretically inspired investigation" based on written and quantifiable sources. See Deryck W. Holdsworth, "Landscape and Archives as Texts" in *Understanding Ordinary Landscapes*, ed. Paul Groth and Todd W. Bressi (New Haven, Conn.: Yale University Press, 1997), 44–55, and "House and Home in Vancouver: Images of West Coast Urbanism, 1886–1929" in *The Canadian City: Essays in Urban History*, ed. Gilbert A. Stelter and Alan F. F. Artibise (Toronto: McClelland & Steward, 1977), 186–211.

In criticizing the approach of cultural geographers, Holdsworth praised a number of works by British and Canadian academics who did not analyze artifacts in their studies of the built environment. Michael J. Doucet and John C. Weaver provided a fine, well-reasoned argument in their "Material Culture and the North American House: The Era of the Common Man, 1870–1920," Journal of American History, 72, no. 3 (December 1985): 560–87. But the essay relied on economic statistics, contemporary journal articles, and secondary sources that described construction practices and technological innovations. The authors did not examine buildings in specific contexts.

I agree with many of their findings, especially their characterization of 1870–1920 as the critical period in the development of the North American house. But I do not place ultimate faith in their observations because I trust the evidence derived from analysis of artifacts more than I trust what people said about artifacts. (Chapter 1 of this text shows that no one can understand the significance of machine tools by reading journals from the 1880s. Physical evidence is essential for understanding woodworking machinery and its products.)

Also, to avoid confusion, I would prefer that studies such as Doucet and Weaver's avoid using the term "material culture." For me, the term suggests a belief that objects convey critical cultural information that can be interpreted reliably. Like Holdsworth, the authors did not share this belief.

Finally, a reliance on theory and a failure to analyze artifacts in their specific contexts can lead to errors in judgment. Holdsworth praised Anthony D. King's study of the bungalow as "a landmark example of how to approach artifacts from a theoretically informed perspective" (Holdsworth, "Landscape and Archives," 54; see King, *The Bungalow: The Production of a Global Culture* [London: Routledge & Kegan Paul, 1984]). King suggested that bungalows, including the types found in Chicago, originated with the British experience in India. The suggestion is implausible, a conclusion derived from a reliance on language describing a house type rather than from a study of houses in their specific context. My fieldwork demonstrated that the Chicago bungalow evolved from a housing form indigenous to the city. The vast majority of bungalows closely resembled an earlier form known as a cottage, which improved steadily over the course of sixty years. While the language for selling houses changed, adopting the romantic term "bungalow," the forms and the methods of construction and sale were related to Chicago's previous real estate traditions.

6. See Eugene S. Ferguson, *Engineering and the Mind's Eye* (Cambridge, Mass.: MIT Press, 1992), xi. Ferguson possesses a remarkable talent for examining the art of engineering. His work provides a clear refutation for those who suggest that the study of artifacts is subjective, irrelevant, and ahistorical. For a similarly elegant analysis, see Henry Petroski, *Invention by Design: How Engineers Get from Thought to Thing* (Cambridge, Mass.: Harvard University Press, 1996.) See also George Basalla, *The Evolution of Technology* (Cambridge: Cambridge University Press, 1988). Tom F. Peters has described the thought process of builders in the nineteenth century in *Building the Nineteenth Century* (Cambridge, Mass.: MIT Press, 1996).

INTRODUCTION

1. Richard L. Bushman, *The Refinement of America: Persons, Houses, Cities* (New York: Alfred A. Knopf, 1992), 410, xii, xv, xvii, 423, 274. In his critique of material culture history, Cary Carson identified *The Refinement of America* as a major work that made explicit the relationship between material life and the themes of mainstream history ("Material Culture History: The Scholarship Nobody Knows" in *American Material Culture: The Shape of the Field*, ed. Ann Smart Martin and J. Ritchie Garrison [Knoxville: University of Tennessee Press, 1997], 417–420).

2. For an assessment of Chicago reformers, see Rivka Shpak Lissak, *Pluralism and Progressives: Hull House and the New Immigrants, 1890–1919* (Chicago: University of Chicago Press, 1989), 62–122, 172–81.

3. See John Higham, *Strangers in the Land: Patterns of American Nativism 1860–1925* (New Brunswick, N.J.: Rutgers University Press, 1955; reprint, New York: Atheneum, 1977), 68–105. For general assessments of the racial views of reformers, see Barbara Miller Solomon, *Ancestors and Immigrants: A Changing New England Tradition* (Boston: Harvard University Press, 1956; reprint, Chicago: University of Chicago Press, 1972), 126–51; and Otis L. Graham, Jr., *The Great Campaigns: Reform and War in America, 1900–1928* (New York: Prentice Hall, 1871; reprint, Malabar, Fla.: Robert E. Krieger Publishing, 1987), 140–43.

4. Francis Amasa Walker, "Immigration and Degradation," *Forum* (August 1891), 644, "Immigration," *Yale Review* 1 (August 1892): 133, and "The Tide of Economic Thought," *Publications of the American Economic Association at the Fourth Annual Meeting* 6 (December 26–30, 1890): 37.

Walker was a seminal figure in American social science. He served as superintendent of the federal census and as president of the Massachusetts Institute of Technology. For two decades, he argued that Americans must prevent the inescapable decline that resulted from allowing the blood of lesser races to gain ascendancy due to a rate of immigration "in comparison with which the invasions under which Rome fell were no more than a series of excursion parties." Repeatedly, Walker asked readers to consider the effects "upon the ambitions and aspirations of our people by contact so foul and loathsome" ("Restriction of Immigration," *Atlantic Monthly* 77 [June 1896]: 828). A generation of social scientists supported this analysis in prominent academic journals. (See Henry Pratt Fairchild, "The Paradox of Immigration," *American Journal of Sociology* 16 [September 1911]: 266–67, and "The Restriction of Immigration," *American Journal of Sociology* 17 [March 1912]: 637–46.)

For histories of Walker's career, see Charles F. Dunbar, "The Career of Francis Amasa Walker," *Quarterly Journal of Economics* 2 (July 1897): 436–48; J. Laurence Laughlin, "Francis Amasa Walker," *Journal of Political Economy* 5 (March 1899): 228–36; Joseph Dorfman, *The Economic Mind in American Civilization*, 5 vols. (New York: Augustus M. Kelly, 1959), 3:101–10; and George M. Fredrickson, *The Inner Civil War: Northern Intellectuals and the Crisis of Union* (New York: Harper, 1968), 203–5.

5. Rosell A. Johnson, "The Eugenics of the City," in *The Urban Community: Selected Papers from the Proceedings of the American Sociological Society, 1925*, ed., Ernest W. Burgess (Chicago: University of Chicago Press, 1926), 90.

6. Hunter expressed his fears of race suicide in his most famous work, *Poverty*, published three years after he completed his survey of Chicago's tenements. Historians who rely on Hunter's tenement survey invariably fail to account for the harsh racial views expressed in *Poverty*. For the influence of Francis Amasa Walker, see Robert Hunter, *Poverty* (New York: Macmillan, 1904; reprint, New York: Harper Torchbooks, 1965), 298–317.

7. Robert Hunter, *Tenement Conditions in Chicago: Report by the Investigating Committee of the City Homes Association* (Chicago: City Homes Association, 1901), 52, 14.

8. Hunter, *Poverty*, 315, 327.

9. Thomas Lee Philpott, *The Slum and the Ghetto: Neighborhood Deterioration and Middle-Class Reform, Chicago, 1880–1930* (New York: Oxford University Press, 1978), 41, 29.

10. Christine Meisner Rosen, *The Limits of Power: Great Fires and the Process of City Growth in America* (Cambridge: Cambridge University Press, 1981), 108, 100.

In *Making a New Deal*, Lizabeth Cohen suggests that Chicago historians have a special advantage because of the city's rich tradition of social science research. She maintains that "so long as their biases are recognized, these contemporary studies of Chicago life can serve social historians like myself as revealing windows into working-class experience." See Lizabeth Cohen, *Making a New Deal: Industrial Workers in Chicago, 1919–1939* (Cambridge: Cambridge University Press, 1990), 7–8. Unfortunately, even the best histories centered in Chicago neighborhoods seldom account for the bias of early twentieth-century investigators.

In criticizing an "extremely positive' narrative about the Back of the Yards, James R. Barrett accepted the extremely negative work of novelists like Upton Sinclair and social scientists like Charles J. Bushnell as "quite accurate, at least so far as the details of physical conditions in the plants and neighborhoods are concerned" ("Local History and Social History 'Back of the Yards,'" *Reviews in American History* 16 [March 1988]: 45). But Bushnell's investigations abetted a highly polemical social science that stressed the need for a trained, native middle class to intercede in the lives of crude and vulgar immigrants. Bushnell assumed that industrial neighborhoods produced "a wild, sodden, sickening, inhuman and infinitely tragical struggle, not only a menace to those finer dreams of a noble, joyous, and beautiful national life, but a threat even to the very essentials of a common and decent civilization" ("Some Social Aspects of the Chicago Stock Yards: Chapter II, The Stock Yard Community at Chicago," *American Journal of Sociology* 7, no. 1 (November 1901): 289.

Both Barrett and Dominic A. Pacyga accepted the objectivity of reformers largely without criticism in their studies of the Back of the Yards. See Barrett, *Work and Community in the Jungle: Chicago's Packinghouse Workers, 1894–1922* (Urbana: University of Illinois Press, 1987), 64–90; and Pacyga, *Polish Immigrants and Industrial Chicago: Workers on the South Side, 1880–1922* (Columbus: Ohio State University Press, 1990), 62–81.

11. Edith Abbott, *Social Welfare and Professional Education* (Chicago: University of Chicago Press, 1942), 149–50. See also Edith Abbott, "Introductory Note," *American Journal of Sociology* 12 (June 1905): 323–24.

12. Hunter, *Tenement Conditions in Chicago*, 21–31, 50, 75, 161–79.

13. Edith Abbott assisted by Sophonisba P. Breckinridge and Other Associates in the School of Social Service Administration of the University of Chicago, *The Tenements of Chicago, 1908–1935* (Chicago: University of Chicago Press, 1936), 8–21. Karen Sawislak and Christine Meisner Rosen described the period following the fire (Sawislak, *Smoldering City: Chicagoans and the Great Fire, 1871–1874* [Chicago: University of Chicago Press, 1995], 69–259; and Rosen, *The Limits of Power*, 93–176).

14. Edith Abbott, "The Wages of Unskilled Labor in the United States, 1850–1900," *Journal of Political Economy* 13 (June 1905): 323–24.

15. Abbott et al., *The Tenements of Chicago*, 363.

16. Ibid., 363–69, 377–92.

17. Ibid., 489, 494–95. Recently, Gail Radford provided a fine analysis of reform proposals for modern housing after 1930; see *Modern Housing for America: Policy Struggles in the New Deal Era* (Chicago: University of Chicago Press, 1996). However, she continued the reform tradition of

dismissing the achievements of working-class groups who participated in the private market. Like most historians, she accepted the views of Hunter and Abbott without reservations.

18. In a fine study of special assessments and local politics, Robin L. Einhorn writes of housing conditions and law from the perspective of reformers, tacitly accepting denunciations of the working-class housing market as universally substandard. Upon considering the work of the few historians who saw benefits to low-cost housing, she writes, "It is questionable whether unhealthy neighborhoods lacking basic physical infrastructure ought to be called 'benefits'" (*Property Rules: Political Economy in Chicago, 1833–1872* [Chicago: University of Chicago Press, 1991], 18–19, 247–67). Her conclusions regarding political economy remain provocative. She also offers an interesting collection of statistics. However, her views regarding the quality of housing lack a basis in detailed research.

For one of the few challenges to the tenement image, see Robert G. Barrows, "Beyond the Tenement: Patterns of American Urban Housing, 1870–1930," *Journal of Urban History* 9 (August 1983): 395. Unfortunately, this work does not examine structures. It was based entirely on statistical analysis.

19. Kenneth T. Jackson, *Crabgrass Frontier: The Suburbanization of the United States* (New York: Oxford University Press, 1985), 11.

20. The first statement of this view was Sam Bass Warner, Jr., *Streetcar Suburbs: The Process of Growth in Boston, 1870–1900* (Cambridge: Harvard University Press, 1962), 46–66. See also Jackson, *Crabgrass Frontier,* 39–44, 103–15. For an overview, see Peter O. Muller, *Contemporary Suburban America* (Englewood Cliffs, N.J.: Prentice-Hall, 1981), 80–116.

21. The term derives from Christopher Lasch, *Haven in a Heartless World* (New York: Harper Colophon, 1977). See also Jackson, *Crabgrass Frontier,* 45–47, 54–61, 72.

22. Jackson, *Crabgrass Frontier,* 190–218, 234–45.

23. C. Wright Mills expressed this view in *White Collar: The American Middle Class* (New York: Oxford University Press, 1953), xv, 11, 54. For a stinging critique of this position, see Olivier Zunz, *Making America Corporate, 1870–1920* (Chicago: University of Chicago Press, 1990), 1–10.

24. Richard Polenberg, *One Nation Divisible: Class, Race, and Ethnicity in the United States since 1938* (New York: Viking Press, 1980), 163, 15. See also David Riesman, *Abundance for What? And Other Essays* (Garden City, N.Y.: Doubleday, 1964), 235.

25. For a brief general discussion of home ownership, see Eric H. Monkkonen, *America Becomes Urban: The Development of U.S. Cities and Towns, 1780–1980* (Berkeley: University of California Press, 1988), 182–205, 296–98.

26. Adna Ferrin Weber offered a brilliant first analysis of this trend in *The Growth of Cities in the Nineteenth Century: A Study in Statistics* (New York: Macmillan Company, 1899; reprint, Ithaca, N.Y.: Cornell University

Press, 1965), 222–29. Later, Graham R. Taylor explored the social and political implications of industrial deconcentration (*Satellite Cities* [New York: D. Appleton & Co., 1915]).

Studies of suburbanization continued to acknowledge the presence of the working class on the periphery until about 1970. These studies suggested the number of working-class residents in the suburbs was at least as large as the number of white-collar, middle-class residents. See William N. Mitchell, *Trends in Industrial Location in the Chicago Region since 1920* (Chicago: University of Chicago Press, 1933), 64–71; Chauncy D. Harris, "Suburbs," *American Journal of Sociology* 49 (July 1943): 1–13; Leo F. Schnore, "The Growth of Metropolitan Suburbs," *American Social Review* 22 (April 1957): 165–73, and *The Urban Scene: Human Ecology and Demography* (New York: Free Press, 1965), 137–51.

27. Olivier Zunz, *The Changing Face of Inequality: Urbanization, Industrial Development, and Immigrants in Detroit, 1880–1920* (Chicago: University of Chicago Press, 1982), 43–45, 161.

See also Roger D. Simon, "Housing And Services in an Immigrant Neighborhood: Milwaukee's Ward 14," *Journal of Urban History* 2 (August 1976): 437–39, 444–47, 454–55, and *The City-Building Process: Housing and Services in New Milwaukee Neighborhoods, 1880–1910*, Transactions of the American Philosophical Society, vol. 68, pt. 5 (Philadelphia: American Philosophical Society, 1978), 40–41.

28. See Abbott et al., *The Tenements of Chicago*, 489, 494–95.

29. Sam Bass Warner, Jr., *The Private City: Philadelphia in Three Periods of Its Growth* (Philadelphia: University of Pennsylvania Press, 1968), ix–xi. For a recent account, by a student of Kenneth Jackson, that continues this perspective, see Radford, *Modern Housing for America*, 85–209.

30. Lewis Mumford provided an early and influential description of the "insensate" industrial city; see his *The Culture of Cities* (New York: Harcourt, Brace & Co., 1938), 142–222, and *The City in History: Its Origins, Its Transformations, and Its Prospects* (New York: Harcourt, Brace & World, 1961), 446–74.

31. Radford, *Modern Housing for America*, 27. Radford provides a fine account of the views of reformers. However, she accepts far too easily their assertions that the low-end housing market failed. Drawing on the work of Edith Abbott, Radford repeated the century-old criticisms of cottage housing. It appears that Radford never studied in any detail a variety of Chicago neighborhoods. Her images of Chicago result from research done in a library. See her chapter "American Housing before the Depression," 7–28.

Having done extensive fieldwork, I do not find Abbott as creditable a source as Radford does. A failed market served the self-interests of reformers since the greater the problem the greater the need for their services. The easy acceptance of the views of professional, academic housing reforms remains a troublesome problem in American history.

32. Henry Glassie expressed this view most forcefully in "Meaningful Things and Appropriate Myths: The Artifact's Place in

American Studies" in *Material Life in America, 1600–1860*, Robert Blair St. George (Boston: Northeastern University Press, 1981), 63–92.

33. Clifford Edward Clark, Jr., *The American Family Home* (Chapel Hill: University of North Carolina Press, 1986), xiii.

34. Gwendolyn Wright, *Moralism and the Model Home: Domestic Architecture and Cultural Conflict in Chicago, 1873–1913* (Chicago: University of Chicago Press, 1980), 231, 254–55.

35. Bushman, *Refinement of America*, 405.

36. David A. Hounshell, *From the American System to Mass Production, 1800–1932* (Baltimore: Johns Hopkins University Press, 1984), 244, 9–12.

37. Carl Smith united each of these events in a single narrative. His work provides a grand, provocative insight into the social tensions affecting Chicago at the turn of the century; see *Urban Disorder and the Shape of Belief: The Great Chicago Fire, the Haymarket Bomb, and the Model Town of Pullman* (Chicago: University of Chicago Press, 1995).

38. For the cultural historian's perspective, see James Gilbert, *Perfect Cities: Chicago's Utopias of 1893* (Chicago: University of Chicago Press, 1991), 131–68.

39. Jane Addams, "A Modern King Lear," in *Satellite Cities*, by Taylor, 68–90. For labor historians, the resolution of the Pullman strike marked the triumph of corporate power in the United States. For the most recent assessment, see Richard Schneirov, Shelton Stromquist, and Nick Salvatore, eds., *The Pullman Strike and the Crisis of the 1890s: Essays on Labor and Politics* (Urbana: University of Illinois Press, 1999).

40. See Lawrence Stone, *The Past and the Present Revisited* (London: Routledge & Kegan Paul, 1987), 82.

41. Specifically, I refer to the work of Olivier Zunz, which expresses the desire for a more contextual narrative history: "Asking how 'people lived the big changes,' we stress the need to uncover the processes of social change over long periods of time and seek to discover patterns of social relations that are truly contextual, not simply deduced from social theory and 'verified' in the records. In doing so, we go beyond conflicting perspectives on major developments, not to mediate between them but instead to locate the simultaneity of significant meanings which interpretative oppositions often mask" (Zunz, "Introduction" in *Reliving the Past: The Worlds of Social History*, ed. Olivier Zunz [Chapel Hill: University of North Carolina Press, 1985], 56). He presents a model study for this method in Zunz, *Making America Corporate*. As we have seen, Cary Carson expressed a similar desire for material cultural histories ("The Scholarship Nobody Knows," 403–4, 413).

42. Zunz, *Making America Corporate*, 18, 24, 35–36, 47, 91.

43. A close relationship existed between cottage housing, home ownership, and community action among Chicago's Germans. For community action within a different context, see Sawislak, *Smoldering City*, 136–62.

44. Nick Salvatore describes this worldview as part of an indigenous democratic tradition by examining the significance of Terre Haute, Indiana, in producing its radical native son, Eugene V. Debs (*Eugene V. Debs: Citizen and Socialist* [Urbana: University of Illinois Press, 1982], 1–87). See also Herbert G. Gutman, *Work, Culture, and Society in Industrializing America: Essays in American Working-Class and Social History* (New York: Vintage Books, 1976), 211–92.

45. Edward R. Kantowicz argued that Poles pursued success in a manner different "from the standard American ideal of an individualist rise to the top in a profession or business" ("Polish Chicago: Survival through Solidarity," in *Ethnic Chicago: A Multicultural Portrait*, ed. Melvin G. Holli and Peter d'A. Jones [Grand Rapids, Mich.: William B. Eerdmans Publishing, 1995], 197). For Polish-Americans, success meant steady work that improved their standard of living and an opportunity for home ownership that allowed them to preserve as well as possible a communal style of life.

Marxists remain highly critical of the political and economic benefits of working-class home ownership. For example, see David Harvey, "Labor, Capital, and Class Struggle around the Built Environment in Advanced Capitalist Societies," in *Urbanization and Conflict in Market Societies*, ed. Kevin R. Cox (Chicago: Maaroufa, 1978), 9–37.

However, David Brody found strong support for unionism among Polish communities in 1919 (*Labor in Crisis: The Steel Strike of 1919* [New York: Harper & Row, 1965; reprint, Urbana: University of Illinois Press, 1987], 130–36, 151, 156–59). Subsequent labor historians have praised community-based labor organizations. See John J. Bukowczyk, "Polish Rural Culture and Immigrant Working Class Formation, 1880–1914," *Polish American Studies* 41 (Autumn, 1984): 23–44; and Barrett, *Work and Community*, 140–41. 176, 195–96.

46. See T. J. Jackson Lears, "From Salvation to Self-Realization: Advertising and the Therapeutic Roots of the Consumer Culture, 1880–1930," in *The Culture of Consumption: Critical Essays in American History, 1880–1980*, ed. Richard Wightman Fox and T. J. Jackson Lears (New York: Pantheon Books, 1983), 7; and Richard Wightman Fox and T. J. Jackson Lears, "Introduction," in Fox and Lears, eds., *Culture of Consumption*, x–xi.

47. Cohen, *Making a New Deal*, 157. See also Ronald Edsforth, *Class Conflict and Cultural Consensus: The Making of a Mass Consumer Society in Flint, Michigan* (New Brunswick, N.J.: Rutgers University Press, 1987), 1–36.

48. In his major study of immigration, John Bodnar provided a large perspective for understanding the relationship between ordinary people and capitalism. Bodnar argued that immigrants confronted capitalism as a calculating people. Pragmatic, they adjusted their life strategies to the imperatives of a steadily changing capitalist economy. While they recognized their inability to alter this transformation, they resisted at various points where they

could assert a measure of control over their lives. See John Bodnar, *The Transplanted: A History of Immigrants in Urban America* (Bloomington: Indiana University Press, 1985), xv–xix, 15–56.

49. John C. Teaford expressed this view in *The Unheralded Triumph: City Government in America, 1870–1900* (Baltimore: Johns Hopkins University Press, 1984), 10.

CHAPTER 1

1. See John M. Van Osdel, "History of Chicago Architecture," *Inland Architect* (April 1886), 35–37. For accounts of the balloon frame, see Walker Field, "A Reexamination into the Invention of the Balloon Frame," *Journal of the Society of Architectural Historians* 2 (October 1942): 3–28; Paul E. Sprague, "Chicago Balloon Frame: The Evolution during the Nineteenth Century of George W. Snow's System for Erecting Light Frame Buildings from Dimension Lumber and Machine-Made Nails," in *The Technology of Historic American Buildings: Studies of the Materials, Craft Processes, and the Mechanization of Building Construction*, ed. H. Ward Jandl (Washington: Foundation for Preservation Technology, 1983), 35–41; and Fred W. Peterson, *Homes in the Heartland: Balloon Frame Farmhouses of the Upper Midwest, 1850–1920* (Lawrence: University Press of Kansas, 1992), 12–15.

Thomas C. Hubka (*Big House, Little House, Back House, Barn: The Connected Farm Buildings of New England* [Hanover, N.H.: University Press of New England, 1984], 44) and Dell Upton ("Traditional Timber Framing," in *Material Culture of the Wooden Age*, ed. Brooke Hindle [Tarrytown, N.Y.: Sleepy Hollow Press, 1981], 88–93) provide more likely accounts.

2. George Kubler, *The Shape of Time: Remarks on the History of Things* (New Haven, Conn.: Yale University Press, 1962), 5–8.

3. Thomas Hubka, "Just Folks Designing: Vernacular Designers and the Generation of Form" in *Common Places: Readings in American Vernacular Architecture*, ed. Dell Upton and John Michael Vlach (Athens: University of Georgia Press, 1986), 426–32.

4. Kubler, *Shape of Time*, 45, 33–39.

5. For an account of Beaubien, see Jacqueline Peterson, "The Founding Fathers: The Absorption of French-Indian Chicago, 1816–1837" in *Ethnic Chicago: A Multicultural Portrait*, ed. Melvin G. Holli and Peter d'A. Jones (Grand Rapids, Mich.: William B. Eerdmans Publishing, 1995), 37–42.

6. The Lisle Park District preserved the Beaubien tavern, moving and restoring the structure when it faced demolition. During the restoration, I examined the structure in detail, benefitting greatly from Ed Land's knowledge. Mr. Land and other volunteers deserve enormous credit for preserving a structure critical for understanding the built environment of metropolitan Chicago.

Another 1830s tavern of timber-frame construction remains in Warrenville, once again saved as a result of the efforts of unpaid volunteers.

7. Upton, "Traditional Timber Framing," 43–44, 65.

8. For an excellent example, see the account of the Colonel Paul Wentworth house in Russell F. Whitehead and Frank Chouteau Brown, eds., *Colonial Architecture in New England* (New York: Arno Press, 1967), 120–33.

9. The Wentworth house was built for a wealthy man. It was not typical of the frames of its era. For description of a more common, simple braced frame of the eighteenth century, see Paul E. Buchanan, "The Eighteenth-Century Frame Houses of Tidewater Virginia," in *Building Early America: Contributions toward the History of a Great Industry*, ed. Charles E. Peterson (Radnor, Pa.: Chilton Book Company, 1976), 54–73.

For a builders' guide with excellent drawings of early twentieth-century frames, as well as many other matters, see Frank D. Graham and Thomas J. Emery, *Audels Carpenters and Builders Guide: A Practical Illustrated Trade Assistant on Modern Construction for Carpenters-Joiners-Builders-Mechanics and All Wood Workers*, 4 vols. (New York: Theodore Audel & Co., 1923), 3:869–71. My copy of this guide originally belonged to a Chicago carpenter.

10. Upton, "Traditional Timber Framing," 57–68.

11. The omission of the central chimney was a major simplification. Without the chimney, carpenters no longer framed a central bay. Consequently, while the Wentworth house has three bays across the front, the tavern has two. Studs framed the doorway. (See figs. 7 and 8.)

12. Hubka, *Big House, Little House*, 32–50.

13. For a very convenient image displaying these forms, see Hubka, *Big House, Little House*, 34. But the interpretation of forms derives from a larger literature. The classic studies are Henry Glassie, *Pattern in the Material Folk Culture of the Eastern United States* (Philadelphia: University of Pennsylvania Press, 1968), 48–55, 64–69, and *Folk Housing in Middle Virginia: A Structural Analysis of Historic Artifacts* (Knoxville: University of Tennessee Press, 1975).

The finest historical essay employing forms remains Cary Carson, Norman F. Barka, William M. Kelso, Garry Wheeler Stone, and Dell Upton, "Impermanent Architecture in the Southern American Colonies," *Winterthur Portfolio* 16 (1981): 136, 143–60. For a bibliographic account of the topic, see Dell Upton, "The Power of Things: Recent Studies in American Vernacular Architecture," *American Quarterly* 35 (1983): 262–79.

14. Genevieve Towsley, *A View of Historic Naperville: A Collection of Articles of Historic Significance from the Sky-Lines*, rev. ed. (Naperville, Ill.: Naperville Sun, 1979), 18–19.

15. The Martin house was destroyed prior to any analysis. However, I examined a similar house built less than one year later by John Stevens. More important, the description applied to a great number of buildings. It is a generalization derived from fieldwork in areas containing houses built before 1850. The object of the fieldwork was to recapture what Henry Glassie described as "a mental event" that occurred in many places simultaneously.

Analyzing common houses will never result in precise studies. As Glassie suggests, "An interpretation of the house's meanings and functions, its possible extensions in context, is, at its most controlled, an essay in probabilities, and, at its least controlled, an act of pure courage. But hypothesis and a bit of scholastic overreaching are better than nothing" (*Folk Housing in Middle Virginia*, 75, 117).

16. See Upton, "Traditional Timber Framing," 91.

17. In Warrenville, a village just north of Naperville and Lisle, Illinois, the inn preserved by the local historical society also employed a timber frame.

18. For example, see Clifford Edward Clark, Jr., *The American Family Home, 1800–1960* (Chapel Hill: University of North Carolina Press, 1986), 18.

19. Carson et al., "Impermanent Architecture," 147; and Upton, "Traditional Timber Framing," 44.

20. Sprague, "Chicago Balloon Frame," 37–39.

21. For descriptions of this type of work, see Industrial School Association, *Wood-Working Tools: How to Use Them: A Manual* (Boston: D. C. Heath, 1887); and Wayne Franklin, *A Rural Carpenter's World: The Craft in a Nineteenth-Century New York Township* (Iowa City: University of Iowa Press, 1990), 76–90, 182–93. Philip A. Korth demonstrated that "regrets over the passing of older hand tools do not disturb the carpenter at work. Few romantic yearnings for the 'good old tools' overpower practical considerations" (*Craftsmanship and the Michigan Union Carpenter* [Bowling Green, Ky.: Bowling Green State University Popular Press, 1991], x; see also 37–39, 49).

22. Hubka, *Big House, Little House*, 37.

23. Visitors to the house should recognize that the original floor boards were removed. The original flooring would have been much wider and irregular in dimension. Lumber mills did not provide a standardized product at this time. The local carpenter probably had to smooth the flooring in his shop (fig. 14). Naper Settlement conveys the lack of uniform building products in the house by exposing a section of wavy, irregularly shaped lath. After 1850 or so, lumber mills cut and sold straight, standard sized lath.

24. Field, "A Reexamination," 21–23.

25. Thomas J. Schlereth, "The New England Presence on the Midwest Landscape" in his *Cultural History and Material Culture: Everyday Life, Landscapes, Museums* (Ann Arbor, Mich.: UMI Research Press, 1990), 196–217; Fred Kniffen and Henry Glassie, "Building in Wood in the Eastern United States: A Time-Place Perspective," *Geographical Review* 56 (1966): 40–65; Fred Kniffen, "Folk Housing: Key to Diffusion," *Annals of the Association of American Geographers* 55 (1965): 549–77; and Pierce F. Lewis, "Common Houses, Cultural Spoor," *Landscape* 19 (1975): 1–22.

26. Lewis, "Common Houses, Cultural Spoor," 8–10, 14–15.

27. Richard L. Bushman, *The Refinement of America: Persons, Houses, Cities* (New York: Alfred A. Knopf, 1992), 262–79.

28. Albert S. Bolles, *Industrial History of the United States from the Earliest Settlements to the Present Time: Being a Complete Survey of American*

Industries (Norwich, Conn.: Henry Bill Publishing, 1881), 500.

29. James Lindsey Hallock, "Woodworking Machinery in Nineteenth-Century America" (M. A. thesis, University of Delaware, 1978), 3, 16. Naper Settlement in Naperville and the West Chicago Historical Society Museum in West Chicago display carpenter's tool chests.

30. Many accounts describe the features of these types. For a guide to styles, see Virginia McAlester and Lee McAlester, *A Field Guide to American Houses* (New York: Alfred A. Knopf, 1986).

31. Herbert Gottfired, "Building the Picture: Trading on the Imagery of Production and Design," *Winterthur Portfolio* 27 (1992): 235–53.

32. Michael J. Ettema, "Technological Innovation and Design Economics in Furniture Manufacture," *Winterthur Portfolio* 16 (1981): 198–203.

33. *Industrial Chicago* (Chicago: Goodspeed Publishing, 1891), 1:680–704.

34. Bolles, *Industrial History of the United States*, 356–57.

35. Ibid., 360.

36. David A. Hounshell explains quantity manufacture with clarity and intelligence. For the British example, see his *From the American System to Mass Production, 1800–1932* (Baltimore: Johns Hopkins University Press, 1984), 35–38.

37. For the developments at the armories, see Merritt Roe Smith, *Harpers Ferry Armory and the New Technology* (Ithaca, N.Y.: Cornell University Press, 1977), 184–251.

38. Hounshell, *From the American System to Mass Production*, 132–51, 172–87.

39. Polly Anne Earl, "Craftsmen and Machines: The Nineteenth-Century Furniture Industry" in *Technological Innovation and the Decorative Arts*, ed. Ian M. G. Quimby and Polly Anne Earl (Charlottesville: University Press of Virginia, 1974), 307–29.

40. Ibid., 309–11, 316–18.

41. For sash, door, and blind factories in Chicago, see *Industrial Chicago*, 318–33. For a range of machines, see F. R. Hutton, "Woodworking Machinery" in *Report on Power and Machinery Employed in Manufactures, Embracing Statistics of Steam and Water Power Used in the Manufacture of Iron and Steel, Machine Tools and Wood-Working Machinery, Wool and Silk Machinery, and Monographs on Pumps and Pumping Engines, Manufacture of Engines and Boilers, Marine Engines and Steam Vessels*, ed. W. P. Trowbridge (Washington, D.C.: Government Printing Office, 1888), 237–41, 267–90.

42. For examples of adapting and redesigning, see Hounshell, *From the American System to Mass Production*, 75–82, 146–51. John Richards described a shift in woodworking machinery by 1870:

> When our manufacturing interests were small and undeveloped, and when machines were regarded as an adjunct or

> auxiliary to hand labor, then a combined machine, capable of doing several kinds of work, had a place to fill in our small shops; but that day is gone, and, as before assumed, it is much better to exercise our ingenuity in separating instead of combining functions in the same machine.
>
> It would, however, be safe to except a single machine in our large shops that would be able to do the "jobbing" without interfering with the standard machines or breaking the system of the shop—a machine that will saw, mould or rebate &c., with the attention of one hand economizes room and expense for jobbing, but on regular manufacturing, the less combination the better.
>
> A friend of the writer some years since devised a machine that performed all the operations needed to complete a carriage wheel, exhibiting great ingenuity and perfect performance, but he was astounded to be told by an extensive manufacturer, who set up his machine, for experiment, that he would require fifty machines to do this work, and advised him to "separate it," in other words to undo what he had done, and leave the machine where he had found it. . . . In fact, everything points to a division of work among as many machines as possible. ("Wood-Working Machinery," *Civil and Mechanical Engineering* 60 [1870]: 392)

43. "Wood-Working Machinery at Philadelphia," *American Builder: A Journal of Industrial Art* 12 (1876): 253–55; "Hollow Chisel Mortising Machine," *Carpentry and Building* (December 1886), 235–36.

44. *Industrial Chicago*, 699.

45. Edward W. Byrn, *The Progress of Invention in the Nineteenth Century* (New York: Munn & Co., 1900), 360. *Industrial Chicago* made this point effectively as well:

> In every city on the American continent those branches of business connected with the lumber trade occupy, by reason of their bearing on other branches of trade, the most prominent positions. In this connection the special branch of the planing mill business, devoted to the manufacture of sash, doors, and kindred articles, is most important, entering, as these products necessarily do, into the construction of all classes of buildings. In times not remote these articles were all made by hand, consequently, while they may have been as good and well made as machine work, the process was slow, and the construction of buildings measurably prolonged and tedious; more hands were required, and more economy and less elaboration rendered necessary in the use of these indispensable requisites. The introduction of machinery revolutionized the business. Sash, doors, and frames were no longer a part of the carpenter's trade. Steam machinery turned out work too rapidly and with such

> perfection that hand work could not compete. . . . The marvelously perfected machinery with which inventive genius has provided the workers in wood, has insured such rapid work and reduced the price of prepared lumber to such a minimum figure that contractors, builders, and those engaged or interested in the construction of buildings have almost universally adopted the comparatively modern methods of placing their orders for such material with firms who are especially prepared to do that character of work. (687, 699)

46. See Philip Scranton, *Figured Tapestry: Production, Markets, and Power in Philadelphia Textiles, 1885–1941* (Cambridge: Cambridge University Press, 1989), 1–7. For analysis of key woodworking industries, see Hounshell, *From the American System to Mass Production*, 125–51.

47. Hounshell, *From the American System to Mass Production*, 168–82.

48. "Ready-Made Houses," *Carpentry and Building* (April 1889), 67.

49. William Cronon, *Nature's Metropolis: Chicago and the Great West* (New York: W. W. Norton & Co., 1991), 200–206.

50. Department of the Interior, *Report on Manufacturing Industries in the United States at the Eleventh Census: 1890*, pt. 2, *Statistics of Cities* (Washington, D.C.: Government Printing Office, 1895), 666–71, and *Census Reports*, vol. 8, *Twelfth Census of the United States, Taken in the Year 1900: Manufactures*, pt. 2, *States and Territories* (Washington, D.C.: U.S. Census Office, 1902), 1071–72.

51. Department of Commerce, *Fourteenth Census of the United States Taken in the Year 1920*, vol. 10, *Manufactures 1919: Reports for Selected Industries* (Washington, D.C.: Government Printing Office, 1922), 422, and *Fifteenth Census of the United States Manufactures: 1929*, vol. 2, *Reports by Industries* (Washington, D.C.: Government Printing Office, 1933), 465, 469–71.

For the irregularity of employment, see Joseph D. Weeks, *Report on the Statistics of Wages in Manufacturing Industries: With Supplementary Reports on the Average Retail Prices or Necessaries of Life, and on Trades, Societies, and Strikes and Lockouts* (Washington, D.C.: Government Printing Office, 1886), 460–500.

For changes within the lumber industry, see William R. Merriam, Director, *Census Reports*, vol. 9, *Twelfth Census of the United States, Taken in the year 1900, Manufactures, pt. 3, Special Reports on Selected Industries* (Washington, D.C.: U.S. Census Office, 1902), 827–97.

For Southern industrialization, see Walter Licht, *Industrializing America: The Nineteenth Century* (Baltimore: Johns Hopkins University Press, 1995), 122–23.

52. Arthur A. Hart, "M. A. Disbrow & Company: Catalogue Architecture," *Palimpsest* 7 (1978): 115–18.

53. See Gordon-Van Tine Company, *Gordon-Van Tine Homes* (Davenport, Iowa: Gordon-Van Tine Co., 1923), 1–2, 6–7. For an account

that emphasized design more than manufacture, see Jan Jennings, "Drawing on the Vernacular Interior," *Winterthur Portfolio* 27 (1992): 260–90.

54. Robert Christie discusses the effects of mechanization on the trade in *Empire in Wood: A History of the Carpenters' Union* (New York: New York State School of Industrial and Labor Relations, 1956), 17–18, 26–30, 79–90, 117–18. See also Frederick Shipp Deibler, "The Amalgamated Wood Workers International Union of America: A Historical Study of Trade Unionism in Its Relation to the Development of an Industry," *Bulletin of the University of Wisconsin: Economics and Political Science Series* 7 (1912): 13–33.

55. "House Joiners versus Cabinet Makers," *Carpentry and Building* (February 1880), 31–32.

56. "Division of Labor," *Carpentry and Building* (August 1881), 147.

57. "Division of Labor in Building Operations," *Carpentry and Building* (February 1880), 36–37.

58. "The Abolition of Apprenticeship," *Carpentry and Building* (August 1879), 142. See Korth, *Craftsmanship and the Michigan Union Carpenter*, 54.

59. "Balloon Framing," *Carpentry and Building*, (August 1885), 144.

60. Solon Robinson, "How to Build a Balloon Frame House," *Transactions of the American Institute of the City of New York, Annual Report* (1854), 403–7.

61. "Balloon Framing," 144.

62. Graham and Emery, *Audels Carpenters and Builders Guide*, 3:916–17.

63. Alfred T. Andreas, *History of Chicago: From the Earliest Period to the Present Time*, 3 vols. (Chicago: A. T. Andreas Co., 1886), 1:373.

64. "Ready-Made Houses," 67.

65. In 1884, T. M. Clark wrote: "The notching or 'sizing' of all beams upon their horizontal supports is made necessary by their inequality in size. Ordinary timbers often vary one-fourth to one-half an inch from their specified dimensions, but by notching them to a uniform distance from the top they will, when laid in place, have their upper sides level ready to receive the floor. The undersides will be uneven, but the subsequent cross-furring will conceal this" (*Building Superintendence: A Manual for Young Architects, Students, and Others Interested in Building Operations as Carried on at the Present Day* [Boston: James R. Osgood & Co., 1884], 133).

66. I found tighter tolerances in houses built after 1885 throughout metropolitan Chicago. For kiln-dried lumber, see E. U. Kettle, *Practical Kiln Drying: A Manual for Dry Kiln Operators, Owners and Superintendents of Woodworking Plants and Vocational Schools* (Grand Rapids, Mich.: Periodical Publishing Co., 1923).

67. Stanley Buder, *Pullman: An Experiment in Industrial Order and Community Planning, 1880–1930* (New York: Oxford University Press, 1967), 38–104. On the architect Solon Beman, see Thomas J. Schlereth, "Solon Spencer Beman, Pullman, and the European Influence on and Interest in

his Chicago Architecture," in *Chicago Architecture, 1872–1922: Birth of a Metropolis*, ed. John Zukowsky (Munich: Prestel-Verlag, 1987), 173–87.

Richard T. Ely questioned corporate beneficence in "Pullman: A Social Study," *Harper's Monthly* 70 (1885): 452–66.

68. Harvey Land Association, *The Town of Harvey, Illinois Manufacturing Suburb of Chicago Aged Two Years* (Chicago: Harvey Land Association, 1892), 4–8, 14–18, 30–38. *Real Estate and Building Journal* reported on the development of Harvey on February 1, 1890; March 22, 1890; April 26, 1890; May 24, 1890; September 6, 1890; October 25, 1890; January 31, 1891; February 7, 1891; February 21, 1891; May 30, 1891; September 5, 1891; October 3, 1891; December 19, 1891.

69. Ann Durkin Keating, *Building Chicago: Suburban Developers and the Creation of a Divided Metropolis* (Columbus: Ohio State University Press, 1988), 64–78. See also Helen Corbin Monchow, *Seventy Years of Real Estate Subdividing in the Region of Chicago*, Northwestern University Studies in the Social Sciences, no. 3 (Evanston, Ill.: Northwestern University, 1939), 1–54, 119–39; and H. Morton Bodfish, "Real Estate Activity in Chicago Accompanying the World's Fair of 1893," *Journal of Land and Public Utility Economics* 4 (1928): 405–15.

70. Keating, *Building Chicago*, 39–50, 61–63.

71. Hubka, *Big House, Little House*, 32–44. Henry Glassie identified this floor plan as a two-thirds Georgian ("Eighteenth-Century Cultural Process in Delaware Valley Folk Building," *Winterthur Portfolio* 7 [1972]: 35–38). British row housing followed the same floor plan; see Stefan Muthesius, *The English Terraced House* (New Haven, Conn.: Yale University Press, 1982), 79–142. For Baltimore, see Natalie W. Shivers, *Those Old Placid Rows: The Aesthetic and Development of the Baltimore Rowhouse* (Baltimore: Maclay & Assoc., 1981), 5–9, 21–39; and Mary Ellen Hayward, "Urban Vernacular Architecture in Nineteenth-Century Baltimore," *Winterthur Portfolio* 16 (Spring 1981): 34–145.

72. Lyman Bridges Company, *Illustrated Catalogue: Lyman Bridges Building Materials and Ready-Made Houses* (Chicago: Rand McNally, 1870).

73. Kenneth L. Ames, "Meaning in Artifacts: Hall Furnishings in Victorian America," *Journal of Interdisciplinary History* 9 (1978): 19–46.

74. See Richard A. Cook, *A History of South Holland, Illinois* (South Holland, Ill.: South Holland Trust & Savings Bank, 1966), 35–57.

75. Gerrit Van Oostenbrugge, "Settlement of South Holland," in *Dutch Immigrant Memoirs and Related Writings*, ed. Henry S. Lucas (Seattle: University of Washington Press, 1955), 62; and Harry Eenigenburg, "Roseland and South Holland," in Lucas, ed., *Dutch Immigrant Memoirs*, 59.

76. South Holland Historical Society, *The House That Peter Built* (South Holland, Ill.: South Holland Historical Society, 1976), 1–5.

77. An extensive survey of South Holland in 1995 discovered 57 structures built before 1870, 173 cottages, 103 bungalows, and 32 stylish, more expensive houses.

78. Linden Seymour Dodson, "The Organizing and Conserving Force of the Church in Social Change in South Holland, Illinois" (Ph.D. diss., University of Chicago, 1932), 46. See also Dodson, *Social Relationships and Institutions in an Established Rurban Community, South Holland, Illinois* (Washington, D.C.: U.S. Department of Agriculture, 1939), 2.

79. The word "bungalow" was a promotional device, an attractive-sounding name for a more stylish but familiar type of house. A great deal of confusion resulted from the use of the term, which entered the English language with the British experience in India. See Anthony King, "The Bungalow," *Architectural Association Quarterly* 5, no. 3 (1973): 6–26. However, it was absurd to suggest that the Chicago bungalow derived in some way from the architecture of India. The basic floor plan existed prior to the use of the name. This was also true in California, where the American bungalow supposedly originated. See Barbara Rubin, "A Chronology of Architecture in Los Angeles," *Annals of the Association of American Geographers* 67, no. 4 (December 1977): 521–27.

80. In Chicago, the oldest portion of the suburban village of Westmont provided the best examples of the minimal distinction between high-end cottages and low-end bungalows. When Germans settled in the village after 1915, they built primarily in these two types. The basic difference was the use of a hip rafter at the front gable-end of the house.

81. Compare "The Princeton," described as a cottage in Aladdin Company, *Aladdin Homes* (Bay City, Mich.: Aladdin Homes, 1917), with the promotion describing the same house as a bungalow two years later in Aladdin Company, *Aladdin Plan of Industrial Housing* (Bay City, Mich.: Aladdin Co., 1919). Accounts that rely exclusively on the study of packaged housing do not provide an accurate depiction of conditions. Whether manufactured by Sears or anyone else, these structures accounted for a tiny portion of the housing market. A company like Aladdin relied on common styles and used alluring language to promote the uniqueness of their product. To understand the development of modern housing, historians must study the local markets that produced the vast majority of houses.

In the nineteenth century, local builders used pattern books for ideas and then adapted the plans. See Dell Upton, "Vernacular Domestic Architecture in Eighteenth-Century Virginia" in Upton and Vlach, eds., *Common Places*, 315–35, and "Pattern Books and Professionalism: Aspects of the Transformation of Domestic Architecture in America, 1800–1860," *Winterthur Portfolio* 19 (1984): 107–50.

82. Although improvements were often minor and incomplete, they were deeply felt. Richard L. Bushman describes these feelings eloquently in *The Refinement of America*, 425–27.

CHAPTER 2

1. Richard L. Bushman, *The Refinement of America: Persons, Houses, Cities* (New York: Alfred A. Knopf, 1992), 15–29, 100–138.

2. Bernard L. Herman, *Architecture and Rural Life in Central*

Delaware, 1700–1900 (Knoxville: University of Tennessee Press, 1987), 232–36, 148–98.

3. For an intelligent, well-considered analysis of the development process, see Ann Durkin Keating, *Building Chicago: Suburban Developers and the Creation of a Divided Metropolis* (Columbus: Ohio State University Press, 1988), esp. chaps. 4 and 5.

4. Richard Jules Oestreicher, *Solidarity and Fragmentation: Working People and Class Consciousness in Detroit, 1875–1900* (Urbana: University of Illinois Press, 1986), xv–xvi, 60–67, 172–214. See also Herbert G. Gutman, *Work, Culture, and Society in Industrializing America: Essays in American Working-Class and Social History* (New York: Vintage Books, 1977), xi.

5. While historians have examined various episodes that give witness to "a culture of opposition," they have not examined the bond between resident, middle-class developers and working-class home owners. Recently, Eric Arnesen argued that cultural studies of the working class have engaged in "open-ended interpretation without the necessary empirical grounding." He called for a more rigorous "reconstructing [of] the social, political, and economic worlds" of a varied working-class population ("Up from Exclusion: Black and White Workers, Race, and the State of Labor History," *Reviews in American History* 26 [1998]: 164–67). No aspect requires more careful study than housing markets. Labor historians have failed to consider the dynamic social consequences of a wealth created by building of working-class communities.

6. After the Great Fire, Chicago's Germans fought for their right to control the built environment. See Karen Sawislak, *Smoldering City: Chicagoans and the Great Fire, 1871–1874* (Chicago: University of Chicago Press, 1995), 121–62.

7. For the role of home ownership in the Homestead strike, see Linda Schneider, "The Citizen Striker: Workers' Ideology in the Homestead Strike of 1892," *Labor History* (23 (1982): 57–59.

8. Various sources have described the founding of Hammond. The best is Hammond Historical Society, *The Hammond Historical Society Presents the Famous 1904 Edition of the "Hammond Daily News"* (Hammond, Ind.: Hammond Historical Society, 1954), 11–16, which appeared originally as "Industrial Edition," *Hammond Daily News*, December 1904. Others include Powell A. Moore, *The Calumet Region: Indiana's Last Frontier* (Indianapolis: Indiana Historical Bureau, 1959), 141–56; Lance Trusty, *Hammond: A Centennial Portrait* (Norfolk, Va.: Donning Co., 1984), 1–18; *Lake County Times* (Indiana), August 8, 1927; Rudolf A. Clemen, *George H. Hammond: Pioneer in Refrigeration Transportation* (New York: Newcomen Society of England American Branch, 1946), 1–16; and *Dictionary of American Biography* (1960), s.v. "Hammond, George Henry."

Partners George Hammond and Marcus Towle were Yankees from, respectively, Fitchburg and Brighton, Massachusetts, just outside Boston. Consequently, they knew firsthand the nature of industrial, residential, and commercial development on the industrial periphery. To understand their urban experience with meatpacking prior to creating Hammond, see Henry C. Binford, *The First Suburbs: Residential Communities on the Boston Periphery, 1815–1860* (Chicago: University of Chicago Press, 1985), 1–79. 220–25.

9. *The Famous 1904 Edition of the "Hammond Daily News,"* 15.

10. For a fine account that places the Hammond Company in a larger context, see Mary Yeager, *Competition and Regulation: The Development of Oligopoly in the Meat Packing Industry* (Greenwich, Conn.: JAI Press, 1981), 49–85.

11. Alfred D. Chandler, Jr., *The Visible Hand: The Managerial Revolution in American Business* (Cambridge, Mass.: Harvard University Press, 1977), 299–302, 391–402.

12. *The Famous 1904 Edition of the "Hammond Daily News,"* 11.

13. Ibid., 11–12.

14. Timothy Horton Ball, *Northwestern Indiana from 1800 to 1900; or A View of Our Region through the Nineteenth Century* (Crown Point, Ind.: n.p., 1900), 303.

15. Timothy Horton Ball, *Encyclopedia of Genealogy and Biography of Lake County, Indiana with a Compendium of History, 1834–1904: A Record of the Achievements of Its People in the Making of a Commonwealth and the Founding of the Nation* (Chicago: Lewis Publishing, 1904), 307–8; William Frederick Howat, ed., *A Standard History of Lake County, Indiana and the Calumet Region*, 2 vols. (Chicago: Lewis Publishing, 1915), 1:293–394; Moore, *Calumet Region*, 154–56.

16. The information derives from analysis of manuscripts from the 1880 federal census. The following table shows the percentage of German, American, and other foreign-born families containing zero, one or two, three or four, and five or more children.

No. of Children	German (%)	American (%)	Other (%)	Total (%)
Zero	19	29	27	24
One or two	27	34	47	33
Three or four	32	29	13	27
Five or more	22	8	13	16

For a Yankee's description of the German population of Lake County, see Solon Robinson, "Notes of Travel in the West," *Albany Cultivator* (March 1845), reprinted in Herbert Anthony Keller, ed., *Solon Robinson Pioneer and Agriculturalist* (Indianapolis: Indiana Historical Bureau, 1936), 402. See also Moore, *Calumet Region*, 78–82, 156–60, 181–88, 342–54.

17. David Nason, "The Diary of David Nason," manuscript, Calumet Room, Hammond Public Library, Hammond, Ind.

18. Hammond was on the Indiana-Illinois state line. Consequently, gambling and prostitution operated without interference from Indiana authorities since they existed on the Illinois side beyond the jurisdiction of the Lake County sheriff.

19. Caroline Hohman, "The Diary of Caroline Hohman," manuscript, Calumet Room, Hammond Public Library, Hammond, Ind.

20. *Lake County Star*, September 1, 1882.

21. "Hammond Items," *Crown Point Register*, August 26, 1886.

22. This information derived from Frank E. Gero, *Frank E. Gero's Hammond City Directory for 1891–1892* (Hammond, Ind.: Calumet Printing & Publishing Co. Printers, 1891).

23. G. A. Garrard, "North Township," in *Counties of Porter and Lake, Indiana, Historical and Biographical*, ed. Weston Arthur Goodspeed and Charles Blanchard (Chicago: Goodspeed Brothers Publishers, 1894), 541–42.

24. "Big Suit against Hammond Estate," *Crown Point Register*, January 22, 1890; Lake County News, April 21, 1898; Gero, *Hammond City Directory for 1891–1892*, 3.

25. Garrard, "North Township," 539.

26. Moore, Calumet Region, 153–62, 414–6; Garrard, "North Township," 539–42; "Hammond Items," *Crown Point Register*, October 21, 1886; *Hammond Daily News*, September 18, 1902.

27. Moore, *Calumet Region*, 216–44; "Another Big Real Estate Deal," *Lake County Star*, May 27, 1887; Homer Hoyt, *One Hundred Years of Land Values in Chicago* (Chicago: University of Chicago Press, 1933), 134–44.

28. Department of the Census, *Census Reports*, vol. 8, Manufactures, pt. 3, *States and Territories* (Washington, D.C.: U.S. Census Office, 1902), 1014, 1018, 1038.

29. See Bureau of the Census, *Fifteenth Census, Manufactures 1929*, vol. 3, *Reports by States, Statistics for Industrial Areas, Counties and Cities* (Washington, D.C.: Government Printing Office, 1933), 162–65.

30. See Olivier Zunz, "Introduction" in *Reliving the Past: The Worlds of Social History*, ed. Olivier Zunz (Chapel Hill: University of North Carolina Press, 1985), 6.

31. *Howat, ed., Standard History of Lake County, Indiana*, 2:554–55.

32. All biographical information comes from the following sources: Goodspeed and Blanchard, eds., *Counties of Porter and Lake*; Ball, *Northwestern Indiana*, and *Encyclopedia of Genealogy and Biography*; Howat, ed., *Standard History of Lake County, Indiana*; and *The Famous 1904 Edition of the "Hammond Daily News."*

County histories provide an especially rich source for Lake County, Indiana, since its small size and relative unimportance in comparison to Chicago and Cook County meant that small businessmen received extensive coverage. Most historical studies of small industrial cities concentrate on the few important local figures. However, the vast majority of prominent men were far less wealthy. These sources potentially reveal a great deal about the values of local capitalism, especially when biographies are combined with analysis of the structures that individuals created.

33. *The Famous 1904 Edition of the "Hammond Daily News,"* 20.

34. This analysis derived from biographical information in local histories as well as a study of occupations and names of persons found in the manuscripts of the 1880 and 1900 federal census as well as in the city directories for 1891 and 1900.

35. Ibid.

36. *The Famous 1904 Edition of the "Hammond Daily News,"* 33.

37. Professionals seldom played roles in local politics. But they assumed roles in the prominent clubs and organizations.

38. The *Hammond Daily News* story about the Minas hardware store was quoted in Howat, ed., *Standard History of Lake County, Indiana*, 578–79; see also "Mamoth Store Opens," *Lake County News*, April 6, 1905.

39. Howat, ed., *Standard History of Lake County, Indiana*, 486–90.

40. Gutman, *Work, Culture, and Society in Industrializing America*, 211–22.

41. For a description of the Hammond plant, see "Beef, Blood, Bones, and Fat," *The Progressive: A Monthly Devoted to the School, the Home, and the Farm* (Hopkinsville, Ky.) (July 1888). For descriptions of labor in the packinghouses, see James R. Barrett, *Work and Community in the Jungle: Chicago's Packinghouse Workers, 1894–1922* (Urbana: University of Illinois Press), 20–31; and Dominic A. Pacyga, *Polish Immigrants and Industrial Chicago: Workers on the South Side, 1880–1922* (Columbus: Ohio State University Press, 1991), 43–62.

42. The larger nature of development was seen most clearly by investments in East Chicago. See Moore, *Calumet Region*, 221–26.

43. "Will Move to Hammond," *Whiting Sun*, February 12, 1898; *Lake County News*, March 10, 1898; *The Famous 1904 Edition of the "Hammond Daily News."*

44. Department of the Interior, *Compendium of the Eleventh Census: 1890*, pt. 1, *Population* (Washington, D.C.: Government Printing Office, 1892), 881.

45. Stephan Thernstrom, *The Other Bostonians: Poverty and Progress in the American Metropolis, 1880–1970* (Cambridge, Mass.: Harvard University Press, 1973), 220–32.

46. This information derived from analysis of Sanborn fire insurance maps for 1887 (Sanborn Map Company). The complete maps are in the Library of Congress in Washington.

47. Richard Harris has published a great deal on persons who built their own homes. However, structures in Hammond do not resemble those he described for Toronto, which, for the most part, appear to be poorly built shacks. For the most complete presentation of his findings, see his *Unplanned Suburbs: Toronto's American Tragedy, 1900 to 1950* (Baltimore: Johns Hopkins University Press, 1996), esp. chap. 8.

48. These figures are derived from analysis of Gero, *Hammond City Directory for 1891–1892*.

49. Fred W. Peterson, *Homes in the Heartland: Balloon Frame Farmhouses of the Upper Midwest, 1850–1920* (Lawrence: University Press of Kansas, 1992), 99–135.

50. Department of the Interior, *Compendium of the Eleventh Census*, 518; and Department of Commerce, Bureau of the Census, *Thirteenth Census*, vol. 2, *Population, 1910* (Washington, D.C.: Government Printing Office, 1913), 568.

51. Department of Commerce, Bureau of the Census, *Fifteenth Census of the United States: 1930, Population*, vol. 11, Families (Washington, D.C.: Government Printing Office, 1932), 424–25.

52. Ibid.

53. Richard T. Ely, "Pullman: A Social Study," *Harper's Monthly* 70 (1885): 465.

CHAPTER 3

1. During the 1870s, Lutherans, Catholics, and Methodists conducted services, but they were irregular since neither a priest nor a minister resided in town. The denominations gathered separately once or twice a month and held services in local residences.

In 1879, Caroline Hohman, an English-born Episcopalian, donated land for Saint Joseph's Catholic Church, while Marcus Towle, a Methodist, donated the money to cover building expenses. After construction of the church, the German parishioners did not receive a priest for four years. When the first pastor arrived, the parish built a rectory costing $3,000 and a school costing $14,000. The histories of Saint Paul Evangelical Lutheran and the First Methodist Churches were similar. Once established, each congregation prospered. By 1889, 200 families belonged to Saint Joseph's, 200 to Saint Paul's, and 100 to First Methodist. See Frederick Howat, ed., *A Standard History of Lake County, Indiana and the Calumet Region*, 2 vols. (Chicago: Lewis Publishing, 1915), 1:361–80.

2. Frank E. Gero, *Frank E. Gero's Hammond City Directory for 1891–1892*, (Hammond, Ind.: Calumet Printing & Publishing Co. Printers, 1891; reprint, Hammond, Ind.: Hammond Historical Society, 1971), 24–28.

3. See George L. Pokos, "The History of Garfield Lodge No. 589," Calumet Room, Hammond Public Library, Hammond, Ind.

4. Gero, *City Directory for 1891–1892*, 25–26.

5. For analysis of the larger debate over temperance, see Karen Sawislak, *Smoldering City: Chicagoans and the Great Fire, 1871–1874* (Chicago: University of Chicago Press, 1995), 217–59.

6. "MC Ry. Wins," *Lake County News*, June 29, 1893.

7. *Lake County News*, July 6, 1893. The cultural division between German immigrants and an American-born middle class was common in Midwestern cities, especially those where both groups vied for political power. Kathleen Neils Conzen developed this theme in her pathbreaking study of Milwaukee, which remains a most valuable text (*Immigrant Milwaukee*,

1836–1860: Accommodation and Community in a Frontier City [Cambridge, Mass.: Harvard University Press, 1976], 154–228). For a more recent version of the conflict between Germans and Americans, see Sawislak, *Smoldering City*, 217–59.

8. The quote about the "hoodoing" of Hammond is from "It's No More," *Lake County News*, December 14, 1893. For accounts of the various fires, see "A Review of Chicago's New Manufacturing Center," *Building and Real Estate Journal*, October 25, 1890; *Drover's Journal*: "The Fire at Hammond," July 12, 1889; "Fire at Hammond," October 24, 1901; October 25, 1901; *Crown Point Register*: "Hammond Items," March 18, 1886; "Hammond Items," September 16, 1886, "Fire Fiend," February 19, 1887; *Lake County News*: November 9, 1893; "It's No More," December 14, 1893; "Fire," January 5, 1894.

9. *Lake County Star*, May 20, 1887; *Lake County News*, November 23, 1893, December 18, 1894.

10. Patrick Reilly later resigned from his position at the slaughterhouse. Like most Hammond leaders, he developed a local business. Reilly became the city's leading plumbing contractor.

11. The Hammond Historical Society provides a list of elected officials in their reprint of Gero, *City Directory for 1891–1892*. The directory also provides information about occupations. For additional reporting, see Crown Point Register, April 22, 1886.

12. "Hammond Items," *Crown Point Register*, April 12, 1886.

13. *Lake County News*: March 22, 1894; "Democratic Ticket," April 19, 1894; April 26, 1894.

14. *Lake County News*: "Questionable Politics," January 18, 1894; "Republican Harmony," March 15, 1894; March 22, 1894; "Republican Powwow," April 5, 1894; "Democratic Ticket," April 19, 1894.

15. "Not in It," *Lake County News*, May 3, 1894.

16. *Lake County News*: April 7, 1898; April 14, 1898; "Victory," April 21, 1898; May 5, 1898.

17. *The Lake County News* published minutes for each city council meeting. A substantial portion of the minutes listed expenditures including the names of persons receiving even trivial amounts of money from the city. They told, for example, that the city spent five dollars on hardware or that a certain three laborers received wages for work done for the city. From these accounts, it must have been clear to small town readers exactly who exercised power. It also must have raised questions of whether power was exercised fairly.

18. Historians have failed to develop adequate analysis of the significance of home ownership and local politics in American cities. However, Eric H. Monkkonen has suggested that "the widespread access to property, especially through home ownership, has made pervasive if not dramatic differences to the nature of American urban life" (*America Becomes Urban: The Development of U.S. Cities and Towns, 1780–1980* [Berkeley: University of California Press, 1988], 186).

19. Stanley Buder, *Pullman: An Experiment in Industrial Order and Community Planning, 1880–1930* (New York: Oxford University Press, 1967), 49–107.

20. Two recent works examine the cultural factors influencing Pullman to build his model town. These works rely on written sources, examining the social worlds of Chicago's elite and the popular press. They document the strong impulses toward social control shared among Chicago's "better" classes. See James Gilbert, *Perfect Cities: Chicago's Utopias of 1893* (Chicago: University of Chicago Press, 1991), 11–19, 131–68; and Carl Smith, *Urban Disorder and the Shape of Belief: The Great Chicago Fire, the Haymarket Bomb, and the Model Town of Pullman* (Chicago: University of Chicago Press, 1995, 209–31, 245–66.

21. Richard T. Ely, "Pullman: A Social Study," *Harper's Monthly* 70 (1885): 457, 460.

22. Ibid., 458–59.

23. For the effect of the strike on George Pullman, see Buder, *Pullman*, 198–201.

24. See Richard T. Ely, "Fundamental Beliefs in My Social Philosophy," *Forum* 17 (1894): 178–79.

25. The best accounts of these events remain Ray Ginger, *The Bending Cross: A Biography of Eugene Victor Debs* (New Brunswick, N.J.: Rutgers University Press, 1949), 92–123; and Almont Lindsey, *The Pullman Strike: The Story of a Unique Experiment and of a Great Labor Upheaval* (Chicago: University of Chicago Press, 1942), 90–107.

26. Ely, "Pullman," 466.

27. Nick Salvatore, *Eugene V. Debs: Citizen and Socialist* (Urbana: University of Illinois Press, 1982), 88–137.

28. Ibid., 125–30.

29. Lindsey, *Pullman Strike*, 107–21.

30. Ginger, *Bending Cross*, 114–25.

31. "The Boycott," *Lake County News*, July 5, 1894. See also "The Strike at Hammond," *Whiting Democrat*, July 5, 1894.

32. "The Boycott."

33. Ibid.

34. *Lake County News*, May 10, 1894, May 31, 1894, June 7, 1894.

35. Lindsey, *Pullman Strike*, 151.

36. "The Situation Here," Lake County News, July 5, 1894; and "The Strike at Hammond."

37. "The Situation Here"; "The Strike at Hammond."

38. "The Situation Here."

39. Ibid.

40. Ibid.

41. Lindsey, *Pullman Strike*, 310–13.

42. *Lake County News*, July 12, 1894.

43. Lindsey, *Pullman Strike*, 148.

44. "Use Caution," *Lake County News*, July 12, 1894.

45. "The Situation Here."

46. *Lake County News*, July 12, 1894

47. *Lake County News*: July 5, 1894; "Whiting Heard From," July 12, 1894; "Resumed Work," July 19, 1894.

48. *Lake County News*, July 12, 1894.

49. Henry Jebsen, Jr., "The Role of Blue Island in the Pullman Strike of 1894," *Journal of the Illinois State Historical Society* 67 (1974): 278–93.

50. Lindsey, *Pullman Strike*, 162.

51. Ibid., 155–75.

52. Altgeld stated his objections precisely two years later in a speech delivered at Cooper Union in New York. See John Peter Altgeld, "Retiring Address as Governor of Illinois," in *The Mind and Spirit of John Peter Altgeld*, ed. Henry M. Christin (Urbana: University of Illinois Press, 1960), 162–63.

53. Lindsey, *Pullman Strike*, 207–8.

54. Ibid., 308–34. For a cautionary note regarding the reporting, see Buder, *Pullman*, 249–50.

55. Frederick Remington, "The Great Strike," *Harper's Weekly* 38 (1894): 680.

56. Ibid., 681.

57. "Troops Here," *Lake County News*, July 12, 1894.

58. Ibid.; and "Troops at Hammond," *Whiting Democrat*, July 12, 1894.

59. David Grayson, *American Chronicle: The Autobiography of Ray Stannard Baker* (New York: Charles Scribner's Sons, 1945), 34–44. See also Lake County News, July 12, 1894; and *Whiting Democrat*, July 12, 1894.

60. "Troops Here."

61. Ibid.; and "Federal Control of Railroads," *Whiting Democrat*, July 12, 1894.

62. "Troops Here"; "Federal Control of Railroads."

63. "Troops Here"; "Federal Control of Railroads."

64. "Troops Here."

65. Ibid.

66. Ibid.

67. Ibid.

68. Buder, *Pullman*, 195–99.

69. Grayson, *American Chronicle*, 41, 43–44. The government offered its findings regarding responsibility for the strike in U.S. Strike Commission, *Report on the Chicago Strike of June–July, 1894*, 53d Cong., 3d

sess., S. Exec. Doc. 7 (Washington, D.C.: Government Printing Office, 1895).

70. "Let Peace Reign," *Lake County News*, August 2, 1894.

71. "Eugene V. Debs," *Railway Times*, November 2, 1896.

72. Salvatore, *Citizen and Socialist*, 342–45. Richard Oestreicher, "Urban Working-Class Political Behavior and Theories of American Electoral Politics, 1870–1940," *Journal of American History* 74 (March 1988): 1260.

73. Oestreicher, "Urban Working-Class Political Behavior," 1283.

74. "Flames Attack Hammond Plant," *Daily Tribune* (Chicago), October 25, 1901; and "Hammond Men Work," *Drovers Journal*, October 25, 1901.

75. Hammond Historical Society, *The Hammond Historical Society Presents the Famous 1904 Edition of the "Hammond Daily News"* (Hammond, Ind.: Hammond Historical Society, 1954), 1. This originally appeared as "Industrial Edition," *Hammond Daily News*, December 1904.

76. Pokos, "The History of Garfield Lodge," 30.

77. *The Famous 1904 Edition of the "Hammond Daily News,"* 1.

78. Ibid.

79. Ibid.

CHAPTER 4

1. John R. Commons, *Races and Immigrants in America* (New York: Macmillan Co., 1907; reprint, New York: Augustus M. Kelly Publishers, 1967), 7, 10–12. Like so many reformers, Commons began and ended his analysis with reference to the theories of Francis Amasa Walker, which he supported as late as 1920. See pages xvi–xix, 198–209.

2. John T. McGreevy, *Parish Boundaries: The Catholic Encounter with Race in the Twentieth-Century Urban North* (Chicago: University of Chicago Press, 1996), 13.

3. For a general discussion of the role of the national parish, see Jay P. Dolan, *The American Catholic Experience: A History from Colonial Times to the Present* (New York: Doubleday & Co., 1985), 127–220. See also Philip Gleason, *Keeping the Faith: American Catholicism Past and Present* (Notre Dame, Ind.: University of Notre Dame Press, 1987), 46–49. For the attitude of the Archdiocese of Chicago from 1880 to 1902, see Charles Shanabruch, *Chicago's Catholics: The Evolution of an American Identity* (Notre Dame, Ind.: University of Notre Dame Press, 1981), 31–53.

4. Edward R. Kantowicz, *Polish-American Politics in Chicago* (Chicago: University of Chicago Press, 1975), 8–9.

5. Edward R. Kantowicz, "Polish Chicago: Survival through Solidarity" in *The Ethnic Frontier: Essays in the History of Group Survival in Chicago and the Midwest*, ed. Melvin G. Holli and Peter d'A. Jones (Grand Rapids, Mich.: William B. Eerdmans Publishing, 1977), 184–91.

6. Quoted in Dolan, *American Catholic Experience*, 181.

7. Ibid., 180–83.

8. John Bodnar describes very well the larger implications of these divisions within immigrant communities. He places these struggles within the context of a middle-class struggle for authority over the larger group (*The Transplanted: A History of Immigrants in Urban America* [Bloomington: Indiana University Press, 1985], 117–43, 156–68).

9. Joseph John Parot, *Polish Catholics in Chicago, 1850–1920: A Religious History* (Dekalb, Ill.: Northern Illinois University Press, 1981), 233–38; Kantowicz, "Polish Chicago," 192–204; and Gleason, *Keeping the Faith*, 52–53.

10. The Resurrectionists responded to the threat of socialism in an increasingly urban world. They believed they could preserve the faith of immigrants by building huge, centralized parish communities that invested all facets of life with a religious dimension. See Parot, *Polish Catholics*, 47–49.

11. Ibid., 47–132. For placing Barzynski in the context of other immigrant leaders, see Victor Greene, "'Becoming American': The Role of Ethnic Leaders—Swedes, Poles, Italians, and Jews," in Holli and d'A. Jones, eds., *Ethnic Frontier*, 144–75.

12. Parot discusses a pact between the Chicago archdiocese and the Resurrectionists in *Polish Catholics*, 46–51.

13. Quoted in ibid., 61.

14. Ibid., 86–90.

15. Conflict between Barzynski and Saint Hedwig's parish led to the excommunication of 1,000 families and the formation of a schismatic church, the Polish National Catholic Church, which did not recognize the authority of Rome. About 5 percent of Polish immigrants became members of the National Church, due largely to conflicts with authoritarian priests who wished to control parish finances. Most immigrants believed excommunication damned eternally the souls of the men, women, and children who joined the schismatic church. See Parot, *Polish Catholics*, 59–132; and Dolan, *American Catholic Experience*, 184.

16. For an account of the Polish south side, see Dominic A. Pacyga, *Polish Immigrants and Industrial Chicago: Workers on the South Side, 1880–1922* (Columbus: Ohio State University Press, 1991).

17. Kantowicz suggests that all estimates of the Polish population in Chicago are educated guesses. His guesses remain as good as any. See Kantowicz, *Polish-American Politics*, 9, 18, 25–26, 165–68, 230, and "Polish Chicago," 181.

18. Gleason, *Keeping the Faith*, 62.

19. For a brief but insightful account of Poles in Philadelphia, see Caroline Golab, "The Polish Experience in Philadelphia: The Migrant Laborers Who Did Not Come," in *The Ethnic Experience in Pennsylvania*, ed. John E. Bodnar (Lewisburg, Pa.: Bucknell University Press, 1973), 39–71.

20. In both Detroit and Toledo, active mayors promoted significant municipal reforms in the twentieth century that enlisted the support of groups

such as the Poles. However, no one understands precisely the relationship among reformers, politicians, and lower-class immigrant home owners. For the situation in Detroit, see Melvin G. Holli, *Reform in Detroit: Hazen S. Pingree and Urban Politics* (New York: Oxford University Press, 1969), 11–18, 61–73, 137–56.

Frederic C. Howe was not intellectually outstanding when compared with the most distinguished progressive reformers. However, he became one of the few with an open mind regarding the lower classes. Howe attributed his personal transformation to the influence of Tom Johnson and the experience of a similar political campaign in Cleveland. Howe describes his feeling with great clarity in his autobiography, one of the great personal statements of the age (*The Confessions of a Reformer* [New York: Charles Scribner's Sons, 1925; reprint, Chicago: Quadrangle Books, 1976], 92–144).

21. The studies of row housing in the United States do not offer much information about low-end markets. However, two sources are useful: see Natalie W. Shivers, *Those Old Placid Rows: The Aesthetic and Development of the Baltimore Rowhouse* (Baltimore: Macclay & Assoc., 1981), 6–39; and, for the English tradition, Stefan Muthesius, *The English Terraced House* (New Haven, Conn.: Yale University Press, 1982), 1–11, 27–37, 69–142.

22. See Roger D. Simon, "Housing and Services in an Immigrant Neighborhood: Milwaukee's Ward 14," *Journal of Urban History* 2 (August 1976): 435–58.

23. Olivier Zunz, *The Changing Face of Inequality: Urbanization, Industrial Development, and Immigrants in Detroit, 1880–1920* (Chicago: University of Chicago Press, 1982), 161–76.

24. Parot, *Polish Catholics*, 39–43.

25. Kantowicz, *Polish-American Politics*, 39–43.

26. Department of Commerce, Bureau of the Census, *Fourteenth Census of the United States*, vol. 2, *Population, 1920: General Report and Analytical Tables* (Washington, D.C.: Government Printing Office, 1922), 1290.

27. Chicago Plan Commission, *Residential Chicago*, vol. 1 of *Report of the Chicago Land Use Survey* (Chicago: Chicago Plan Commission, 1942), 16.

28. Ibid., 14, 199–216.

29. Ibid., 227–46.

CHAPTER 5

1. James Gilbert examines the critical relationship between elite and popular culture at the fair in *Perfect Cities, Chicago's Utopias of 1893* (Chicago: University of Chicago Press, 1991), 73–130.

2. See Ellen Corbin Monchow, *Seventy Years of Real Estate Subdividing in the Region of Chicago* (Evanston, Ill.: Northwestern University Press, 1939), 128–46; H. Morton Bodfish, "Real Estate Activity in Chicago Accompanying the World's Fair of 1893," *Journal of Land and Public Utility*

Economics 4 (November 1928): 403–16; Ann Durkin Keating, *Building Chicago: Suburban Developers and the Creation of a Divided Metropolis* (Columbus: Ohio State University Press, 1988), 33–63.

3. Gwendolyn Wright, *Moralism and the Modern Home: Domestic Architecture and Cultural Conflict in Chicago* (Chicago: University of Chicago Press, 1980), 40–45. See also Homer Hoyt, *One Hundred Years of Land Values in Chicago* (Chicago: University of Chicago Press, 1933), 71.

Since Wright published *Moralism and the Modern Home* twenty years ago, various histories have mentioned the bonfires and parades that characterized the efforts of Samuel Eberly Gross. But no historians have bothered to go the next step and examine the houses he built or the people who purchased them. The omission of this information speaks volumes about the failure of historians to employ the methods of social history to develop a context for understanding urban home ownership.

4. Hoyt, *One Hundred Years of Land Values in Chicago*, 130, 167–68.

5. Ibid., 311–16, 232, 276, 369–423.

6. Upton Sinclair, *The Jungle* (New York: Doubleday Page, 1906; reprint, New York: Bantam Books, 1981), 44.

7. Ibid., 44–47.

8. Ibid., 49.

9. "A New Settlement Near Hammond," *Real Estate and Building Journal* (November 22, 1890).

10. Monchow, *Seventy Years of Real Estate Subdividing*, 128–29, 142–48.

11. "A New Settlement Near Hammond."

12. Hoyt, *One Hundred Years of Land Values in Chicago*, 130–22, 139, 161–73.

13. Bodfish, "Real Estate Activity in Chicago Accompanying the World's Fair of 1893," 408–9.

14. Monchow, *Seventy Years of Real Estate Subdividing*, 143–48.

15. See Thomas Lee Philpott, *The Slum and the Ghetto: Neighborhood Deterioration and Middle-Class Reform, Chicago, 1880–1930* (New York: Oxford University Press, 1978), 19–20, 12–13.

16. The information describing Stachowicz derives from my analysis of manuscripts from the federal census for 1900 for West Hammond, Illinois, as well as city directories for Chicago.

In 1797, Poland disappeared from the map of Europe, its territories divided between Prussia, Austria, and Russia. The partition continued until World War I. Consequently, census figures related to Polish immigration in the United States can be confusing since Poland did not exist politically as a European nation. Fortunately, in the Calumet region, census takers identified Poles as having immigrated from one of the three partitions. Distinctions between German, Austrian, and Russian Poles allowed for a more precise analysis of West Hammond's population.

17. Archdiocese of Chicago, *Antecedents and Developments* (Des Plaines, Ill.: St. Mary's Training School Press, 1920), 552.

18. The account of real estate activities derives from advertisements appearing in *Dziennik Chicagoski* on the following dates in 1891: February 7, May 7, May 20, June 4, June 29, July 15, July 18, July 30, August 19, September 3, September 9, September 15, September 25, October 3, November 14, 1891, April 15, April 22, May 11, June 8, June 15, July 6, August 17, October 13, October 14, November 2, November 12, December 21, 1892.

19. Ibid., February 7, 1891.

20. Ibid., April 25, 1891.

21. Ibid., May 9, 1891.

22. Ibid., July 15, 1891.

23. Ibid., April 12, 1892.

24. Ibid., October 24, 1892; May 23, 1893; August 17, 1893.

25. Ibid., May 11, 1892.

26. Archdiocese of Chicago, *Antecedents and Developments*, 552–53. See also Saint Andrew the Apostle Church, *Diamond Jubilee, 1892–1967, November 5, 1967, Saint Andrew the Apostle Church, Calumet City, Illinois* (Calumet City, Ill.: Saint Andrew the Apostle Church, 1968).

27. *Dziennik Chicagoski*, November 10, 1893.

28. The names appeared in the *Real Estate and Building Journal* (January 1893–December 1897). However, these lists do not appear to be complete. To determine who settled in West Hammond, the names were checked against the manuscripts for the 1900 and 1910 federal censuses for West Hammond as well as the city directories for these years. It was possible as well that some families settled in West Hammond but then moved. Nevertheless, in all likelihood, at least half of those who purchased lots originally were not able to settle in West Hammond.

29. *Diamond Jubilee, 1892–1967*.

30. Lawrence Stone, *The Past and the Present Revisited* (London: Routledge & Kegan Paul, 1987), 30.

31. The information regarding East Chicago and West Hammond in 1900 and 1910 derived from very careful analysis of manuscripts for the federal censuses. As Stone advised, the work was accomplished with a hand calculator and a concern for narrative. I read these documents much as I would any written text. For example, it mattered that Polish residents of the communities recorded the data for the census. In all likelihood, a resident of such a small community provided fairly accurate information. He knew many if not most of the people he surveyed. So I trusted both the West Hammond and East Chicago enumerators when they identified the partition of Poland from which the immigrants derived.

Readers should notice the numbers representing the range of ages of heads of families were rounded. Historians too often provide statistical data and imply degrees of accuracy that are absurd. As a profession, we must understand the implications of saying that "39.43 percent" of heads of households were in their thirties. At no point in this study would I claim accuracy to the hundredths of 1 percent, no matter what a computer or a calculator tells me. Given the data, anyone who makes this suggestion is one of two things: ignorant or a liar. I worked very hard to acquire figures "in the ballpark." This is not an apology for the roughness of my data. Indeed, I think many fellow academics, especially those in the social sciences, would benefit from being able to determine the appropriate tool for measurement. It makes no sense to use a micrometer when a yardstick will do.

32. William Frederick Howat, ed., *A Standard History of Lake County, Indiana and the Calumet Region*, 2 vols. (Chicago: Lewis Publishing, 1915), 1:620–21, 515–16.

33. See Daniel D. Luria, "Wealth, Capital, and Power: The Social Meaning of Home Ownership," *Journal of Interdisciplinary History* 2 (Autumn 1976): 267–69.

34. The generalizations derive from analysis of the 1898 and 1911 Sanborn maps for West Hammond and for similar maps of East Chicago.

35. Olivier Zunz examined similar circumstances in Detroit. Unlike others, Zunz found complex circumstances that defined immigrant neighborhoods. His study remains the finest of its type. See Zunz, *The Changing Face of Inequality: Urbanization, Industrial Development, and Immigrants in Detroit, 1880–1920* (Chicago: University of Chicago Press, 1982), 252–58, 173–95.

CHAPTER 6

1. E. Palma Beaudette-Neil, ed., *Thornton Township, Cook County, Illinois: A Brief Sketch of the Township's Prominent Men and Industrial Establishments* (Hammond, Ind.: Neil Publishing, 1920), 63–66.

2. "Escapes from a Dive," *Lake County Times*, December 10, 1907.

3. *Lake County News*: "Democratic Ticket, Republican Ticket," April 5, 1894; "West Hammond Election," April 19, 1894; "West Hammond Politics," March 25, 1897; "West Hammond Ticket," April 8, 1897; November 22, 1897; "West Hammond Election," April 21, 1898. See also "J. J. Flynn's Successor," *Lake County Times*, December 10, 1907.

4. "West Hammond Has a Hotly Contested Election," *Lake County News*, April 19, 1900.

5. Theodore Dreiser, *Sister Carrie* (New York: Doubleday, Page & Co., 1900; reprint, Boston: Houghton Mifflin Company, 1959), 13–16.

6. "West Hammond," *Lake County News*, April 20, 1900.

7. "West Hammond Election," *Lake County News*, April 21, 1901.

8. Ibid.; *Lake County News*: "Citizens Win Out," April 17, 1902; "Election Approaches," April 2, 1903; "Three Tickets in Field," April 14, 1904; "Democratic Ticket Wins," April 21, 1904; "Citizens Ticket Named,"

March 29, 1906; "Surprise in Village," April 19, 1906.

9. "West Hammond Democratic Ticket Will Have Opposition," *Lake County News*, March 28, 1907.

10. *Lake County News*: "West Hammond Election," April 10, 1907; "Election Situation at Fever Heat," April 15, 1907; "West Hammond Teems with Voters," April 16, 1907; "West Hammond Man Popular," April 11, 1907; "Citizen Ticket Defeated," April 18, 1907.

11. *Lake County Times*: "WH Primary," April 16, 1908; "Finneran Easy Winner," April 22, 1908; "Hold Election," Lake County News, April 28, 1908.

12. *Lake County Times*: "Village Holds First Primary," March 10, 1909; "Election Held," April 9, 1909; "Many Elections in Village," April 16, 1909; "West Hammond Election Eve," April 19, 1909; "Big Surprise in West Hammond Election," April 21, 1909.

13. Markam was profiled in Beaudette-Neil, ed., *Thornton Township, Cook County, Illinois*, 69. For Nowakowski's role in a land syndicate, see *Lake County Times*: "Markam Is Now Out," May 29, 1907; "Big Deal across State Line," March 10, 1910. For articles discussing improvements to the village, see *Lake County Times*: "Village Board Meets," April 5, 1907; "Hard Blow to Dives," May 7, 1907; "Village Is Ready for Event," July 9, 1910.

14. "Surprise in Village." For additional accounts of corruption, see *Lake County Times*: "Village to Become a City Soon," July 22, 1910; "Finneran Makes Fast Reply," July 28, 1910; "Clerk Takes Exception," August 13, 1910; "Villagers Swarm to Gathering," January 26, 1911.

15. *Lake County News*: January 18, 1894; March 15, 1894; March 22, 1894; "Republican Powwow," April 5, 1894; April 19, 1894; April 26, 1894.

16. Eric Monkkonen, *America Becomes Urban: The Development of U.S. Cities and Towns, 1780–1980* (Berkeley: University of California Press, 1988), 138–44.

17. *Lake County Times*: "Village Ready for Hot Fight," March 15, 1910; "Finneran Defeated," March 16, 1910; "Village Clerk Will Not Contest," March 17, 1910; "Interest Great," April 11, 1910; "Defeat of Martin Finneran," *Lake County News*, March 17, 1910.

18. *Lake County Times*: "Trustees Angry," November 25, 1910; "Markam Describes Process," December 3, 1910.

19. "Election Is Thwarted by a Girl," *Lake County Times*, December 28, 1910.

20. "Village Bell in New Role," *Lake County Times*, December 29, 1910.

21. "Election Is Thwarted by a Girl."

22. "Villagers Swarm to Gathering," *Lake County Times*, January 26, 1911.

23. "Lays Blame for Vice on Hammond," *Lake County Times*, January 26, 1911.

24. "Miss Brooks Completes a Most Strenuous Campaign," *Lake County Times*, January 31, 1911.

25. "Miss Brooks Lead Crowd of Women," *Lake County News*, March 30, 1911; "Riot in Village; Girl Is Jailed," *Lake County Times*, March 25, 1911.

26. "Village Excited," *Lake County Times*, August 14, 1911.

27. *Lake County Times*: "Virginia Brooks," January 26, 1922; "Comments," January 30, 1911.

28. *Lake County Times*: "Village to Become City in May," February 1, 1911; "News Jars the Village Last Night," February 8, 1911.

29. "Name Has Unsavory Sounds," *Lake County News*, July 27, 1911.

30. "West Hammond to Hold Election, *Lake County News*, November 25, 1911.

31. "Complex Situation in Village," *Lake County News*, April 12, 1911.

32. "Mayor Defeated by Nine Votes," *Lake County News*, April 19, 1911.

33. William Frederick Howat, ed., *A Standard History of Lake County, Indiana and the Calumet Region*, 2 vols. (Chicago: Lewis Publishing, 1915), 1:620–21, 515–16.

34. *Lake County Times*: "Board Amazes West Hammond," August 8, 1911; "Board Holds Second Secret Session," August 9, 1911.

35. "Brooks Gets Into Fight," *Lake County Times*, August 11, 1911.

36. "Mass Meeting at Columbia Hall," *Lake County Times*, August 14, 1911.

37. "Riotous Session of the Village Board," *Lake County Times*, October 14, 1911.

38. "Putting One Over on the Dear Public," *Lake County Times*, December 29, 1911.

39. *Lake County Times*: "Village on Qui Vive," December 29, 1911; February 26, 1912; "Drunken Disturbers Beaten," March 4, 1912; "Times Is Roundly Condemned," March 11, 1912; "Reform Triumphant in West Hammond," March 13, 1912; "Pledged to Reform New City," April 17, 1912; "People's Ticket Won Out," *Lake County News*, March 14, 1912.

40. *Lake County Times*: "Time Roundly Condemned," March 12, 1913; "Reform Triumphant in West Hammond," March 13, 1912.

41. "Women at Work," *National Municipal Review* 2 (July 1912): 504; "How One Girl Cleaned a Town," *Literary Digest* (August 10, 1912). See also *Lake County Times*, July 26, 1912.

42. *Lake County Times*: "Women Attack Miss Brooks," January 17, 1913; "Now What Did Virginia Dance," January 18, 1913; "Brooks Disappointed," January 2, 1911; "Owners to Be Posted on Streets," November 15, 1911.

43. Lloyd Wendt and Herman Kogan, *Bosses in Lusty Chicago: The Story of Bathhouse John and Hinky Dink* (Bloomington: Indiana University Press, 1967), 282–314.

44. *Lake County Times*: "Young Reformer Lectures," April 24, 1912; "Reformer Misquoted," April 25, 1912.

45. "Miss Virginia Brooks of West Hammond Takes Lead at Indiana Convention," *Lake County News*, April 11, 1912.

Brooks encountered her greatest opportunity when John Messmaker, a railroad engineer, died mysteriously in Henry Foss's dive. Messmaker's wife claimed foul play. But nothing could be proved until Brooks received a letter telling of the location of Frankie Ford, a twenty-year-old prostitute who was with Messmaker the night he died. Ford testified that Foss had given Messmaker an overdose of morphine and sent her out of town to cover up his involvement. Ford also told police of Esther Harrison, a prostitute who died of "a terrible affliction that made her a menace to the entire community during her life and made death come as a welcome relief" (*Lake County Times*, April 11, 1912).

Following these disclosures, the newspapers reported a "plague in West Hammond." Appalled, a wealthy Chicago woman provided funds for a detective to search for additional witnesses to Messmaker's death. Within a week, a second woman testified that Frankie Ford was a morphine addict who had given Messmaker an overdose while attempting to steal his money. She did the same to Esther Harrison. Of course, the new disclosures made equally sensational headlines. See *Lake County Times*: "Girl Lays Bare West Hammond Death," September 5, 1912; "Revolting Conditions Revealed," September 9, 1912; "Witness Scared," September 10, 1912; "Too Hot for Them," September 11, 1912.

46. *Lake County News*: "West Hammond Is Happy," April 13, 1905; "West Hammond Man Is Held Up," April 4, 1907; *Lake County Times*: "In West Hammond's Reeking Slums," August 21, 1906; "Wicked, Wicked West Hammond," April 19, 1907; "Dives Hold Three New Victims," April 20, 1907; "Only One More Day to Go," April 30, 1907; "Men Caught in Dive Raid," May 28, 1907; "Hard Blow to Dives," May 7, 1907; "West Hammond Diveless," May 10, 1907; "Flynn Collects Small Fines," May 13, 1907; "All Quiet," May 14, 1907; "Dives Open?" May 17, 1907; "Shots Fail to halt Girls," May 18, 1907; "Can't They," May 21, 1907; "Dive Inmates in a Barn," May 22, 1907; "What Became of Dive Keepers," May 24, 1907; "Raid Dives," May 25, 1907; "Dive Cases Go Over," May 28, 1907; "Con Moor Gets License," September 13, 1907. For an account of the behaviors associated with prostitution, see Ruth Rosen, *The Lost Sisterhood: Prostitution in America, 1900–1918* (Baltimore: Johns Hopkins University Press, 1982), 69–136; and Timothy J. Gilfoyle, *City of Eros: New York City, Prostitution, and the Commercialization of Sex, 1790–1920* (New York: W. W. Norton & Com., 1992), 197–223, 251–97.

47. "Invaded by Vices," *Lake County Times*, October 22, 1909.

48. *Lake County Times*: "Citizen Enters Complaint," April 12, 1910; "Village Faces an Injunction," May 3, 1910. For the best account of conditions

in the dives during the reign of the old gang, see "There Is No Lid in West Hammond," *Lake County Times*, August 30, 1911. The *Times* estimated the dives employed fifty prostitutes.

49. "Council Passes Drastic Ordinance," *Lake County Times*, May 7, 1912.

50. *Lake County Times*: "Return Administration after W. Hammond Dives," June 4, 1912; "Kulcyk Loses His Job," September 17, 1912.

51. "W. Hammond Takes State Line Action," *Lake County Times*, July 28, 1912.

52. "Last of Old Gang Is Ousted," *Lake County Times*, March 12, 1913.

53. *Lake County Times*: "Reformer Cannot Run Now," March 4, 1913; "Stachowitz States His Position," March 5, 1913; "Last of Old Gang Is Ousted," March 12, 1913.

Later the next year, Nowakowski encountered the anger of his parishioners once again. The pastor's "housekeeper" of ten years (i.e., his mistress—a fact confirmed by oral interviews) offended many members of the parish. Because of a "long curdling dislike and distrust of the woman," the parishioners held an "indignation meeting" and elected a committee of five to tell the woman to "vacate her housekeeping of the rectory." The committee provided five reasons: she was too extravagant; she was a poor housekeeper; she talked too much and too often; she thought she owned the rectory; and she "snubbed" members of the church and callers. When she refused to leave, the parishioners encouraged Nowakowski to persuade her otherwise. She remained. So Nowakowski visited Chicago, leaving "the drastic resolution of the problem to the members of his congregation."

Two hundred parishioners gathered outside the rectory. When Police Chief Joseph Okraj and Police Magistrate Adam Stachowicz arrived, the crowd, equipped with a key, stormed the rectory. Hearing their approach, the housekeeper ran to her bedroom, locked the door, and refused to admit the angry parishioners. Undaunted, the crowd broke down the door, gathered the woman's belongings, and evicted her from the rectory. Clearly, paying for churches, schools and rectories, like paying taxes, gave the Poles a sense of ownership and rights within their community. *Lake County Times*, December 30, 1914.

54. *Lake County Times*: "Last of Old Gang Is Ousted," March 12, 1913; April 16, 1913. Reformer Jacob Czaszewicz did not face opposition for treasurer. But Adam Stachowicz ran against Frank Green and another Polish candidate. In the primary, Stachowicz did not receive a majority of the vote because of the division in the Polish community. However, one month later in a head-to-head race against Green, Stachowicz received 69 percent of the vote, 80 percent from the south side and 57 percent from the north side.

55. *Lake County Times*: "Reformer Gets Cold Shoulder," March 13, 1913; "Virginia Brooks Weds," April 4, 1913; "Says Lonesomeness Is Cause of Many Girls' Fall," March 15, 1913; "Virginia Will Not Spend Life in Lifting West Hammond's Fallen," *Lake County News*, April 10, 1913.

56. Charles Washburne, *Come into My Parlor: A Biography of the Aristocratic Everleigh Sisters of Chicago* (New York: National Library Press, 1936), 241–43. Also see Rosen, *Lost Sisterhood*, 112–36.

57. "Indianapolis Papers Flay Virginia Brooks," *Lake County News*, September 25, 1913.

58. Twenty-years later, Brooks's ex-husband Charles Washburne described the play as "the first of the 'white slave' plays, timely, open-faced, and popular-priced. . . . It was all show, all 1913, all chambermaid" (*Come Into My Parlor*, 242–43).

59. "Virginia Brooks Asks Decree," *Lake County Times*, October 19, 1915.

CHAPTER 7

1. The account of Frank Wachewicz's career derives from a study of real estate advertisements that appeared in the *Lake County Times* and from examination of the neighborhoods Wachewicz built. Advertisements appeared on the following dates: September 24, 1912; June 20, 1913; May 1, 1915; September 19, 1916; October 19, 1917; March 2, 1918; March 15, 1918; March 20, 1918; May 17, 1918; December 31, 1918; August 30, 1919; September 3, 1919; September 16, 1921; May 10, 1922; May 10, 1923; May 11, 1923; May 12, 1923; May 25, 1923; July 31, 1923; August 11, 1923; August 14, 1923; October 10, 1923; October 19, 1923; October 27, 1923; March 28, 1924; July 18, 1924; July 19, 1924; August 12, 1924; August 28, 1924; September 12, 1924; September 13, 1924; September 25, 1924; October 2, 1924; October 13, 1924; March 31, 1925; September 11, 1925; September 26, 1925; May 22, 1926; June 4, 1927; August 12, 1927; August 18, 1927; September 3, 1927; September 9, 1927; October 12, 1927; January 8, 1928; March 7, 1928; March 7, 1928; March 10, 1928; March 20, 1928; April 13, 1928; April 17, 1928; April 18, 1928; April 20, 1928; April 25, 1928; April 27, 1928. Articles describing the Wachewicz agency may be found in the *Lake County Times*: "Frank J. Wachewicz Has Eighteen Dwellings Started," May 17, 1918; "Building Operations Cross Line," August 24, 1921; "Wachewicz Organization Breaks All Records," January 30, 1925; "Big Building Program for Calumet City," November 19, 1926; "Calumet City Preserves to Be Developed," July 21, 1927; "Construction Program for Calumet City," July 3, 1928; "Commerce Directors Endorsed Project," February 1, 1929.

2. See E. Palma Beaudette-Neil, ed., *Thornton Township, Cook County, Illinois: A Brief Sketch of the Township's Prominent Men and Industrial Establishments* (Hammond, Ind.: Neil Publishing, 1920), 60–65.

3. "West Hammond Building Boom," *Lake County Times*, January 9, 1917.

4. Most old blocks were divided into twenty-five-foot lot frontages. Fifty-foot lots resulted when buyers purchased two lots. If two buyers purchased three lots, than they could divide the property into thirty-seven-and-one-half-foot lots. These lots were especially common when members of a

family built houses next to each other.

5. This information derived from two full-page newspaper advertisements that listed all of the properties for sale by Wachewicz. Such advertisements by realtors provide a general sense of the market and its range. See *Lake County Times*, October 19, 1917; March 7, 1918.

6. See the advertisement for P. Thullen Homes in Beaudette-Neil, ed., *Thornton Township, Cook County, Illinois*.

7. *Lake County Times*, August 29, 1921; January 30, 1924.

8. John Bodnar describes the increasing diversity among the immigrant middle class in *The Transplanted: A History of Immigrants in Urban America* (Bloomington: Indiana University Press, 1985), 138–39.

9. West Hammond, now Calumet City, provided neighborhoods that clearly demonstrated distinctions between Poles and Germans, between immigrants and the second generation. The neighborhoods remain as evidence for those wishing to see the distinctions for themselves. However, as in much of Chicago, demolition is taking its toll. If historians do not develop sophisticated means for recording and analyzing housing types, history will be the loser. As it stands, most projects that survey neighborhoods are worthless. Inadequately trained, poorly paid, and oblivious to the larger concerns of social history, persons conducting these surveys blithely identify the styles of housing in a neighborhood, following the example of the various books that distinguish Italianate from Queen Anne. Following this pattern, one survey of the Calumet region failed to identify cottages as a housing type, let alone a critical one, even though they dominated large sections of the built environment. One only need look at any such survey or visit most house museums to experience our failure to interpret the wonders of the built environment.

Of course, my criticism relates to urban housing, especially in the Midwest. The quality of research and presentation at places like Colonial Williamsburg constitutes a national treasure. Judged by these standards, urban historians have failed miserably in their efforts to interpret nineteenth- and twentieth-century cities.

10. "Neighbor Seeks New Foundation," *Lake County Times*, May 8, 1914.

11. Ibid.; *Lake County Times*: "Coming Election Discussed," April 17, 1915; "Platform of the Democratic Party," April 19, 1915; "Seeks New Methods to Pay Debts," February 14, 1916.

12. *Lake County Times*: "Neighbor Seeks New Foundation," May 8, 1914; "Outline Program from 1916," January 7, 1916; "City Divided into Two Camps," January 24, 1916; "Letters Tell of Coming Campaign," January 27, 1916.

13. "Seeks New Method to Pay Debts."

14. *Lake County Times*: "Will West Hammond Vote Wet," April 6, 1914; "Bitter Fight on over There," March 27, 1914.

15. *Lake County Times*: "Women Suffragettes to Gather," March 4, 1914; "Object to Hammond Women," March 11, 1914; "Fearful Row over

Canvas," March 21, 1914; "Women Accuse the Chief," March 23, 1914; "Dry-Wet Fight Nears End," April 3, 1914.

16. Politicians understood the importance of enfranchising women, for in a minor election held one month prior to the local option vote, women voters altered the balance of power in West Hammond. In that election, women accounted for only 27 percent of all voters. The turnout was especially low among Polish women. They accounted for only one of every three women, while Polish men represented three of every five male voters. If the vote had included only men as in all previous elections, Poles would have accounted for 57 percent of all voters. However, with the low turnout among Polish women, Poles accounted for only 50 percent of voters. Clearly, Polish women had to exercise their right to vote if the city wished to keep Thornton Township wet and if Poles wished to remain the dominant faction in city elections. See "Object to Hammond Women."

17. "Will West Hammond Vote Wet," *Lake County Times*, April 6, 1914.

18. *Lake County Times*: "Saloons Fate at Polls," April 7, 1924; "Wets Put Ticket Across," April 8, 1914.

19. "Will West Hammond Vote Wet."

20. *Lake County Times*: "Finneran for Mayor," February 18, 1915; "Platform of the Democratic Party," April 19, 1915.

21. "Corruption Not Wanted in W. Hammond," *Lake County Times*, April 16, 1915.

22. "Finneran for Mayor"; "Platform of the Democratic Party."

23. "Corruption Not Wanted in W. Hammond."

24. *Lake County Times*: "Both Sides Claiming Victory," April 20, 1915; "How the Election Came Out," April 21, 1915.

25. "How the Election Came Out."

26. "W. H. Platforms," *Lake County Times*, February 14, 1915.

27. *Lake County Times*: "Big Things for West Hammond," February 22, 1917; "West Hammond Mecca for Saloonmen," March 22, 1917.

28. "Big Things for West Hammond."

29. "West Hammond Isn't Worrying," *Lake County Times*, February 10, 1917.

30. "West Hammond Mecca for Saloonmen"; *Lake County Times*: "Kamradt Named," March 14, 1917; "Kamradt Re-Elected," April 18, 1917.

31. "Saloon License History," *Lake County Times*, March 6, 1919.

32. "Want Clean City," *Lake County Times*, May 30, 1918.

33. "Saloon License History."

34. *Lake County Times*: "Saloonmen Must Pay in Advance," April 25, 1919; "No Orgies Says council," June 13, 1919; "Financial Crisis Stirs W. Hammond," July 2, 1920; "West Hammond Discusses Taxation," July 12, 1920; "West Hammond to Have Bond Election," August 11, 1921.

35. "Difficulty May Be Adjusted Shortly," *Lake County Times*, November 25, 1929.

36. The *Times* explained the unique circumstances that allowed West Hammond to circumvent the law:

> The little city just across the state line is possessed of features peculiar to herself, which are not to be found anywhere else in this country, and probably not in the world. Depending as she does entirely on Hammond for her public utilities, her mercantile establishments and her railroad terminals, at the same time she is outside the jurisdiction of Hammond and Indiana authorities. Chicago officials are too busy to clean up the scores of wide open saloons and even should they find time to do it, the many repeated visits that would be necessary to thoroughly finish the job are beyond the realms of possibility. ("Millennium May Make It Dry," *Lake County Times*, August 19, 1921)

37. *Lake County Times*: "West Hammond to Have Bond Election," August 11, 1921; "Building Operations Cross Line," August 24, 1921.

38. For a general description of the period, see Paul L. Murphy, *World War I and the Origin of Civil Liberties in the United States* (New York: W. W. Norton & Co., 1979), 71–132. For events in the Calumet region, see *Lake County Times*, October 3, 1918; April 5, 1917; May 28, 1921; May 3, 1921; May 7, 1919; May 9, 1919. For the significance of the region as a site in the larger national crisis, see David Brody, *Labor in Crisis: The Steel Strike of 1919* (Philadelphia: J. B. Lippincott, 1965), 36–159.

39. *Lake County Times*: "Polish People Patriotic," April 11, 1918; "Wheels a Barrow and Buys $1,000," April 25, 1919; "Remains of Soldier Brought from France," August 6, 1921.

40. "Polish People Patriotic"; "Wheels a Barrow and Buys $1,000."

41. *Lake County Times*: "Welcome Home Day Is Celebrated," November 11, 1919; "Welcome Home Stirs Multitude," November 12, 1919.

42. "J. Lietzan Body Ends Long Trip," *Lake County Times*, April 2, 1921.

43. A German Catholic raised on West Hammond's north side, Lietzan did not attend Saint Andrew's. He received an education at the German parochial school in Hammond (*Lake County Times*: "Sale of Polish Library Bonds Dragging," July 1, 1920; "West Hammond Wants Park," July 11, 1917; "West Hammond Wants Soldiers' Community," April 8, 1919; "Pushing Memorial Campaign," June 5, 1919; "W. Hammond to Vote on Memorial," August 22, 1919; "Memorial Meeting Today," August 27, 1919; "West Hammond Carries Proposition," September 11, 1919).

44. *Lake County Times*: "West hammond's New Swimming Pool Ready," July 28, 1922; "Hundreds Enjoy Pool," July 29, 1922.

45. *Lake County Times*: "Two Cities Have Joint Celebration," November 9, 1922; "Program Fixed," November 10, 1922; "Twin City

Celebration One-Sided," November 13, 1922.

46. *Lake County Times*: "W. Hammond City Beautiful," May 1, 1919; "W. Hammond's new Athletic Director," March 10, 1923; "West Hammond Welfare Association," October 17, 1923; "Calumet City to Join Parade," May 19, 1924; "Calumet City Parade Opens," May 21, 1924; "Trash Fires," May 22, 1924; "Calumet City Ends Clean-Up Week," May 23, 1924; "Two Thousand at Health Show," May 27, 1926; "Spotless City," May 29, 1926; "Clinic at Calumet City," January 18, 1927; "Mayor Issues Edict," May 5, 1927; "Clean-Up Campaign," May 6, 1927; "Calumet City Will Have New Press," May 13, 1927; "Calumet City Clean-Up," May 16, 1927; "Calumet City Nurses Aid," September 13, 1927; "Miss Bailey Reports," August 23, 1928; "Calumet City Holds Pre-School Exams," July 17, 1929.

47. *Lake County Times*: "New City Hall for W. Hammond," October 31, 1922; "Calumet City to Have $75,000 City Hall," July 28, 1924; "Calumet City Officials on Junket," August 2, 1924; "Plans Finished for Calumet City Municipal Building," September 3, 1924; "New Buildings Planned," September 11, 1924; "Populace Sees City Hall Opening," August 22, 1925; "New City Building Dedicated," August 24, 1925.

48. *Lake County Times*: "Calumet City to Have New English Church," January 12, 1925; "Cardinal to Dedicate New School," November 5, 1927. In the United States, the Catholic church established both territorial and national parishes. Under normal conditions, the church expected people within a particular geographic region to attend their territorial parish. However, exceptions were made for national parishes, which were formed for the members of a particular ethnic group. These parishes allowed for membership regardless of geographic boundaries.

49. *Lake County Times*: "Sobieski Changed to Lincoln," October 7, 1924; "Lincoln School Dedicated," March 30, 1925.

50. *Lake County Times*: "Calumet City to Have New School," May 12, 1924; "Thornton High School Boasts 450 Students," September 26, 1929. Figure 113 shows the second high school. The first building was destroyed by fire in 1934. The second school was completed in 1936.

51. U.S. Department of Commerce, Bureau of the Census, *Fifteenth Census of the United States, 1930, Population, vol. 6, Families* (Washington, D.C.: Government Printing Office, 1932), 424–25.

52. Students of Thornton Fractional North, *Chronoscope 1938* (Calumet City, Ill.: Thornton Fractional Township High School, 1938), 6–7.

53. U.S. Department of Commerce, Bureau of Census, *Fifteenth Census, of the United States, 1930*, 424–25.

54. Oscar Handlin, *The American People in the Twentieth Century* (Cambridge, Mass.: Harvard University Press, 1954), 86–108, and *The Uprooted: The Epic Story of the Great Migrations That Made the American People* (Boston: Little, Brown & Co., 1951), 258.

55. See Bodnar, *The Transplanted*, 117–43.

56. "Pledge to Build Church," *Lake County Times*, April 30, 1912; and "Magnificent Edifice," *Lake County News*, May 2, 1912.

57. *Lake County Times*: "Bishop of Rhode Dedicates School Building," June 8, 1914; "Church Dedicated Tomorrow," June 6, 1914.

58. "W. Hammond Church Burns to Ground," *Lake County Times*, January 28, 1918.

59. *Lake County Times*: "Mundelein to Dedicate Cal City Edifice," October 17, 1931; "Beautiful Church Dedicated," October 18, 1931.

60. See Richard Wightman Fox and T. J. Jackson Lears, "Introduction" in *The Culture of Consumption: Critical Essays in American History, 1880–1980*, ed. Richard Wightman Fox and T.J. Jackson Lears (New York: Pantheon Books, 1983), xiii. Fox and Lears assume that advertising is "the central institution of consumer culture." Their assumption fails to account for manufacture as an equally significant contributor to consumer culture. Moreover, such critics continue to suggest that advertising in national mass circulation magazines is more worthy of study than advertisements in local newspapers. But as a group, local advertisers directed their efforts at a larger and more varied audience than did middle-class magazines. They provide a superior source for understanding the range of the market.

For an alternative interpretation to Fox and Lears, see Lizabeth Cohen, *Making a New Deal: Industrial Workers in Chicago, 1919–1939* (Cambridge: Cambridge University Press, 1990), 99–158.

61. See Mary N. Stone, "The Plumbing Paradox: American Attitudes toward Late Nineteenth-Century Domestic Sanitary Arrangements," *Winterthur Portfolio* 14, no. 3 (Autumn 1979): 300. See also Maureen Ogle, "Domestic Reform and American Household Plumbing, 1840–1870," *Winterthur Portfolio* 28, no. 1 (Spring 1993): 33–58.

62. See Gail Caskey Winkler, "Introduction" in *The Well-Appointed Bath: Authentic Plans and Fixtures from the Early 1900s*, ed. Charles E. Fisher III (Washington, D.C.: Preservation Press, 1989), 1, 17–22.

63. For an exceptional record of the problems manufacturing sanitary ware, see Thomas Maddock's Sons Company, *Pottery: A History of the Pottery Industry and Its Evolution as Applied to Sanitation with Unique Specimens and Facsimile Marks from Ancient to Modern Foreign and American Wares* (Philadelphia: [Thomas Maddock's Sons Company, printed by Dando], [1910]), 131–78.

64. Cohen, *Making A New Deal*, 83–90. Her account relied heavily on Joseph John Parot, *Polish Catholics in Chicago, 1850–1920: A Religious History* (Dekalb: Northern Illinois University Press, 1981), 179–214. For an alternative view, see Bodnar, *The Transplanted*, 156–68.

65. My grandmother, a second-generation Pole whose family originated from the German partition, made this point clear to me when I was a child. A friend of mine was the son of a tavern owner, whose family she believed possessed greater wealth than ours. One summer, when the child

spoke of the air conditioning at his house, my grandmother bristled. We used fans. After the child went home, my grandmother explained the situation. She said the child's grandfather, who had established the tavern, was "hunky John, and he didn't speak good English."

66. See *Lake County Times*: "Federal Men Hit Cal City," July 14, 1929; "Beer Flats Expected Now," November 12, 1929; "Cal City Police Raid Beer Flats," August 29, 1930.

67. "Residents Tired of Carnivals," *Lake County Times*, July 11, 1924.

68. Al Capone's rise and fall affected the city's reputation. The events surrounding his conviction for tax evasion were specially significant. See *Lake County Times*: "Federal Agents Make Foray," June 27, 1930; "Report Cal City Raided," August 22, 1930; "Arrest Dealers, Owners, Bookies," September 3, 1930; "Detectives Visit Soft Drink Parlors," September 26, 1930; "Chicago Raiders Work on Big Scalp," February 14, 1931; "Agents Raid Cal City," March 31, 1931; June 4, 1931; "Calumet City Evidence before Federal Jury," June 5, 1931; "Not a Rift in Calumet City Cloud of Doom," June 6, 1931; "Federal Grand Jury Silent," June 13, 1931; "Guilty Capone," June 16, 1931; "Operator of Saloon Shot Down," July 10, 1931; "Burnham Woods Sees Al Capone," August 18, 1931; "Zick Roils Mayor John," April 18, 1935.

69. "*Life* Spends Saturday Night in Calumet City," *Life*, January 20, 1941, 74–79.

70. "Life," *Lake County Times*, January 22, 1941.

CONCLUSION

1. Robert Wiebe, *The Search For Order, 1877–1920*, (New York: Hill & Wang, 1967), 2–7, 302.

2. For an attempt to measure the wealth created by an urban real estate market, see Davil L. Wickens, *Residential Real Estate: Its Economic Position as Shown by Values, Rents, Family Incomes, Financing, and Construction, Together with Estimates for All Real Estate* (New York: National Bureau of Economic Research, 1941).

INDEX